More Advance Praise for *Managing Your Inheritance*

"Knowing what to do with an inheritance is not as simple as it might seem. How to make it grow, produce the income you may need, or transfer it efficiently to the next generation requires precise planning. *Managing Your Inheritance* explains how to accomplish your goals. It's an excellent resource."

—Joseph H. Bragdon,
general partner, Conservest Management Company

"This book provides an excellent road map for the recipient of any size inheritance. When you inherit assets, you are faced with making financial and emotional decisions you never before had to make. This comprehensive set of guidelines is essential in making the right choices throughout this transitional stage of your life."

—Gale Anne Hurd,
producer (*Terminator, Aliens, The Abyss*)

"Not only is this an excellent and readable primer on inheritance, but the stress on preparation *now*, in a socially responsible context, is outstanding. The authors' advice is invaluable in addressing the emotional and financial issues of inheritance, including women's issues, how best to manage your advisors, and sustaining a win-win approach through the whole process."

—Susan Davis,
president, Capital Missions Company

"*Managing Your Inheritance* contains an important combination of the basics that persons with new inheritances should know. It is a helpful blend of the practical and the philosophical, the should-do and the can-do. It also reminds us that inheriting wealth can not only help meet personal goals but also contribute to larger social objectives."

—Tim Smith,
executive director, Interfaith Center on Corporate Responsibility

"Too often, we leave financial planning to others. My mother had been urging me to become involved in intergenerational planning, so I was delighted to sit down with my daughter to take control of our future together. Card and Miller's book really helped. It is perfect for anyone who wants a painless and easy-to-follow guide through a daunting process."

—Lynda Johnson Robb

Managing Your Inheritance

MANAGING YOUR INHERITANCE

GETTING IT,
KEEPING IT, GROWING IT—
MAKING THE MOST OF
ANY SIZE INHERITANCE

Emily W. Card and Adam L. Miller

TIMES BUSINESS

RANDOM HOUSE

All the characters in this book, with the exception of public figures, are fictitious.

Library of Congress Cataloging-in-Publication Data

Card, Emily.
Managing your inheritance : getting it, keeping it, growing it—
making the most of any size inheritance / Emily Card and Adam Miller.—
1st ed.
p.   cm.
Includes index.
ISBN 0-8129-2600-5
1. Finance, Personal.   2. Inheritance and succession—Economic aspects.
3. Wealth.   I. Miller, Adam (Adam L.)   II. Title.
HG179.C3278   1995
332.024—dc20   95-13765

Manufactured in the United States of America
9 8 7 6 5 4 3 2
First Edition
Designed by Robert C. Olsson

Acknowledgments

No book can be written without the help of many people in many ways. The following are some of those people to whom thanks are owed:

Denise Marcil, for her faith and support in this project, and her steadfast persistence as an agent and friend.

Karl Weber, for his receptiveness, insight, and helpful suggestions.

Christie Kelly, for her thorough and astute research. She added depth to the book that we would have lost without her help.

Nancy Inglis and Anne Haas for their thorough copyediting.

Kimberly McGlaughlin, for willingly accepting the arduous task of line editing the entire manuscript.

Roz Kilner and Erin Fulfer, who have helped in too many ways to recount.

Perry Wallack and Larry Witzer, for sharing their accounting expertise and, along with Andy Millard, their homes.

Donovan Campbell and Elizabeth Howard, for lending their general expertise in this area of the law.

Sandra Chan of Perkins Coie in Los Angeles and Los Angeles attorney Earl O. Bender for their expert review of the estate planning material.

Joanne and Dave Gibson, for sharing their part of America with two wandering writers.

Lamar Card for his constant encouragement.

Dean Susan Praeger of the UCLA School of Law for nurturing the diverse community where the two of us studied law; Professors George McGovern, Eric Zolt, and Jesse Dukeminier for their teaching; and William McGeary for keeping us connected.

A special thank-you is owed to libraries that went beyond the call of duty: the County Library at Marina del Rey, Santa Monica Library, and UCLA's Anderson School of Management Library.

Waldo Card-Brosveen, for being patient and entertaining during the long hours of our work.

On a personal level, Emily would like to thank the Newcomb College Center for Women for its continued support of her work; Kent Brosveen for fostering creativity; John Felice and Jason Felice for moral and physical support; and her mother, Anne Dempsey Watts, who had the courage to prepare for her own transition.

Adam would especially like to thank Ilene Miller for her lifetime help correcting his grammar and Steven Miller for continuing to correct his math; Marci Miller for her unwavering advocacy; Terry Newbold and Celeste Smith for encouraging his writing way back when; Brian Culot for his steadfast support despite an intense writing schedule; and his grandfathers, Henry Weinstein and Gus Miller, for sharing the wonders of a generation past.

To all our other relatives and friends, for putting up with the late nights, retreats, and the constant distraction of writing.

And special thanks to Jim Morrison and the Doors, whose music kept the creative juices flowing day in and day out.

Note

The tax system is constantly changing. Consequently, the tax discussions in this book have been designed for general applicability. But note: Pending legislation may increase the unified estate tax credit, which will significantly affect any estate planning advice herein regarding the current $600,000 exclusion. Recent proposals support raising the exemption equivalent amount to $750,000 and phasing in the change over several years.

This book has been written for a lay audience. The technical legal definitions of certain terms, such as "heirs" (intestate distributees determinable solely upon the death of the decedent) and "beneficiaries," have been forgone in favor of the more common, connotative meanings of the words.

This publication is designed to provide accurate and authoritative information in regard to the subject matter covered. It is published with the understanding that the publisher and author are not engaged in rendering legal, accounting, or other professional service. If legal advice or other professional advice, including financial, is required, the services of a competent professional person should be sought. (From a Declaration of Principles, jointly adopted by a committee of the American Bar Association and a committee of publishers.)

Contents

MANAGING YOUR INHERITANCE

INTRODUCTION

—○—

THE BASICS OF INHERITED WEALTH

Maybe you have just faced a personal tragedy. You have somehow found the strength to pick up this book and begin a most important transition in your life.

Or maybe you simply want to be prepared when your time of transition comes. You might not see yourself as an heir, but think again. One hundred and fifteen million Americans will leave bequests averaging $90,000 over the next decades, ranging in size from modest to multimillion-dollar estates. Consider the following:

1. Do your parents own a home?
2. Is their home paid for?
3. Do your parents own stocks, bonds, mutual funds, or have IRA accounts?
4. Does your state law provide an inheritance for children as well as spouses if there is no will?

If you answered yes to any of these questions, you may be among the "new heirs"—baby boomer children of the first large-scale middle class in history—who stand to inherit almost $11 *trillion* from their savings-oriented, depression-era parents. These savings, combined with the twin effects of Reagan-era tax cutting and an economic boom in the 1980s, form the unprecedented projected transfer of wealth.

Inheriting money doesn't sound like a problem, so you're probably thinking: Why do I need a book to find out how to spend my inheritance? But *spending* your inheritance is exactly what you shouldn't do.

Here's the problem: Unlike their frugal parents, boomers have exhibited the lowest savings rate in recent U.S. history, only about 3 percent of income. In addition, this generation—you know who you are—has amassed the highest debt in history, $722 billion, not counting mortgage and credit card debt.

Your twin temptations: pay off debt and then create new debt. Old habits die hard, so our challenge is to help you understand how to conserve and grow your new assets.

But even before you inherit, or while you are in the process of going through probate (the formal transfer of your inheritance), you'll face many new issues, from dealing with executors to conquering the complexities of estate planning.

We designed this book to carry you through the process.

THE NEW HEIRS' PRIMER

The management of inherited wealth can be organized around three basic concepts:

- Inheriting the past,
- Maximizing the present, and
- Providing for the future.

New heirs often inherit more than money; tremendous psychological implications are typically bundled with inherited wealth. As an heir, you may have to deal with feelings of guilt and responsibility, as well as family "silver strings" which tie the inheritor to the grantor. You must control the temptation to immediately replace your current lifestyle with the inheritance. And as a new heir, you will be confronted with a variety of complex legal and tax issues at an emotionally distraught time.

Once the estate is settled, you should develop an asset management plan which will maximize the current and future value of your inheritance. Managing a lump-sum transfer raises asset allocation and capital preservation concerns that differ in focus from typical personal finance issues.

Finally, your inheritance presents you with both opportunity and responsibility. The receipt of an inheritance marks a change in your life, in terms of your family, your finances, or both. As a result, you now need to consider your own estate plan and the way you want to use your capital to provide for the future of your family and our society.

In the three main parts of the book, we will explore each of these concepts.

Although most of us think of heirs and heiresses as the celebrated super-rich, during the coming decades we will see a new type of inheritor. Many will be middle-aged or even nearing retirement. Some will be younger baby boomers with a propensity to spend. Other inheritors will be restricted by trusts, such as those set up for college education or those established for control of family members' access to assets.

Together you are the "new heirs." You face the prospect of managing lump sums of inherited money although you may never have learned good money management habits for yourself. Your challenge: To preserve and grow the inheritance rather than squander it.

HOW MUCH IS MUCH?

All inheritances are not created equal. Although current predictions show the average inheritance at $90,000, the amount any new heir actually receives can vary dramatically. As a result, the

THE 4M FORMULA

Here's a brief example of differences based on the size of the inheritance, or what we call our 4M Formula:

—•—

Modest *(Less than $50,000)*

Probate: May not be required.
Lifestyle: Minimum changes.
Estate Plan: Living trust, will or will substitutes, and living will.
Action: Secure your retirement and your children's education.
Investments: IRA, home, and educational trust.

—•—

MODERATE *($50,000–$250,000)*

Probate: Probate or living trust.
Lifestyle: Ease some of your cash flow concerns, but do not retire. Consider your tax position and your estate plan.
Estate Plan: Living trust and living will.
Action: Develop a conservative asset allocation plan.
Investments: IRA, home, mutual fund, and tax-free bonds.

—•—

MAJOR *($250,000–$1,000,000)*

Probate: You are probably the beneficiary of a complex estate plan, and now you need to create one of your own.
Lifestyle: Even if you cannot yet retire, these resources may allow you to change careers or engage in other pursuits you've dreamed about.
Estate Plan: Living trust and living will. If your estate is over $600,000, and you are married, preserve the $600,000 exemption from estate tax for both you and your spouse, consider an irrevocable insurance trust, and give annual gifts.
Action: Plan for taxes, allocate your assets, and maximize your inheritance. Seek professional advice.
Investments: Real estate, stocks, bonds, IRA, metals, and international funds.

---•---

MILLIONS *(Over $1,000,000)*
Probate: You have probably been part of the estate planning process as a trust beneficiary or the recipient of cash gifts for most of your life.
Lifestyle: Many options await.
Estate Plan: Set up an irrevocable trust funded by exempt annual $10,000 gifts to each of your children and grandchildren.
Action: Work closely with a team of advisors to develop your estate plan, allocate your assets, and minimize your tax liability. You can flow your capital to socially responsible venture capital and charitable organizations. Be wary, the positive opportunities provided by wealth can have equally powerful costs.
Investments: Real estate, growth stocks, bonds, international funds, metals, minerals, and venture capital.

right advice to follow depends on whether your inheritance is modest or in the millions. To apply the general rules to your specific situation, "4M Formula" checklists appear throughout the book. The 4M Formula summarizes advice according to the size of your inheritance. Our cutoff points follow—but, of course, what you consider "modest" or "major" depends on you.

- Modest *(less than $50,000)*
- Moderate ($50,000–$250,000)
- Major ($250,000–$1,000,000)
- Millions *(over $1,000,000)*

If you have been living a high lifestyle, even an inheritance of $200,000 may seem fairly modest; conversely, if your inheritance is significantly more than your family's annual income, its effects could be major, regardless of its size.

THE FIRST YEAR

The challenges and dangers facing new heirs are especially strong immediately after inheriting. By avoiding temptation and planning ahead, you can successfully navigate the transition.

Be aware of emotional pitfalls. Acknowledge and deal with the emotional aspects of inherited wealth, especially the wealth of your parents. Examine how susceptible you may be at an emotionally charged time to solicitations for your money that don't best suit your needs.

Look out for silver strings which bind inheritors to their wealth. Dealing with the psychological aspects of inheritance is critical to successfully managing the wealth. The emotional family ties that inherited wealth represents can take their toll. If parents were overbearing, middle-aged "children" may rebel by spending their parents' money. A wise inheritor learns to focus on his or her own needs rather than allow the family strings to tug.

Be prepared when you receive your inheritance. If you believe your parents, spouse, or relatives will leave you money, it's prudent, not ghoulish, to know the basics beforehand.

The New Heir's Checklist

Here is a quick list of suggestions for beginning to manage your inheritance successfully, especially during your first year as a new heir.

- Be aware of emotional pitfalls.
- Be aware of psychological silver strings.
- Plan ahead for inheritance.
- Learn to deal with trusts.
- Focus on preserving your capital.
- Work to minimize taxes.

- Be a conservative investor.
- Protect your capital from inflation.
- Start good habits now.

By familiarizing yourself with the estate settlement process now, you will be better able to discuss estate plans with your family. You can even fantasize about what you might do with a given amount of money; e.g., so much to pay off debts, so much to college funds, so much to investments, and so much to charity. Then, commit your thoughts to paper and tuck them away so that you'll have a plan prepared at a contemplative, rather than emotional time.

Dealing with trusts can present special challenges. If your property is held in trust, you'll want to stay as active as you can in the management of the trusts, even if only on an informal basis. If you are an income beneficiary, try to get the income disbursed every year in full. Do not leave it to accumulate, because undistributed income becomes *corpus*, or principal, and will not be available for your use unless the trust specifically allows for its distribution.

Focus on preserving your capital, especially for the first year or two after you inherit. Even if you spend the income from the assets, preserve the capital base for growth in the future. If you spend the inheritance now, without planning, you will regret it later.

Work to minimize taxes, both for the estate, if you can, and on your earnings from the estate. If your family politics allow, try to help your parents structure their estate to the best advantage to minimize estate taxes. Estates worth less than $600,000 are free of federal taxes to the heirs. For larger estates try working with your parents, if they're willing, to develop trust and gift programs to achieve lower estate tax costs.

Be a conservative investor. You should pause before undertaking any investment or other activity that would put your capital at risk. For example, if you have $200,000 and you put it in a safe but long-term investment it might earn $20,000 a year. Depending on where you live and whether you own a home, you could retire on that amount. You could also easily run through $200,000 in a year-long spending spree and be left with nothing.

Protect your capital from inflation with solid growth-oriented investments, rather than looking to "make a killing" in high-risk, high-growth investments. The myriad of deals that entrepreneurs offer provide enticements for the newly moneyed. We would all like to find the next Apple Computer or Reebok Shoes to invest in, but the reality is, for all but the most sophisticated and active investor, the most prudent path is to diversify with conservative, growth-oriented opportunities.

Financial Decision Making

To ease decision making, your finances should be approached in terms of the following investment issues (discussed fully in Chapter 6):

- *Cash Flow:* The timing of cash inflows, whether your income or disbursements (income and dividends) from your investments, and outflows, or payments.
- *Taxes:* The potential tax consequences, which can improve or hamper the expected return from your income or an investment.
- *Growth:* The expected returns on an investment and the opportunity for an investment to grow the capital base, such as the increase in the value of real estate held over time.
- *Risk:* Simply put, the potential for loss related to an investment. Risk is typically inversely related to growth or expected return. Risk can be further divided into two types: systematic risk related to the holding of a specific asset, such as AT&T stock; and nonsystematic risk, relating to overall market performance, such as the entire stock market.

- *Liquidity:* The ease of converting an investment to cash, such as the difference between the time it takes to withdraw money from your savings account and selling your home.
- *Diversification:* The mix of assets that comprise the investor's total wealth. An asset base consisting only of local real estate investments is poorly diversified because the entire base is subject to loss from a downturn in that real estate market.
- *Personal Preference:* To prevent investors from regretting even rational business decisions, it is imperative that inheritors take their personal desires and preferences into account, such as the desire to retain a particular piece of property because of its high sentimental value despite a low market value.

New heirs face the additional challenge of considering these investment parameters when combining their existing assets—however scant—with their inheritances.

EMOTIONAL WEALTH

When we meet our inherited fortunes, often in those vulnerable months following the death of a parent, we are usually least equipped to deal with them. Whether one has lived a lifetime with the expectation of inheriting resources or the possibility is a new one, preparation can save emotional, as well as financial, expense.

To be ready when your inheritance comes, incorporate good budgeting, savings, spending, and investment habits now. These habits, along with a plan, will pave the way for positively managing your inheritance.

In addition, you may want to consider the privileges of wealth. According to the old school, "noblesse oblige," or the obligations of wealth, included using the money to create good, generally through philanthropy. But the new school has a better idea, to direct the economy toward positive change through the *socially responsible use of capital.*

While an inheritance offers you personal benefits, your new money also affords you the opportunity to make a difference. Just look at how the environmental movement has reached down to the checkout line, where many times when you buy groceries, you're queried, "Paper or plastic?" Consider what would happen if every new heir put 10 percent of her or his inheritance into investments that underwrote positive social goals—that would mean $1.1 trillion forging a new path.

The possibilities have barely been contemplated by policy makers. From views on the meaning of wealth to the effects on their own children, the $11 trillion transfer of wealth can make change agents of a vast new group of inheritors. The baby boom generation has changed everything it's touched. With capital in hand, this generation could well reset personal, social, and political priorities for decades to come. As a new heir, you can join them.

A New Heir's Challenges

1. Avoid the temptation to change your lifestyle immediately, and recognize that there are both obvious and subtle psychological implications of inheriting wealth.

2. Try to talk about estate planning with your family. Remember that you are not the only one who may face problems with parents or siblings and learn from the experiences of others.

3. Gain an understanding of the estate process before you are forced to deal with executors and trustees at emotional times.

4. Learn the fundamentals of cash flow, budgeting, retirement planning, and taxes to stay in control of your new and old assets.

5. If you are the beneficiary of a trust, learn to deal with the special challenges of trusts.

6. Plan your estate. Even if you already have a will, the addition of your inheritance is cause enough to reexamine your estate and consider the multitude of options available to you.

7.   Develop a professional team to advise you on your legal, financial, and other affairs.

8.   Consider the trade-offs of risk, growth, liquidity, and diversification in allocating your assets.

9.   Learn from the successes and failures of other new heirs trying to manage their inheritances.

10.   Take control of your wealth and direct the flow of capital to socially responsible uses.

—◯—

PART I

INHERITING THE PAST

Of comfort no man speak:
Let's talk of graves, of worms, and epitaphs;
Make dust our paper, and with rainy eyes
Write sorrow on the bosom of the earth.
Let's choose executors, and talk of wills.
— Shakespeare, *King Richard II*

1

---◯---

AVOIDING INHERITANCE PITFALLS

So YOU JUST GOT an inheritance. Time to get rid of that old car sitting in the driveway, or maybe time to get a new driveway. Tired of eating at those same restaurants and wearing those same old outfits? Already planning a trip to Europe? Not so fast! The temptations that come with the windfall of an inheritance are like those facing a lottery winner. Like the lottery winner, to make the most of what you get, avoiding the temptation to make overnight changes is key.

Unless your money is in trust, unlike the lottery winner, you'll receive your inheritance in a lump sum. So before you run out to buy a new wardrobe or a new car, let's take a quick look at the difference, even without inflationary effects, between buying a $100,000 Mercedes 500 SL convertible and putting the same money in an equity mutual fund earning an average of 7 percent over the next ten years:

	500SL	Mutual Fund
Day 1	$100,000	$100,000
Day 2	90,000	100,019
Year 2	75,000	114,981
Year 5	55,000	141,763
Year 10	30,000	200,966

If you can't resist the temptation to spend some of the money immediately, then at least do it systematically. A few suggestions:

1. *Take 5 percent of your inheritance and go crazy.* Buy something you always wanted, take a trip, get some new clothes, pick out some nice presents for your family, throw a party—you get the idea. The point is, get it out of your system, but keep it under control. (With a large inheritance, don't spend the entire five percent at once. Put it in a special savings account and consider it your discretionary money, to use with or without discretion.)

2. *Pay off your expensive debts.* Credit card debts and other debts with 14-percent-plus interest rates cost more than an investment will normally earn you. It is safe to assume that you'll save money if you retire such expensive debts. Paying off these debts serves two purposes: You're relieved of the psychological burden of having the debt, and you've made a financially rational decision since the debt costs more than you can safely earn with the same money.

Two cautions apply. First, if you've been a habitual overuser of credit, simply paying the bills won't solve the problem. You'll have to retire most of your cards and stringently examine the causes and solutions to overspending.

Second, if you have a mortgage or other less long-term, lower interest obligations, don't pay them immediately. Examine whether you can achieve higher returns from investments than the cost of interest on the debt. Don't forget to take taxes into account. Unless the investment is tax-exempt, you'll owe income taxes on dividends, interest, or other income earned. And, if you retire your mortgage, you'll lose your income tax deduction for the interest portion of the payment.

Although you may later decide to exchange less costly debt for freedom, don't do so immediately. Having the bank as your co-investor in property can save your finances in a market downturn or natural disaster. If your state provides *nonrecourse* mortgages for residences, which limit losses on default to the property mortgaged, think very carefully before retiring mortgage credit. Of course, the upside of retiring the debt is that the interest paid on the life of a loan can double the cost of the house.

3. *Consider starting or increasing savings for your retirement.* Building your retirement accounts provides multiple benefits. First, a pledge to a retirement account is a conscious commitment to save for the future. Second, if you qualify for tax savings (employed or self-employed), you can defer income taxes on the funds placed in an IRA, Keogh, or 401(k) plan. Third, if you've put off retirement planning, the new resources allow you to take this important step now. Or, if you've underfunded your retirement plan, you can now use the resources to pay in the maximum allowed by law. Fourth, because of early withdrawal penalties associated with retirement accounts, you'll have a built-in incentive not to withdraw funds, as compared to a savings or money market account. Fifth, these funds will grow on a pre-tax basis; therefore, retirement savings earn compound interest for you on money that would otherwise go to taxes. Even if all of your other investments turn sour, with a solid retirement account, you won't starve in your old age, as long as you leave the retirement funds intact.

4. *Set up an educational fund for your children.* If you have children and have not started saving for their education, now's the time to put aside money specifically for this purpose. If your inheritance provides enough money to educate your children, but college is a few years off, you can set up an educational trust for each child, funded each year with your $10,000 gift-tax exclusion per child.

Each of these suggestions is a safe way to let off some spending steam without causing you to hastily mismanage your inheritance, to your later regret. The technicalities of money management, taxes, asset allocation, trusts, and estate planning are explained in Parts Two and Three of the book, where these and other choices for the management of your wealth are discussed in detail. First, it's important that you get into the proper mindset by dealing with the psychological aspects of inheriting wealth.

THE ROLE OF THE INHERITANCE IN *YOUR* LIFE

Just because you have new assets does not necessarily mean that you have a new life. When the inheritance arrives, or even before it gets to you, you need to consider the effect the inheritance *could* have on your life. Is it enough to have a good time tomorrow? Is it enough for your future retirement? Is it enough to retire now?

To identify the potential role of the inheritance in your life, begin a journal, allowing yourself to list your dreams, however far-fetched. Order your dreams and aspirations in terms of your personal sense of priorities. Pick the top three or four and see whether the money you have inherited will allow you to realize these goals.

Not all dreams can be attained through wealth, but you may be able to revitalize some long-forgotten desires. Allow your imagination free rein before you check it against practical reality. Then ask if you have provided for your children, your future? Do you have political, charitable, or socially responsible activities that you want to support? Dream your dreams, but do a reality check before you start spending.

Why Bother Managing?

What is the point of all this talk about responsibly managing your inheritance anyway? It is *your* inheritance, so what's the big deal if you spend the whole thing tomorrow for a good time? Good reasons exist to manage the inheritance for yourself, and if not for yourself, for future generations.

Yourself

If you spend an entire inheritance to have a good time, a modest amount won't last long, and then you'll be back where you started. However, the inheritance will continue to grow if you use your current income to maintain your current lifestyle. If you are now forty and achieve 8 percent returns compounded annually on $50,000 until you're sixty-five, you will have $367,009 to live out the rest of your nonworking life, not to mention any other savings or retirement benefits (and social security payments) that you might receive. Even if you assume 4 percent inflation, the present value of the amount is $135,688. That thought alone should provide you with longer-term relief and happiness than any short-lived spending spree.

If you inherit a large amount of money, then you inherit opportunity, the opportunity to control the flow of capital. By responsibly managing this control, you can improve your life, the lives of your family members, and the world around you. Not only do you have the opportunity to save for your future, but you can supplement your current income to support activities and causes of interest to you. You also can learn to face the challenges of inherited wealth before they darken an otherwise bright outlook on life.

Society

If the personal argument isn't convincing enough, let's try the socially responsible approach. Imagine if every new heir mismanaged or squandered his or her inheritance. The cumulative effect of such irresponsibility on a nation already burdened with $4 trillion in debt could be devastating. In effect, past savings would be spent presently at the cost of the future.

Of course, you might argue that it is virtually impossible that all $11 trillion of the inheritance boom would be simultaneously mismanaged. But if you do it, why shouldn't the next guy, and his sister, and her friend. Just remember that every well-planned investment decision that you make not only provides for yourself but is an investment in the future of our economy.

THE 4M FORMULA FOR LIFESTYLE

——o——

MODEST

Follow the advice in this chapter closely. The majority of your inheritance should be going toward your children's education and/or your retirement plan.

——o——

MODERATE

Depending on the size of your inheritance, you may be able to supplement your current income nicely, prepare for your family's future, and enjoy less of a cash flow crunch. Follow the advice in this chapter.

——o——

MAJOR

You have many options and opportunities. You can supplement your income and improve your standard of living, or you can take the opportunity to make a transition to a new career or a new location. You should follow the advice in this chapter, but then focus on your asset allocation discussed in Part Two of this book.

——o——

MILLIONS

Don't run out and quit your job yet. You have been given the opportunity to revisit dreams that may now be attainable; but remember, the income of one million dollars, after taxes and inflationary effects, might not provide the living standard of a high-paying career. Seriously consider your alternatives, expected cash flows, and your asset allocation. Age plays a role as well, since having money is no substitute for the psychic rewards of career competence. Do enjoy some of your discretionary money while you're planning.

PUTTING THE INHERITANCE IN PERSPECTIVE

A common pitfall for new inheritors, especially those who have grown accustomed to living from paycheck to paycheck, is to exaggerate the extent of their inherited wealth. Even with a lump-sum inheritance, most modest and moderate heirs cannot afford to stop working or to radically adjust their lifestyles, but some mistakenly assume they can. Better: Establish a preliminary budget and gain a clear picture of the changes in your tax position in light of your inheritance before you make any rash decisions. With a "quick and dirty" budget, you can immediately see whether the inheritance will simply supplement your lifestyle or replace it.

For most working heirs, given the projected average "baby boom" inheritance of $90,000, the primary use should be for retirement funds. In particular, if a salaried person has enjoyed a "live today, pay tomorrow," high-cash-flow life, the inheritance could spell the difference between a difficult retirement and a secure one.

Far too many new heirs have squandered their inheritances. One new heir spent her entire inheritance on a "desperately needed" winter trip to Hawaii. Within two weeks of returning, her prior stress level had returned, her income had not improved, and her retirement account remained virtually empty. Had she invested the funds, she could have taken a more modest summer vacation and grown the assets to maintain her current lifestyle after she retired. Instead, she acted as if the inheritance represented a permanent change in her income that she would enjoy every year and let it vanish forever in short-term satisfaction.

For some fortunate heirs at the upper end of the inheritance scale, the inheritance serves as a new source of income which replaces the need to work. As is the case with many wealthy inheritors, the heir may already have been enjoying a steady income from trusts or family gifts. With the added funds, the new heir now has the opportunity to focus on favorite causes; set up a charitable giving budget; or enter the world of political giving, with the associated heady access to the powerful and famous. These heirs should take time to understand the special issues related to dealing with trusts; creating sophisticated estate plans (for estates over $600,000); and making socially responsible venture capital investments.

For other heirs, whose position falls somewhere in the middle, the inheritance is large enough to use some of the income or principal now, but too small to replace a salary. The extra flexibility provided by the supplemental income may be enough to allow the heir to choose a new job or a new career. Or these heirs could consider reducing their work time to enjoy more free time. One study has found that 18 percent of people inheriting more than $150,000 stop working, as compared to less than 5 percent of those receiving modest inheritances.

WEALTH

If it has not affected you already, inheriting money, especially if it is a lot of money, will change your life in both obvious and subtle ways. An awareness of these potential effects, whether or not they actually do apply to you, will help you to confront or avoid them. Although in our culture it's commonplace to assume "the more money the better," a writer once observed, "To suppose, as we all suppose, that we could be rich and not behave the way the rich behave, is like saying that we could drink all day and stay sober."

Wealth has been the obsession of writers, musicians, psychologists, and sociologists for decades. Although these few have warned of the futility of wealth, "enough money" remains the elusive Holy Grail of many.

Often inherited wealth, granted without discipline, unearned except by birthright, leaves a person crippled emotionally or intellectually. Michael Crichton expressed this idea in *Jurassic Park* in a monologue of the fictional scientist Ian Malcolm:

> "I will tell you what I am talking about," he said. "Most kinds of power require a substantial sacrifice by whoever wants the power. There is an apprenticeship, a discipline lasting many years. Whatever kind of power you want. President of the company. Black belt in karate. Spiritual guru. Whatever it is you seek, you have to put in the time, the practice, the effort. You must give up a lot to get it. It has to be very important to you. And once you have attained it, it is your power. It can't be given away: it resides in you. It is literally the result of your discipline.
>
> "Now, what is interesting about this process is that, by the time someone has acquired the ability to kill with his bare hands, he has also matured to the point where he won't use it unwisely. So that kind of power has built-in control. The discipline of getting the power changes you so that you won't abuse it.
>
> "But scientific power is like inherited wealth: attained without discipline."

This lack of discipline has differentiated many dilettante heirs from successful investors and entrepreneurs. Heirs all too often develop a distorted sense of themselves and others, not having experienced the effort, cultivated the relationships, or attained the leadership associated with achieving the wealth firsthand.

Distorted perception is not the only shortcoming of wealth. Others have warned of the inability of money to satisfy the most basic of human desires—love. The Beatles express the sentiment in "Can't Buy Me Love" and Bruce Springsteen sings about it in "Ain't Got You." Money, they warn, is not the answer to a satisfying life.

But it could obviously provide you with some of the comforts on the way. As attributed to J. P. Morgan, "Money, young man, is good for the nerves." It would be foolish to suggest that in today's society there are no benefits to having money. Money can bring comfort, opportunity, and power. For the right price, fine dining, fast cars, and exquisite service await. Even legal and health care delivery are affected by wealth. In fact, control of the flow of capital provides the ability to affect industry, create opportunity for others, and better the community. And it certainly may help you to achieve your personal goals.

But beware, the stream of control between you and money flows both ways. Should the day come when the money controls you, all the benefits of wealth are soon washed away.

Some heirs resent their wealth. Having already won the game society scores with wealth, they feel they have nothing left to compete or strive for. In *The Fountainhead*, Ayn Rand describes this phenomenon best through the monologue of a fictional wealthy New York heir, Mitch Layton, who attacks the publisher of a newspaper empire on whose board Mitch sits:

> . . . I come to a meeting of stockholders and he treats us like flunkies. Isn't my money as good as his? Don't I own a hunk of his damn paper? I could teach him a thing or two about journalism. I have ideas. What's he so damn arrogant about? Just because he made that fortune himself? Does he have to be such a damn snob just because he came from Hell's Kitchen? It isn't other people's fault if they weren't lucky enough to be born in Hell's Kitchen to rise out of! Nobody understands what a terrible handicap it is to be born rich. Because people just take for granted that because you were born that way you'd just be no good if you weren't. What I mean is if I'd had [his] breaks, I'd be twice as rich as he is by now and three times as famous. But he's so conceited he doesn't realize this at all!

This warped perspective can arise from insecurity common among young heirs. They judge themselves, as others do, by wealth, and yet they never truly feel it is their own. Karl Marx argued that because they did not share in the creation of the wealth, a sense of alienation accompanies the wealth. With wealth as the prime measure of accomplishment, they can find no basis for an unbiased evaluation of their own self-worth. Whether it tends to bring happiness or despair, money, a mere material object, has its limits. As Henry David Thoreau observed, "Superfluous wealth can buy superfluities only. Money is not required to buy one necessity of the soul." Your wealth may give you the time to paint, but it will not make you a great painter.

PSYCHOLOGICAL PITFALLS

Heirs have historically been thought to deal with their wealth as do princes, in luxurious enjoyment. But recent research has focused on the negative psychological effects associated with inheriting substantial sums of money. Although responses vary with each case, you are better prepared for your own inheritance if you are aware of the psychological responses common to many of the heirs.

Regret

A common response among first-generation heirs of entrepreneurial wealth is regret—regret that the parent creating the business focused so much on monetary issues and not enough on life. These heirs often wish that they had been given at least a portion of the value of their inheritance in the form of attention and wisdom. This response is particularly acute where families have defined themselves by their wealth.

Immaturity

In families with more than one child, inheriting wealth almost inevitably involves settling outstanding emotional and family positional issues along with settling the wealth. Unfortunately, many families with high net worth suffer from various disfunctionalities that compound this emotionally fraught period. The problem is that in such wealthy families, the money is frequently substituted for expressions of love or achievement as the token of exchange.

In some cases, the expectation and fact of substantial inheritance results in delayed (sometimes permanently) emotional development. In others, money insulates heirs from many of life's challenges and everyday problems, but consequently inhibits their full growth as personalities. For this reason, some heirs act as though they are four even when they are forty-year-old private investors.

Some second generation inheritors—faced with a seemingly limitless number of options when money is not a constraint—may also have difficulties with self-discipline. Although they may never face the need to choose a career path, self-discipline is necessary not only for work, but also for building significant relationships.

Boredom

Inheritors also often experience boredom. They miss seeing real-life challenges because wealth brings so many available options. In fact, the same challenges facing others also face the heirs. The difference is that the heirs may have more immediate resources available to meet those challenges or seek new ones.

The other reaction to the flood of decisions suddenly available to new heirs is paralysis, the inability to make life choices because of the multitude of options. Heirs find themselves unable to plan a career or even a weekend because decisions seem impossible in the face of so many options.

In reality, plans must be made the same way they were made before the inheritance, hopefully with added creativity. Now more of the plans you make may be realistic, but time, if not money, limits us all, even the wealthy.

Authoritarianism

Some heirs unknowingly develop a distorted view of their own power and an exaggerated self-esteem, basing their relationships with other people on the experience they might have had with servants or the deference afforded to their families when they were younger because they were rich. These habits, in turn, result in the heir having problems with the use of power. With the positional power afforded in our society to those with wealth, heirs too often become petty tyrants without realizing it. Like celebrities, rich people rarely hear the truth from others.

As expressed by Michael Crichton, when heirs receive wealth without the discipline ordinarily required to create it, situations arise where personalities have power, in the form of wealth, but lack the personal power and control to exercise it wisely.

It is important to recognize that money alone will not gain you true respect. If you do acquire power through your inherited wealth, remember that although money may afford control over others, people, in the end, respond to people.

Paranoia

The attention often afforded to wealth makes some heirs feel at once guilty and paranoid. Since they are so often the targets of others' material desires, relationships become difficult to establish because of feelings of mistrust. In addition, women inheritors may face other problems, from the difficulty of finding a suitable mate to the fact that they are left out of family business and investment decision making. These feelings often accompany and exaggerate the other negative emotions facing the heirs.

This fear may be overcome by maintaining control over your wealth. If you do not flaunt your wealth or make it a defining characteristic of yourself, then people will more likely respond to you rather than your money. In this sense, paranoia about your highly visible wealth may be a self-fulfilling prophecy.

Inadequacy

Autonomy and identity are often hard to establish and maintain when a family has so defined itself by its wealth, rather than by its accomplishments. Studies show that among the wealthy, self-esteem is often inadequate. Inheritors often fear failure, especially in the area of vocation, since they've never been forced to earn their own living and don't really know whether they could.

Where so much emphasis is put on money, it becomes the only measure of worth. And there is always someone more worthy because there is always someone more wealthy.

AWARENESS ENABLES AVOIDANCE

While these experiences are drawn primarily from the very wealthy, even more modest inheritors will experience some of these feelings, especially in a society where poverty and hopelessness abound.

Though hopefully not all new heirs will be overcome by temptation or experience all of the above problems (especially since the amounts most inherit will be modest compared to great third or fourth generation fortunes), the problems that wealthy inheritors experience could color your relationship to your inheritance and to others.

The happiness and despair borne by wealth have been well documented. The polarity of possible outcomes makes clear that the money itself is not the determining factor. Rather, your attitude and the fullness of your being will define the effects of your inheritance on your life.

2

---○---

FAMILY MATTERS

The Inheritors, The Movie

Act I, Scene 1

INT.—KITCHEN—1958—CHRISTMAS

[Fade in:]

[JOAN runs to kiss FATHER hello while STEVE tries to cover up his report card.]

> FATHER
>
> Hi, honey pie, straight A's again?

[He reaches into his pocket with one hand.]

> FATHER
>
> [Cont.]
>
> Steve?

[Steve reluctantly hands over his report card, hangs in the doorway. Father hands Joan two dollars as he studies Steve's grades. He tucks his wallet back into his pocket.]

> FATHER
>
> [Cont.]
>
> Well, at least you got one B—in P.E.

[CUT TO:]

INT.—PARENTS' HOUSE—PRESENT

[Dressed in black, Steve and Joan sit at the kitchen table, holding copies of their dad's will.]

STEVE

Why am I surprised he left you the house and stocks and me the Mercedes and his library? He was always shelling out dollars to you.

JOAN

I earned that money. Besides, I can't help it if I was a better student.

STEVE

It doesn't take a genius to see he always favored you—about four times as much.

[He holds up the will.]

JOAN

Steve, he knew you love collecting—you can't place a value on that.

[Steve throws the will on the table, rises.]

STEVE

Excuse me. I've got to get started boxing up my inheritance—two hundred old *National Geographics*.

[FADE OUT.]

The nonfiction reality is that death often catches us by surprise. The grieving heirs are often called upon to confront one another around property issues, discussions of which all too often substitute for much-needed, healthy grieving, and as a result, conflict ensues.

Whatever the previous family dynamic, roles are written large at death. In families that dealt poorly with conflict when the parent was alive, property struggles often break out. One family fought over a used toaster at a will reading. In another, a father had his contentious children flip coins for every object of personal property, from used clothes to antique furniture, that any of them wanted.

No matter the financial position of the family—from working class to wealthy—the control of money represents power and control within the family. In that respect, the family mirrors society. In some families, this power and control may be shared in a model of functional family management. In others, money is mistakenly substituted for love, leading to disfunctionalities and miscommunications.

The level of family trust will also govern the extent to which the family is able to cope with preparing in advance for the death of a parent. Parents who maturely face the fact that life on earth is limited and set about to square up their financial affairs leave their children in a better financial position than parents who deny their own mortality and delay settling their affairs.

The ideal model involves a parent who is willing to discuss estate plans openly, including children in their thinking. Two-thirds of parents surveyed said that they already discussed their wills with their children or meant to. If children are allowed to give their points of view directly to their parents while parents are still alive, parents are empowering children to carry on as the next generation in the family. According to one survey of potential heirs, 58 percent thought prior knowledge of an inheritance's detail would avoid conflict and controversy later.

But inheritance often replicates lifetime family patterns of dealing with money. Financial secrets represent financial control. In families where children have learned only the minimum about family finances, aging parents aren't likely to suddenly become spouting sources of information as they approach death.

In fact, one reason so many people die *intestate*, without any will or estate plan, is their inability or unwillingness to face up to their own mortality. In addition, as long as a parent can dangle the possibility of "prospects," the parent can keep the child's attention. As middle-aged people struggle with their own often precarious existences and face coping with the demands of aging parents, sometimes, it's sad to say, parents feel that only the prospect of getting their money keeps the kids coming home.

By contrast, there is an implicit, though not often articulated, promise between generations that if the younger generation cares for the older one, then the younger generation can expect to inherit. Unfortunately, as marriage and family life have eroded, introducing second and even third spouses, new parameters must be considered. Studies show that most people plan to leave the bulk of their estate to their spouses; if a parent has remarried, children often fear being left out in the cold.

Families can approach intergenerational issues proactively, sitting down and sharing the details so that there are no surprises after the funeral.

Or, they can follow the movie script model, where in addition to death, property arrangements are a grab-bag of surprises, often unpleasant.

PROACTIVE FAMILY ESTATE PLANNING

PARENTAL WILLINGNESS TO DISCUSS THEIR PLANS

A fundamental issue that must be addressed is how to get a family to talk about death and property. While some families do it by the book, sitting down and tackling the tough issues involved in discussing mortality and the succession of generations, don't be surprised if your request to talk about your parents' estate plans (or even their estate) is met with stony silence or even anger.

While everyone knows that they will eventually die, most want to put off thinking about the specifics of time. How often have you heard the phrase, "If I should die"?—as if there were an alternative!

Preparing an estate plan confronts even the most practical and worldly adults with teary-eyed issues. Parents have been known to shudder at the thought of their otherwise capable and respected children taking over the family business.

So, while the ideal scenario involves a rational discussion of key issues—the location of the will, the choice of executor, the

designation of beneficiaries, and the preparation of a tax plan—
the reality is often different. You may have to be satisfied with
knowing little or nothing of your parents' plans. Or, at best, bits
and pieces may emerge over the years as you visit other family
graves or discuss the deaths of family members.

By contrast, older people increasingly share their thoughts
about taking extraordinary life-saving measures in the event of lingering illness. Because of modern medical technology and the
specter of lingering indefinitely, the preparation of living wills or
other instructions regarding medical decisions has become commonplace. Alumni associations, church groups, and community
hospitals hold how-to seminars that help individuals to commit
their wishes regarding life support and other medical decisions to
legally binding instructions in the form of both durable powers of
attorney and living wills.

Even though your parents may resist discussing the money
and executor portions of their estate wishes, you may find them
more receptive if you express your concern about their well-being
in the end. But don't press these delicate issues or use health issues as a wedge to open the estate discussion. Often, as people approach death or sense that their time is passing, they will
undertake preparing their estate plans, a most private and personal activity. They may not necessarily want to discuss these
plans with their children.

One estate recipient shared her experience:

> My own mother loved life too much to relish planning for
> her end. But after losing two brothers, she was motivated to put
> her affairs in order. When Mama died, she managed to go in
> style. She hadn't done everything by the book, but she had
> taken sufficient steps so that her children could manage closing
> her affairs.
>
> California allows holographic, or completely handwritten,
> wills. Mother took great care to prepare a properly drawn holo-

graphic will, complete with the disposition of most of her property. In retrospect, I realized that she had been preparing her estate plan for about two years, as her many questions about family heirlooms suggested. She had subtly established who wanted what, then made sure her plans fairly distributed the various items. Whenever she wasn't sure, especially about more modern objects, she had instructions such as: "Children, draw straws for my television."

This case illustrates the privacy that some caring parents feel they need to have to go in peace. The case also shows that a mother's concern for equity among her children becomes evident to all concerned. Even though the estate was small, each child felt included.

In traditional families, the father controlled the family finances. For many baby boomers, Robert Young's family in *Father Knows Best* was the archetype. *Bonanza*, where the mother had disappeared and a loving but authoritarian father was in complete control, presented the artistic extreme. The Bradys were the *Father Knows Best* for the 1970s, giving the children of divorce a fantasy family to focus on. *The Brady Bunch* featured the wife, Carol, shopping with the maid, Alice, while the father was off at work.

While we want to avoid stereotyping sex roles in the family, baby boomers, depending upon their ages, have grown up with images of lifestyles that have long since disappeared. But these images play into the behavior of parents planning their estates. Robert Young, who changed into his smoking jacket from his suit jacket when he arrived home each night, would hardly sit down and discuss the disposition of his bank account with his three children, even though he was forthcoming on other issues. The Brady Bunch didn't spend much time talking about family money.

But the baby boom generation spanned the birth of the women's movement and upheaval of the 1960s. Family roles and expectations have completely changed. So it's not surprising that the generation primarily passing the estates is applying values that clash with those of the generation primarily receiving the estates. A typical situation involves a taciturn father holding back financial information, which the children unsuccessfully try to elicit from time to time. One client told of walking over land that had been in the family since just after the Civil War, trying to find out what her father's plans for the place were. All she could learn from this conversation was that the father hoped he could preserve a particular forty-acre lot that held much family sentimental value for the four children. Later, in a separate conversation, she learned that her father planned to leave all his money to his second wife. When the daughter suggested leaving a life estate so that the land could be preserved for his children after his second wife's death, the father stopped discussing the topic. At yet another date, when his executor had a heart attack, the father admitted that he was considering changing executors. But he wouldn't reveal who the new executor was to be. The daughter asked, "Who should we call to locate your will, then?" Stony silence was the only response.

By contrast, another family openly discussed its land. In particular, the Gibsons readily talked about their concern with keeping the family farm intact in the face of estate taxes. The land had been in the family for one hundred years, and the entire Gibson family worked together to establish plans that would provide a large enough piece of land to keep the ranching operation intact.

The older generation of Gibsons had thus openly faced the challenge together with the younger generation. Conversely, in the former, noncommunicative family, property control had always been a tightly held source of family control. The daughter remembered her eighty-five-year-old grandmother driving across her lands, pointing them out, boundary marks and all. On the topic of inheritance, the only subject that was specifically discussed was who would get the heirloom quilts.

Experiencing the death of a parent can be somewhat less traumatic if you've prepared for the financial and legal obligations you'll assume. If you are unable to talk about these questions with your parents, at least familiarize yourself with the steps of the estate closure process in advance so that it all doesn't come as a mystery complicating an already difficult period of loss.

Below are some types of reactive estate receipts you may encounter or prevent.

REACTIVE ESTATE RECEIPTS

CONTROL BY FAMILY MALES

In families with several children, men have historically dominated family business affairs. Although women's roles have changed in many areas of life, women still are playing financial catch-up. Women also have tended not to be as familiar with the fine points of financial strategy as men, so when the going gets tough, men tend to assume control. Even after he died, the traditional male made sure that his money was in good hands by leaving everything in trust for his wife, specifically (and intentionally) with bank trust departments run by men.

While attitudes about women's roles in the workplace have helped change attitudes about women's roles in the family, gender conflict is likely to emerge in times of family stress, including during the estate process.

SIBLING RIVALRY

In a family with more than one child, inheritance often involves settling outstanding emotional issues along with settling the property. This case is particularly acute with high-net-worth families in which money is frequently substituted for expressions of love.

Although rivalry among siblings is normal, the receipt or potential receipt of money is likely to heighten the antagonism. For example, in one family, two brothers, John and Anthony Jones, were co-beneficiaries of a trust fund that gave them discretionary income for life, with the remainder to be distributed to their children. The older brother, John, had no children, but his younger brother, Anthony, who had two children, pressed the trust department not to distribute any income to the current generation. If the trust department followed Anthony's instructions, the trust would grow for the benefit of his children at the expense of his brother.

The Mitchells, who run a family business, have three children, Aron, Bernice, and Carol. Aron had married into a family with a business of their own and had become involved there. Carol had shown she was not management material. With her MBA, Bernice was the logical heir to the family business. Even though Carol had no realistic hope of running a successful business, she became resentful when faced with the reality that she would be cut out of active management, while Bernice would run the company.

THE SURVIVING SPOUSE

In most marriages, one spouse will predecease the other, leaving questions about how to manage the estate that's been planned together and left to one.

Facing bereavement and building a new life, sometimes after nursing the spouse through a long illness, is difficult enough. Added to that burden, dealing with financial issues can be especially intimidating to women of the past generation. Many women whose major adult years were spent in single-earner marriages will now face managing substantial estates during the period from the death of their husbands until they die. The skills for such an endeavor don't appear overnight, yet these women are among the new heirs.

Nothing can fully prepare you for the shock of your spouse's death. Worse still, widows of entrepreneurs are often expected to rise to the challenge of taking the helm of a company or protecting the family's interest at the worst possible time. In one case, a woman was left battling with embittered business partners, each vying for control of her husband's clothing company. While fighting among themselves for managerial control, all were united on one front: attempting to undervalue the interest of the deceased partner to their mutual gain. The widow was sufficiently astute to hire an attorney to protect her interest and finally won a drawn-out lawsuit that divided the company's assets. In another case, the widow was forced to make critical decisions about her husband's car service company left to her. Instincts eventually proved correct, but there were losses in the interim.

One way to reduce these risks is to stay informed about your spouse's business. Another is to be educated about financial matters. The requisite money management information to help you face these tasks is here in this book, and other reading can be found in the sources section at the end of the book.

Another task may also await you as a surviving spouse: contending with middle-aged children whose own expectations often don't match their material prospects. As the older generation's savings have begun to shrink—many attributing this change to the consumption of the savings for medical needs and the expenses of longer lives—children watch their presumed inheritances dwindle.

This situation is bound to create tension between the generations. It is the job of the surviving spouse to protect herself or himself first, preserving the hard-won life savings so that funds will not run short. As pressing as the needs of the younger generation seem—whether they are private schools for the grandchildren in today's tough urban environments or down payments for homes never bought—unless ample funds are available to the surviving spouse, he or she must be very conservative in sharing wealth. Unfortunately, the sad but true case is that the children may not have money should you need it, and worse yet, if they have it, you may not be able to count on them to share.

On the other hand, if anticipated nursing-home expenses will eradicate your hard-won savings, you may want to create an irrevocable trust or gift-giving program to ensure that at least a portion of your savings are enjoyed by your children. Consult a professional for further advice in this area.

FAMILY BUSINESSES

When family businesses are involved, more than jealousy and bereavement can enter the picture. From the smallest companies to major financial empires, sustaining the family business after the death of the first or second generation often proves impossible.

The Bingham family press empire, widely reported in the media, provides a case in point. As the aging parents turned over control to their children, the "boys" in the family were given executive positions in the family string of newspapers, valued at over $300 million. The "girls" were given allowances. One of the daughters decided that she wanted more control or she wanted out. Sally Bingham's decision, in the face of recalcitrant male siblings, eventually led to the breakup of the media empire. In forcing the family to sell the newspapers, Sally Bingham was taking the only step left open to her. All other avenues for gaining control of her own money, in her opinion, had been closed by her family members.

In another case, a manufacturing family with two children gave their son, the younger child, the important responsibility of functioning as president of the firm. The older child, the daughter, even though better educated and with a much firmer grasp of finances, essentially functioned only as her father's assistant. When the parent died, the son's lack of business savvy spelled the end of the family business.

STEPPARENTS

With the increase in second and third marriages, a major problem facing families occurs when children come into conflict with stepparents. When the family nest egg has been built up by the original couple, one set of children is bound to feel deprived when they see their mother or father's money left to the stepparent rather than themselves. Even if the second husband or wife is only given lifetime rights to the property in the form of a life estate, children realize they may never see any inheritance if the provisions allow for discretionary use of all the funds. If expensive medical costs are incurred or if a stepparent lives it up, children may be left nothing of either parent's assets.

This specter has been all too real in several celebrated cases. Pamela Churchill Harriman was sued by her stepchildren in a multimillion-dollar lawsuit over her management of the trust left by her wealthy husband.

PARENTAL MISTRUST

Not all children turn out according to parental expectations. From long experience the parents have learned that their children are not financially responsible. Or, in other cases, well-meaning parents create will or trust provisions that effectively limit their children's options. In either case, these arrangements reflect parental mistrust of the children they have raised. Listed below are some tools that parents have used.

Spendthrift Trusts

Spendthrift trusts are designed to limit access to children's inheritances by placing them off-limits to creditors. In this scenario, funds are left in a trust with the specific provision that no debts can be paid from the income or corpus of the trust. While the spendthrift trust provides income to the beneficiary each year, the beneficiary's creditors cannot attach the property, but can take income. The beneficiary cannot receive any more than the annual income allowance.

Silver Strings

In other cases, parents bind their children with silver strings long after their deaths. Without tax or other incentives, leaving funds in trust for healthy mature adults is tantamount to keeping them as emotional and financial dependents for their lifetimes. Their message is clearly "We want you to have the money, but with conditions." These conditions include whatever the trust provides. For example, a standard of living might be specified and limited. A trust might cease to distribute income if a child is engaged in certain unacceptable career choices. Or, the trust might only pay for certain items, such as education or medical expenses, leaving heirs to characterize travel cruises as "education" and personal trainers as "medical expenses."

Family Legacies

Without believing in ghosts, we can still see the effect of the dead long after their last breath. With the disposition of property, the deceased impose their values and affect lives for generations to come.

Popular literature has often traced the influence of families on protagonists, and psychoanalysis has centered on conscious recognition and rejection of these influences. Who can forget Scarlett O'Hara calling for her mother years after her death, or the echoes of her father, "Land is the only thing in the world that amounts to anything . . . for 'tis the only thing in this world that lasts."

When powerful figures die, those left living are often cast adrift. Suppressed feelings may surface after death, adding to the emotional confusion, especially if there was unsettled business between parent and child.

The question of the disposition of material possessions adds fuel to the flame. When these possessions have been used as surrogates for expressed love and approval, their disposition can deeply affect the heirs.

On a *policy* level, our world is controlled by the living (for example, wills requiring marriage to inherit have been ruled as against public policy); but on an *emotional* level, reconciling the death and the disposition often challenge even the most emotionally mature.

GREAT EXPECTATIONS

A principal feature of inheritance is that there are legally no heirs until someone dies. Potential heirs only have *expectancy*. Unless the will-maker is mentally incompetent, a valid will can be changed many times. The dissonance between expectancy and actuality gives rise to many post-death traumas, not to mention celebrated court cases, most often where children are "disinherited" by an intervening third party, usually a second wife or husband or a charity.

Generally speaking, a person can dispose of her or his wealth however they wish. (Two exceptions concern spouses and children born after the will was made.) Yet, disappointed heirs apparent continue to seek relief in the courts. Three highly visible cases illustrate the gap between expectations and will-makers' choices.

In 1986, five of the six children of J. Steward Johnson, of Johnson & Johnson, the pharmaceutical firm, were omitted from their father's will, which left his $500-million estate to his former nurse, whom he married. The children sued, charging undue influence on the part of the nurse, but Mrs. Barbara Johnson prevailed.

In another celebrated case, the four stepchildren of Virginia Kraft Payson battled her over control of the late Charles Shipman Payson's $70 million estate. His estate had been inherited from his wife, Joan Whitney, whose financier father Payne Whitney had left her half of his $194 million estate. Joan had launched the New York Mets in 1962, had five children, and died in 1975, leaving $7.5 million in trust for each living child and the rest of her $100 million estate to her husband. When Charles died, his will left everything (except the trusts) to his second wife Virginia. After a thirteen-week trial in 1986, a jury sided with Virginia. The children decided not to appeal, but planned to lobby for a law that ensures children their "right" to inherit. In fact, surveys show that most Americans plan to leave everything to their spouses. Children's rights of inheritance are primarily limited to certain technical circumstances when there is a will to the contrary.

In another publicized tale of greed, Anne Catherine Getty, granddaughter to Jean Paul Getty, the oil billionaire who died in 1976, sued to overturn the twenty-first codicil to his will. Previously the will had left the residue or remainder of his estate to a trust, after specific bequests including twelve to women with whom he had been romantically linked. The income of the trust was to go to the Getty museum in Los Angeles. The twenty-first and last codicil eliminated the trust under the will as recipient of the residue of his estate and left the museum as the direct beneficiary. Anne Getty, a potential trustee under the pre-twenty-first codicils, sued to invalidate the twenty-first on the grounds of lack of mental capacity. Her motive was the desire to serve as a trustee for the $700 million legacy and receive associated trustee fees. Anne Getty lost because the court found she did not have standing (the legal ability) to sue; however, the case does illustrate the lengths to which family members will go when substantial sums of money are involved. Jesse Dukeminier, in his classic textbook on wills, trusts, and estates, notes:

> In this book we deal with people, the quick as well as the dead. There is nothing like the death of a moneyed member of the family to show persons as they really are, virtuous or conniving, generous or grasping. Many a family has been torn apart by a botched-up will. Each case is a drama in human relationships.

Ambrose Bierce reputedly observed, "Death is not the end; there remains the litigation." This maxim represents the exception, not the rule. The media and even the law professors tend to focus on the exceptional, the unusual rather than the ordinary course of events. But for most families the reality of a death in the family is often far less dramatic than the media images of celebrated cases. Unless you have experienced a death, your images may be of high drama rather than the predominant feeling of numb grief. What drama there is tends to be petty, unless you are dealing with a young person dying unexpectedly or the extraordinary wealth illustrated in the above examples. Family members with time on their hands awaiting funerals notoriously choose that time to pick fights. Or, they divert their time focusing on the details of the funeral.

In any case, once the funeral is over and visiting relatives have returned home, the long process of closing the deceased's affairs begins.

Steps to Follow When a Close Relative Dies

1. Determine funeral, memorial service, and burial or cremation wishes.
2. Notify the newspapers and/or call friends to let them know

the details of the service and whether flowers or donations to a favorite charity are preferred by the family.

3. Establish whether burial insurance or a burial policy through a particular funeral home exists. If so, try to learn what provisions it contains before the final funeral instructions are given to the mortuary. For example, some policies pay for one type of casket but not another.

4. If the deceased served in the military, determine whether any military honors are desired. Veterans Affairs (V.A.) provides for a flag, which covers the coffin during the burial service (and is then given to the family). The funeral director will obtain the flag, if the family so wishes. Limited burial and plot allowances also apply for those receiving V.A. compensation. A $300 burial benefit plus a $150 plot allowance is available if the deceased is buried in other than a state or national cemetery. For those with service-related disabilities or who died during active duty, the amount is $1,500. State and national cemetery burial is available to any honorably discharged veteran, depending upon availability. For more information, call the V.A. at 800/827-1000.

5. Social security pays a one-time $255 allowance to the spouse or minor children of the deceased who are living with the deceased at the time of death. For more information, call the Social Security Administration at 800/772-1213.

6. If there are no burial benefits or insurance, remember that someone from the family will have to pay in cash or by credit card before the final ceremony. To an already grieving family, several thousand dollars for unanticipated funeral costs can add a weighty burden, especially if out-of-state travel is also involved.

7. Take time to deal with your own grief and to visit with family members, especially those that have traveled from distant locations, before addressing the details of the estate.

8. Locate the will or family trust document, especially if burial instructions are not found. But do not try to cope with all the provisions of the will before the funeral.

9. Explain to the likely heirs that the will review or reading will take place after the funeral and that copies will be provided for those under time pressure to leave.

10. Insist that an inventory be taken before any personal effects are removed from the home of the deceased. Especially where a family has jewelry and other valuable objects in the home, would-be heirs have a tendency to snatch items that they have coveted. Or, more positively, items of sentimental significance may be carted off by grieving relatives. Bottom line: Neither behavior is acceptable. Many items will have been enumerated in the will, and family schisms created by hasty actions during a funeral will haunt a family for years.

11. Make sure to receive an ample supply of certified death certificates from the funeral home and put the original, if any, in a secure location. The certificate will be required for many aspects of closing the estate, from selling an automobile to deferring payment of the decedent's debts.

12. Identify the executor or executrix (i.e., personal representative of the deceased after death) named in the will and/or the trustee of any living trust, to commence any probate or other administration and assure that the decedent's wishes are carried out.

13. Be sure the executor or trustee handles all outstanding mortgages and other debts. Do not pay off credit cards and other debts from your own funds. First, beneficiaries are not responsible for such debts, and should the debts exceed the assets, the creditor must cancel the debt. Second, the estate is taxed on net assets. To the extent you reduce debts from nonestate funds, you will lose the benefit of the deduction and increase the taxes.

14. Don't expect the estate to be settled quickly. *Do not commit funds you haven't yet received.* For example, do not use an anticipated inheritance to purchase a home by signing a purchase contract because you might not have the required money at closing.

15. Give yourself time. Don't do anything rash in the first year after a parent's death. In one case, an heiress became engaged twice, fired all her advisors, and took over the management of her complex affairs in the year when she should have mourned her parental loss and kept a less stressful schedule.

Although these problems are most acute in wealthy families, every heir is challenged by the pitfalls of inheritance. By recognizing the potentially damaging effects of an inheritance, you and your family are better prepared to maximize the benefits of your gifts.

Whatever the dynamics, pre- or post-death, the point inevitably comes when the family must face the loss of a parent or one spouse the loss of the other. As Publius Syrus said many centuries ago, "Anyone can hold the helm when the sea is calm." Your challenge—and that of your family—is to survive the transition in as calm and orderly a fashion as possible, hopefully with family goodwill intact.

3

---○---

ACCEPTING THE
INHERITANCE

GETTING YOUR INHERITANCE is much more complicated than withdrawing the cash from an ATM machine. Rooted in tradition and state law, the estate transfer process involves many legal and procedural formalities that can serve as both safeguards and obstacles for new heirs. Aside from dealing with your family, you are likely to encounter executors, accountants, lawyers, and even bankers.

Unfortunately, too many people die without making plans. *Sixty percent* of all adults in the U.S. die without a will. Unless there are will substitutes in place, these estates transfer in accordance with state intestacy laws, which vary by state and generally provide for the order of inheritance among the closest living relatives. In this instance, usually the heirs know who they are; in the extreme case, if no relatives qualified to take under the state intestacy laws are found, the estate passes to the state treasury. Moderate and larger estates are more likely to be distributed according to a formal estate plan prepared by the deceased. Both tax considerations and the desire to protect relatives usually drive people to make estate plans, but even loving and otherwise efficient people find it hard to formalize their own demise on paper.

First we'll discuss the usual case of intestacy, the norm for 60 percent of the population. Then we'll talk about the "unusual" case, the parent or relative who dies with an estate plan—wills and nonprobate transfers—in place.

The rising use of living trusts and other will substitutes has made probate avoidance and the elimination of its corresponding formalities, delays, and fees, more commonplace among those heirs benefiting from a formal estate plan. But one billion dollars still pass through the probate process each year.

WHAT ACTUALLY HAPPENS AFTER THE FUNERAL?

Once you have dealt with the funeral, the first thing that needs to be determined, if you don't know already, is how your parent or relative left his or her affairs. The older and richer a person is, the greater the likelihood of a will. Most people have trouble coming to grips with their own mortality and the formalities of the legal system, both out of fear and expense. So don't be surprised if your otherwise well-organized parent had a less-than-perfect estate plan.

No matter what arrangements you encounter, the brief sketch below should prepare you for what's ahead. The stresses will be reduced if you, as a new heir, understand the process you are about to go through. That process will be determined by a mix of three key factors:

• The *document or other legal framework*, such as property ownership or intestacy;

• The *size* of the estate, which affects both the probate process and the tax position; and

• The *state law* that governs. For property held in more than one state, special rules apply, and each state has different rules.

THE USUAL CASE: INTESTACY

If your relative falls into the intestate category, you'll need to determine the provisions of your state law by talking to an attor-

ney or referring to another knowledgeable source, such as your
state attorney general's office. These provisions, called intestacy
laws, will determine who will inherit. In general, one third to one
half of the estate will go to the surviving spouse, with the rest
being divided equally among the children.

When the family tree includes a child who predeceased the
parent, the states differ in how the estate gets distributed. In some
states, the grandchildren each share their parent's portion of the
estate only (*per stirpes*). In others, the inheritance is distributed
equally according to the number of surviving direct descendants
of the deceased, regardless if they are children, grandchildren or
great-grandchildren (*per capita*). Still other states follow a modification known as *per capita by each generation*.

Let's take an example to understand the distinction. (Be
warned: Legal examples tend to be as confusing as the concept is
complex.)

Aaron dies intestate. He had three children, Bolton, Erin, and
Hugh, and five grandchildren, Chris, Dean, Fran, Ilene, and
Joseph. Graphically, the family tree looks like this:

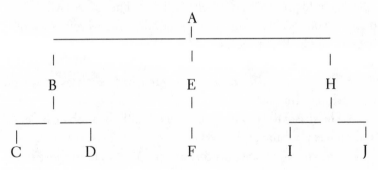

If we assume Aaron had outlived Bolton, Erin, and his wife,
but everyone else was living at Aaron's death, then Chris, Dean,
Fran, and Hugh would inherit Aaron's estate under state intestacy
statutes as follows:

	Chris	Dean	Fran	Hugh
Per capita	1/4	1/4	1/4	1/4
Per stirpes	1/6	1/6	1/3	1/3
Per capita at each generation	2/9	2/9	2/9	1/3

Where no spouse or children are living, the inheritance is determined according to a complex network of familial relations. You could be first in line to inherit from your great uncle, depending upon the laws of the state he lived in and the number of, and genealogical distance between, relatives still alive. Had he lived in another state you might receive nothing.

Depending on the size of the estate involved and your relation to the decedent, you may wish to consult local counsel to determine whether or not you have a valid claim to the property. Unless you stay in touch with your family, you may not even know of a potential inheritance. The administrator must make every effort to find known heirs, but it pays to stay in touch!

In certain cases, otherwise qualified persons under the intestacy laws will be disinherited. These include potential recipients that the state deems "unworthy," such as "killer benes" (those who killed their benefactors) and parents who have abandoned their minor children.

A person can also voluntarily disqualify himself or herself. For example, a child may release a parent from inheritance rights by taking a gift during the parent's lifetime and signing a document that provides for such a release. Or, as far-fetched as it may seem to many of us, a person can actually *disclaim* or formally refuse to take an inheritance.

A disclaimer is typically made to avoid creditors threatening to levy (or take) the inheritance or to achieve certain tax savings. Under most estate plans and most state intestacy laws, the intended beneficiary's children take the inheritance in the place of the disclaiming beneficiary, preventing the intended beneficiary's creditors from reaching the gift. If you are thinking about disclaiming, be aware that each state has formal requirements to make an effective disclaimer, so consult local counsel.

Timelines: Deadlines to Watch

Although the executor is ultimately responsible for meeting the required deadlines on behalf of the estate, you should be aware of the various timelines involved in the estate transfer process.

1. Entering the will for probate: Varies state by state. Some estates are passed entirely outside of probate, other estates are held up in probate court for years.

2. Listing the estate contents: Generally, ninety days after death.

3. Federal tax return: Nine months after death (if the estate is over $600,000; no return required if the estate is under $600,000).

4. Disclaimer: Usually nine months after death.

5. Contesting the will: Varies state by state.

THE UNUSUAL SCENARIO: SUCCESSION BY WILL

The first document you will need after a parent or relative dies is the will or living trust document. If you find a will, once it's read (and it may never be read aloud), a number of steps will invariably follow.

Probate

Shortly after the funeral, and within the framework provided by state law, the will is normally admitted to a probate court, a special court designed to deal exclusively with estates.

The will names the *executor* (or another person in charge of carrying out the details of the will and property disbursement) who is ultimately responsible for filing the appropriate legal paperwork. Within ninety days in most jurisdictions, the executor must file an inventory and appraisal of all assets with the probate court. The list must account for everything from jewelry to bank deposits.

Executors, Administrators, Personal Representatives, and Trustees

Unless you act as the executor, you will have to deal with the executor (a person appointed by a testator to carry out the directions and requests in his or her will), *administrator* (a person appointed by the court to manage the assets and liabilities of a decedent), *personal representative* (either executor or administrator), and/or *trustee* (a person appointed to control the investment and distribution of a trust) during the settlement period.

These functions can be carried out by either individuals or institutions, such as banks. If you do not already know the executor or the bank's representatives, get to know them. While these people have a strict fiduciary duty to execute the terms of the will or trust, if you get on their wrong side they'll make life tougher for you. If you don't like the will, don't take your frustration out on the executor. You may need his or her help. For example, if you are out of money and the estate is likely to have adequate funds, the executor can apply to the probate court to release some funds through probate. Depending on the state, the executor can provide for the family without seeking court approval and preliminary distributions are possible if the estate is solvent.

Fees

The executor receives fees or "reasonable compensation," usually set by state law. The average amounts vary significantly by state (see Table 3-1).

TABLE 3-1: SAMPLE EXECUTOR FEES

State	Estate of $500,000	$5 Million
California	11,150	61,150*
New Jersey	20,500	118,000*
New York	19,000	134,000
Ohio	15,000	105,000*
Texas	5% of cash disbursements and receipts	

*May be raised by probate court.
Source: Frum, David, "How to Die Cheap," Forbes, June 21, 1993, pp. 164–165.

When You Are the Executor

While it may save fees for you or another family member to serve as executor (executor fees can be, and often are, waived by executors who are related to the deceased), remember that being in the position of executing a parent's will can be trying, adding legal deadlines to the pressures of the grieving process. In addition, the fees are taxable as income; however, many advisors note that for large estates, if relatives who are also beneficiaries serve as executors, and thus effectively receive a portion of their inheritance in the form of fees, the income tax on the fees may be lower than the estate tax on the same amount.

Your decision about taking the role of executor is not one that should be made solely on financial grounds. Executors must appear in court, and the procedure sometimes takes months or even years, depending on the size of the estate and the complexity of the legal issues involved. In addition, executors have significant fiduciary obligations to the other beneficiaries of the testator. Family tensions can get magnified when one child is accorded control over the money, even temporarily.

Of course, the process of going through papers, many of them relating to the deceased person's entire history, can be cathartic. Early childhood diaries and belongings may provide insights into a past long gone and forgotten.

Whether you have a choice in the matter is another issue. You may be named as executor without your knowledge. Your response to whether or not you are named the executor may depend on how much you like to be in control, even during an emotionally fraught time. In addition, family relationships will play a major role in determining how the executor position is filled. Typically, in a family with several children, parents pick the most "responsible" child, continuing life patterns set long ago in childhood. This choice may in turn lead to a reemergence of sibling conflicts as old childhood issues are revisited in the context of the death.

Administration

The probate court authorizes the executor or appoints an administrator to *administer* the estate. The length of the administration period varies. A complex estate with many holdings may require considerable administration, while an estate with only a few assets should require little or no administrative activity.

Administering the estate consists of gathering all the assets and debts, locating and notifying creditors of their need to file claims, determining whether assets must be sold to satisfy debts, and finally distributing the estate to the heirs or beneficiaries. In most states, the administrator works under the jurisdiction of the court, but in some states the administrator works independently.

The assets of the estate are used, first, to pay funeral expenses, estate administration expenses, debts or claims against the estate, and mortgages. The remaining amount, the *net estate*, is then taxed. The taxes must be paid before the estate is distributed to the heirs. Under some circumstances monies can be disbursed during the probate period. For example, a widow whose assets have been frozen may ask the court for an allowance.

Not all estates are subject to formal probate administration. Studies have shown that about three-fourths of all estates skip the probate administration phase. In this case, the estate assets are used to pay the taxes and debts, if any, and then the estate is immediately distributed.

Estate Tax Returns

For estates over $600,000, a federal estate tax return must be filed within nine months of the date of death. Depending on state law and the size of the estate, a state estate tax return may have to be filed at the same time. Probate may extend far beyond this nine-month period, particularly if the estate is complex, heirs cannot be located, or the will is contested.

Debts

Debts are generally paid from the estate during the settlement process. At the onset, the executor will contact creditors and inform them of the death. While many creditors extend grace periods of six to eight months before taking action, most won't waive their right to interest payments, although some states limit the accrual of interest after death. If the estate has cash, it's a good idea to have the executor pay outstanding bills from the estate's cash supply before the estate is settled to avoid the interest charges.

In any case, debts and estate taxes typically are paid before beneficiaries receive their full distribution. In situations where debts exceed assets, the beneficiaries are *not* responsible for paying outstanding sums. The personal debts of the decedent are just that—personal. If the estate cannot cover the debts, the creditors have no further recourse. The only exception is under *universal succession*, the direct taking of the inheritance, which operates in

Georgia in a modified form, and in Louisiana. Otherwise, if the estate is insolvent, the claim is simply dropped, so you normally should not pay the estate's debts out of your own pocket.

When the family home is the main asset, being able to assume the mortgage without a new loan application and new rates also becomes an issue. Some banks allow the transfer of collateral to the next generation. But be forewarned: You may have to negotiate a new loan, especially if interest rates have risen significantly since the terms of the original loan were set. If the house must be sold to pay off a debt, you usually won't have to meet mortgage payments until the estate is settled. Chances are that the bank will wait it out, since repayment of the loan is guaranteed and lawsuits can be costly. However, don't take chances. Be sure to check, and recheck.

Closing the Estate

The estate is expected to be closed as promptly as possible. Real and personal property must be sold, taxes must be paid, and the returns must be accepted. But, the court must grant a discharge before the personal representative is relieved of responsibility. Only then is the estate formally closed.

THE REALLY UNUSUAL CASES: CONTESTED WILLS

While most estates are settled according to the scenario presented above, with no illegitimate children or omitted spouses appearing to challenge the will or trust, the unusual cases provide grist for the media and legal mills.

The formalities required to properly execute a will allow potential heirs dissatisfied with the terms of the will to contest its validity. Three problems can raise challenges to the validity of a will during probate:

- The will is invalid because of lack of mental capacity, the exertion of undue influence on the will-maker by family, friends, or lawyers, or fraud.
- The will is improperly signed or executed, usually because of a lack of proper witnesses or witnessing ceremonies in accordance with state law.
- The will has been revoked by the maker.

Will contests typically arise for one of two reasons. First, if a distributee (a relative who would receive a share of the estate under state intestacy laws, such as a child) is cut out of the will, that person has a strong incentive to argue that the will is not valid. If the will was not properly signed or witnessed, or if the testator did not have sufficient mental capacity to understand what he or she was doing, the will is invalid. Without a valid will, the estate is distributed according to intestacy laws, and the dissatisfied contestant becomes a happy heir.

The second likely reason for will contests is even more intriguing. During your lifetime, you can make unlimited changes to your will, as long as the formalities for valid execution are properly followed. Many people are private about their wills, and most people are consistent in their choice of beneficiaries. In some rare cases, however, neither is true. The original named beneficiaries knew about the first will, but a second will is presented for probate. Individuals named in the first will but left out of the second will are motivated to deny the second will and argue that the first will was never revoked. Oftentimes in these cases, the disappointed beneficiaries of the first will argue that a major beneficiary of the second will used his or her power and influence to cause the change. Sometimes it is a new lawyer who causes the unwitting testator to include him or her in the revised will. Other times, a live-in nurse suddenly takes the majority of what would've been the children's share.

The most highly publicized incident of declaring a will invalid occurred when the will of billionaire Howard Hughes was challenged as a forgery.

Some states allow *no-contest clauses* to minimize the likelihood of a will contest. With a no-contest clause in the will, if a named beneficiary in the will contests its validity (because she would be entitled to a larger share if the will is invalid) and loses the contest, she may receive absolutely nothing. No-contest clauses help prevent frivolous will contests.

High costs, delay, rigid formalities, and the risk of will contests have brought the probate process into disfavor. In recent years, more families have turned to will substitutes and revocable trusts as ways to avoid probate. In the next chapter, we discuss the issues confronting trust beneficiaries. Then in Part Three, we will examine the use of trusts in estate planning.

SUCCESSION BY WILL SUBSTITUTES: JOINT TENANCY AND LIFE INSURANCE

Living trusts have become the most popular and flexible form of nonprobate property. We'll discuss them in detail in Chapter 4. Other nonprobate assets, including *joint tenancy* and life insurance, are also widely used to ease the estate transfer process by passing directly to the survivor or named beneficiary.

Joint Tenancy

Joint tenancy with the right of survivorship, where the survivor automatically gains ownership of the entire property upon the death of the co-owner, used to be the most popular form of probate avoidance. Then two changes occurred almost simultaneously: growth in the popularity of living trusts, which provide much more flexibility and control, and changes in the tax code that eliminated estate taxes for transfers between spouses.

Most couples hold their homes either in joint tenancy or in one of the two marital forms of ownership (tenancy by the entirety and community property). But a joint tenant cannot will his or her half to another person. In second marriages, this feature prevents a parent from leaving his or her share to children from a first marriage. Bank accounts and other assets can also be held in joint tenancy.

Another aspect of joint tenancy is that creditors cannot attach the property for debts after the joint tenant/debtor has died. Unless the creditor has moved to attach the property before the debtor dies, the creditor will have no recourse. For example, if a business goes sour and the husband dies, leaving the home in joint tenancy to the wife, the creditor has lost out, unless the business was community property. However, if the mortgagor attaches the property during the lifetime of the debtor, the joint tenancy is severed or ended and the property title converts to a tenancy in common. In this case, the property could now be attached by other creditors as well.

Life Insurance

Although subject to estate taxes, life insurance passes outside of probate, directly from the insurance company to the named beneficiaries. Special irrevocable insurance trusts may be used to avoid estate taxes as well. These trusts follow specific rules, which are discussed in Chapter 10.

THE SPECIAL CASE OF SMALL ESTATES

Even without living trusts, not all estates are subject to probate. States provide special exemptions from probate and administrative formalities for small estates, usually requiring only a sworn statement (affidavit) by the heirs or the executor. Forms can be presented to the bank, the department of motor vehicles, and other agencies, and the property can be claimed or transferred. The size of what qualifies as a "small" estate varies from $10,000 to $100,000, depending upon state law. In addition, some states do not require full probate administration for any estate that passes directly to the surviving spouse.

UNIVERSAL SUCCESSION

The ancient Romans followed the less complicated system of universal succession (the direct taking of the inheritance). The heirs "step into the shoes" of the deceased, assuming all assets and liabilities. Many European nations still follow this system today. There are no executors, no administrators, and no probate. The heirs must distribute property according to the will, and they are personally liable if they do not.

Although there is a strong trend toward less formalistic and legally involved estate transfer, universal succession is only available in limited ways in the United States. Louisiana is the only state that has fully adopted a system of universal succession. In California, a surviving spouse can assume the assets and liabilities and forgo administration, thereby electing to avoid probate. In Georgia, a modified form of universal succession is recognized, allowing the heirs to petition for an order stating that no administration is necessary because the estate owes no debts and the heirs agree upon the division of the estate.

Despite the limited availability of universal succession in the United States, the use of non-probate transfers has become widespread. P.O.D. (payable on death) bank accounts, mutual funds, pension plans, and life insurance represent an increasingly significant portion of today's estates. Combined with the availability of living trusts, probate is becoming a smaller, though still significant, form of estate management.

TAKE CARE OF YOURSELF

Paying bills in the interim is only one of many questions that will confront you if you suddenly find yourself as an heir. What about your own money? Time? Decisions you postponed, especially if a family member's lingering illness had been restraining you?

Don't let the estate process keep you from attending to your own life. If you obsess about the details rather than pay attention to your own needs, you'll end up making the grieving process harder on yourself.

Sooner or later, the estate will be settled, and you will face a new set of challenges. Your concern should shift from the details of closing the estate to managing your new money. The next steps you make will probably be among the most important financial decisions of your life.

4

---○---

BENEFITING FROM A TRUST

WHEN DEALING WITH INHERITANCE, most of us will fall into the category of middle income, middle class, baby boom inheritors, for whom the expectation and experience of inheritance is a new one. But there is another class of readers, the high-end inheritors—whether baby boomers, trust-fund babies, or widows—whose fortunes are substantial and whose challenges match the size of their fortunes.

In almost every case, the fortunes of these major estates are passed in trust through the generations. As a result, we will focus here on the special case of receiving a trust.

TRUST TERMS

Trusts have language and rules all their own. They are the legal expression of the control of wealth, both materially and psychologically. A brief overview of trust terms is helpful to begin.

- *Trust:* A separate legal entity created to hold and manage property for the benefit of one or more individuals or other entities, such as charities.
- *Grantor or Benefactor:* The person who sets up the trust and provides the funds.
- *Trustee:* The trustee is the person who takes legal title to the trust property and holds the property for the benefit of the trust's

beneficiaries. The trustee has a fiduciary or financial duty to follow the intentions of the trust creator as set out in the will or trust instrument. Often a bank trust department serves as the trustee, but attorneys, family friends, and even the trust creator, in the case of a living trust, can be the trustee.

A trustee's duties include administering the trust according to the trust document's provisions, in the interest of the beneficiaries; preserving the trust property; and ensuring that the trust's assets are protected.

• *Beneficiary:* The person or persons for whom the trust is created. Beneficiaries may include recipients on more than one generational level. A secondary beneficiary is second in line to benefit from the trust, a tertiary beneficiary is third in line to benefit from the trust and so on until the trust dissolves.

• *Remainderman:* The person or persons who will receive the body of the trust when it is dissolved. While charitable trusts may continue indefinitely, private trusts are limited in duration by the Rule Against Perpetuities (see below).

• *Revocable Trust:* The grantor of a revocable trust retains the right to revoke a trust or change its terms at any time. Consequently, revocable trusts, also known as living trusts, receive no special tax treatment.

• *Irrevocable Trust:* Once created, an irrevocable trust cannot be terminated by the grantor. As a result, the irrevocable trust is a separate entity for both legal and tax purposes.

• *Trust Principal or Corpus:* Both trust and tax law treat the corpus (from the Latin for "body") or principal of the trust differently from the income, or earnings, that the capital produces. In trust law, the corpus consists of the original funds plus capital gains or appreciation of the underlying amount originally placed in trust by the grantor.

• *Trust Income:* The trust income is generally the interest, dividends, and rents that the trust holdings or corpus produces. Generally if not distributed in the tax year of the trust plus sixty-five days, the income reverts to corpus.

• *Trust Capital Gains:* While income may be disbursed to the beneficiary or trust recipient, often at the discretion of the trustees, capital gains, such as those produced by the growth in value of stocks or real estate (unless the trust specifically provides otherwise), are not considered income for trust purposes. These funds remain with the corpus, growing the body of the trust.

• *Trust Income Tax:* In tax law, the income is taxed either to the trust or beneficiaries, while capital gains generally remain in the trust and receive lower, more favorable tax treatment. Income tax rates range from 15 to 39.6 percent on a tax rate schedule which climbs more steeply than individual rates and reaches 39.6 percent for the trust at a taxable income of $7,650. By comparison, the same rate is reached for a single person at $256,500, illustrating the financial benefit of distributing trust income rather than keeping it in trust to be taxed at a much higher rate. Realized capital gains from the trust are taxed at 28 percent.

• *Rule Against Perpetuities:* To ensure that property did not pass indefinitely from one generation to the next forever under the control of a "dead hand," a standard was created in a 1681 English court ruling called "the Duke of Norfolk's case," which finds its modern legal expression as follows: Any future interest must vest, if at all, within a life in being plus twenty-one years plus the gestation period (that is, nine months). In other words, even well-drafted trusts are restricted in duration to an outer limit of approximately one hundred years (assuming a trust measured by the life of a baby who lives eighty years). In practical terms, most trusts are now further limited by tax laws imposed in 1986.

• *Generation-Skipping Tax (GST):* Before 1986, grantors could make use of a loophole to avoid double estate taxation. Instead of being taxed on the conveyance of the estate from parents to children and then taxed on the conveyance from the children to their grandchildren, the parents would convey directly to their grandchildren. The GST plugs this tax loophole, forcing taxation at each generation of the family.

Under current law there is an exemption from the GST for conveyances of up to $1 million by an individual or $2 million by a married couple. Aggregate generation skipping conveyances in excess of these amounts are subject to the generation skipping tax at a flat 55 *percent* rate. Trusts that were irrevocable on September 25, 1986 (with no later gifts added) are fully exempt from the GST, so old family money has an estate planning advantage over new money.

• *Charitable Trusts:* Charitable trusts can continue indefinitely, and money left to a properly IRS-qualified charitable organization or institution is estate tax free. Money can be left outright to an existing charity, or a charitable trust can be created. The tax break has prompted charitable and educational institutions to prepare complex estate planning packages to induce charitable giving. The central feature is a gift to the charity that provides lifetime benefits to the donor, with the remainder passing to the institution.

THE REVOCABLE LIVING TRUST

Setting up a family *living trust* requires family trust of the personal, emotional sort. In other words, by signing the document, your parents have already sanctioned your managing their money during their lifetime under certain circumstances, including their incapacity. Or the trust may provide for co-management between the two generations. While a key impetus for creating such trusts is eliminating the need for the probate process, a byproduct is that the next generation is empowered by being drawn into their parents' affairs prior to death. Of course, a parent could set up a living trust without informing the children, but this is usually impractical. Making the children co-trustees without informing them would defeat many of the reasons for creating a trust, including the desire to provide some transition in case of incapacity.

Both probate fees and the probate process can be largely circumvented in most states if your parents agree to place their estate in trust.

Revocable trusts, also called revocable living trusts, have become increasingly popular. They flourished almost overnight after the publication of Norman Dacey's 1965 book *How to Avoid Probate*. While Dacey, a nonlawyer, had effectively challenged the probate system in his book, a case ten years earlier had set the stage. Lawyers were initially outraged with Dacey. The New York County Lawyers' Association sought an injunction to ban the sale of the book as the unauthorized practice of the law. However, after denouncing the book, the legal profession capitulated. Now many states have statutes dealing with the revocable trust and related issues.

These trusts literally change property ownership from the grantor to the trust, with the grantor retaining the right to change it back. A revocable trust is largely a "legal fiction" since the grantor (you or your parent) is usually the trustee.

For example, today your car is in your driveway. Tomorrow morning you create a revocable living trust. Tomorrow afternoon you go to the Department of Motor Vehicles and transfer the title of the car to yourself as trustee of your trust (i.e., Bill Smith, Trustee, for the Smith Family Trust). Tomorrow night the car is still in your driveway and you still have the keys, but now the car is in trust. Can you feel the change? No, but now the car will not have to go through probate to pass to your trust's beneficiary. The law sees a change even where you see an illusion; thus, lawyers call it legal fiction.

All assets can be transferred into a revocable living trust. For example, ownership of Bill Smith's home could be transferred to "The Smith Family Trust." The trust is then run by Bill Smith as trustee along with alternate or co-trustee family members. If you are attempting to encourage your parents to create a trust and your parents seem hesitant to entrust their finances to you as the alternate or co-trustee, suggest that they consider a neutral party, such as another relative or a bank trust department.

Check the actual numbers in your state to see the comparative costs of third-party trust administration and state probate costs. Outside trustee fees could actually exceed probate fees. These fees cover administrative expenses, such as registering a change of title on real estate, cars, securities or other property. If you are the trustee, some of these fees can be saved, but a lawyer will still be required to draw up the trust document. (Even though family members often volunteer to serve as executor or trustee without taking customary fees, the administrative burden can be higher than originally imagined; consider having the family member rewarded if matters are complex.)

The fictional Jensen family illustrates how a trusting family can simplify transitions. Anita Jensen, an astute businesswoman now in her midseventies, decided to include her son and daughter in her estate plan a decade earlier. With a revocable trust drawn up by her attorney, she shared management of her business and personal affairs with the children. In addition, she systematically transferred assets to them annually, thereby reducing the potential estate tax bite considerably. While Anita is still alive and healthy, she is assured that when she does depart, her children will not face the additional torture of settling a messy estate that less well-grounded families can experience.

As one judge noted, "The best way to avoid a probate contest is to sit down with members of your family and discuss what you intend to do" before a will or trust is drawn up. Such discussions accomplish four important goals:

• Eliminate the element of surprise resulting from plans becoming known only after death;

• Enable family members to see that the writer of the will is of sound mind which lessens the chance of challenges to the will;

• Enable families to sort out differences through discussion and informal negotiation, rather than squaring off later in court; and

• Allow an opportunity to explain if children are not to be treated equally.

By contrast, if injustices are perceived, conflict will ensue.

When You Are the Beneficiary of a Living Trust

While the will holds many a final secret, the living or revocable trust is most often done in open cooperation between the generations. Thus, if you are at the receiving end of a living trust, the strong likelihood is that you know about it already. (Interestingly enough, the will actually becomes a public record once probated, whereas the trust document does not. So even though the trust is often dealt with openly during life, its contents can remain a family secret.) Living trusts are set up while the grantor or trust creator is still alive. They can be given any name, such as "The Levin Family Trust," and the grantor can act as one trustee with one or more family members as co-trustees or alternate trustees.

To create a trust, real or personal property must be involved. The title to that property is transferred by the original owner to the trust, which holds the property for the benefit of the trust beneficiaries. The trustees are given control over the property.

With irrevocable trusts, once the trust's creator and donor has given up title to the property, that person loses control over the property in the trust. But the living trust, as it now has been popularized, defies this rule. The grantor retains not only the right to revoke the trust, but the right to use the property in the trust. The income can be used for his or her benefit. That power is relinquished only at death (or incapacitation if the trust contains such a clause). At that point, the alternate trustees would take over, and depending upon the instructions in the trust documents, would now use or dispose of the property in the trust.

Let's return to the Levin Family Trust. Ralph Levin, a widower, owns a home, some jewelry that he inherited from this late wife, a small portfolio of stocks and bonds, two bank accounts, and various furniture and other items in the house. His total estate is worth $450,000. Ralph has two children, Jane and Ned, and he decides that to avoid probate he will create a living trust, leaving all his property to them.

The steps are fairly simple. A trust document is drawn up according to the requirements of his state, preferably by an attorney. (Although there are do-it-yourself will and trust documents, mistakes can be costly; and if you do make a mistake, you won't be able to fix it from the grave.) Then all the assets to which one normally holds formal title—including the home, securities, and bonds—are transferred to the Levin Family Trust. The deed to the residence is re-recorded with the county clerk or registrar. The stocks and bonds are reissued to the trust. Other items, such as the jewelry and furniture, are usually listed in the trust document, and a "general assignment," or a general clause that gives all residuary or remaining property to the trust, is also included.

Ralph can appoint himself as trustee. He can change the terms or revoke the trust as long as he is alive, provided he has the capacity to reorganize his affairs. When Ralph dies, the children can dissolve the Levin Family Trust and the property can be disbursed to them. If they prefer, Jane and Ned can continue the trust for the benefit of their own children.

If you are the beneficiary of a living trust, you will likely become trustee or co-trustee when your parent dies. You and your siblings, guided by any direction in the trust document itself, will dispose of the property which is now yours to handle as trustees.

Administration Under the Living Trust

The trustees will administer the trust, paying any debts that come due. Since the property has already been passed out of the donor's estate to the trust, *no probate court is involved. There are no probate delays and no probate fees.* Creditors can reach the assets of a living trust during the creator's life or even at his death. One problem with living trusts is that there is no closing, so debts theoretically can be presented by creditors for an indefinite period of time, although all debts would be subject to statute of limitation rules, which vary by state. To solve this problem, some states such as California have recently enacted procedures for a four-month cutoff of debts, provided correct procedures are followed, with an absolute limit of a year.

Because of the potential creditor problem, a living trust works best with less-complicated estates. An entrepreneur with several risky business ventures wouldn't make this sort of arrangement as it might subject her heirs to creditors' claims for years to come.

Fees

The living trust may provide for fees for the trustees, but unlike probate fees, they are not set by state law.

Taxes and the Living Trust

With a living trust, an estate tax return normally needs to be filed only if the gross estate is over $600,000. The trust will continue to be subject to income taxes during the course of its existence.

The living trust does *not* save estate taxes, it only avoids associated probate costs; therefore, if the gross estate is worth over $600,000, taxes will still be owed, just as with a will.

Closing the Living Trust

Unlike probate, the timing of trust closure varies tremendously. The trust can close immediately after the assets are divided. Or the trust document could prevent beneficiaries from receiving their shares until they reach a certain age, say thirty. Some trusts may actually last a great while before being required to close. Therefore, unlike the case of intestacy, the living trust's provisions can vary widely.

IRREVOCABLE TRUSTS

In past generations, much of the family wealth of the country was tied up in irrevocable trusts. Typically, when a wealthy patriarch died, he left his fortune in trust for his spouse and children. With old family fortunes, the money was often tied up for several generations, the only restriction being a complex legal limit—the Rule Against Perpetuities (see definition, page 67). The rule was created in England in the 1600s to prevent property being tied up perpetually. Practically speaking, a trust could continue about one hundred years, assuming one of the measuring lives lived to his or her eighties.

In Boston, traditionally the center of old money management, specialized firms, some dating back two centuries, devote themselves to managing family money and family members. Most major banks have trust departments that do the same thing.

Irrevocable trusts traditionally have served to perpetuate patriarchy. In the last twenty years, however, changing social attitudes and changing women's roles have undermined the grip of trust departments on widows' lives. Many women now earn their own money and spouses of wealthy men demand more of their money be left out of trust. Before the husband would often leave not only his own estate, but his wife's funds as well, tied up in trust so as to "protect the little lady" from the vulgarities of finance.

Translation: so no other man will get his hands on hubby's hard-earned money.

WHAT TO DO IF YOU ARE THE RECIPIENT OF AN IRREVOCABLE TRUST

If you find yourself at the receiving end of a trust, you'll have a number of concerns. First and foremost is the issue of what is yours and what is not. To resolve this issue, you need to understand several points about trusts. First, irrevocable trusts are a separate legal entity with a bundle of property rights. Just as a ball may be wound with several strands of different-colored twine, the rights to a trust can be untwined and given to different people. Or, only one or two colors can be untwined, with the remaining ball later becoming the property of yet another person or entity.

Second, irrevocable trusts have their own separate tax identity. Trust law and tax law are so closely interwoven that we cannot discuss one without the other. Even the types of trusts are defined in tax-related terms. Of all the areas of tax law, trust tax law is one of the most complex. Our goal here is to make you aware of a variety of issues that could affect you. Don't expect to become an expert by reading this chapter; do expect to be able to ask experts questions without feeling embarrassed. And don't be surprised if experts reply, "I'll have to look that up." That's the way trust tax law is. It even challenges the experts.

TRUST TYPES

Simple trusts are those that pay out all the trust income to one or more individual beneficiaries every year. Believe it or not, these simple trusts are covered by different Internal Revenue Code rules than *complex trusts*.

Complex trusts include those where income can be accumulated to be paid out later, those where corpus can be distributed currently, and those where there are charitable beneficiaries.

Some trusts provide income until a certain point when the trust ends and the beneficiary receives the principal or corpus. Other trusts provide only a benefit for a person's lifetime, with the principal going to others designated in the document setting up the trust. Another model provides income only, but under certain circumstances, such as illness, the trustees may invade the principal.

An Irrevocable Trust Checklist

1. *Look at the trust document.* A surprising number of heirs fail to take the simple step of studying the trust document, or even more shocking, fail to ask for the document in the first place. Once you are the beneficiary of a trust, you have the right to see the document. Families often try to hide the information from heirs. If you cannot obtain the document from your family attorney with a simple phone call, hire an attorney to make the next call for you. The bank or trustee should also have a copy.

2. *Look at the quarterly or monthly trust report.* Without reviewing the performance of your trust, you'll be unable to judge whether the trust investments are working for your needs. If you are a life beneficiary, you want to ensure that there is adequate income flowing from the trust. If the trust is heavily invested in nonrental real estate, that works to the remainderman's advantage, as do growth stocks and other long-term growth investments.

3. *Keep informed about distributable net income.* Obtain, either directly or through your attorney or accountant, the trust accounting income statements on which the income available to distribute (distributable net income) is calculated. Be sure that the income due you is, in fact, being paid and that amounts held back are not excessive.

4. *Negotiate trustee fees.* Before sitting down to negotiate, research the typical trustee rates at your local banks. You may find a trustee's chart of set fees, but if your trust is sizeable, certainly if over $1,000,000, there is room for fee adjustment. The larger the trust, the more room for negotiation.

5. *Get on good terms with the trust officers.* Trust officers are not the enemy. They are typically middle-income employees, and they take pride in managing large amounts of wealth. Of course, it is to the trust officer's benefit to manage a larger portfolio, both in terms of fees for the bank and job esteem for the officer. Sometimes trust officers treat the money as if it were their own. (Legally it actually is the property of the trustee, but not to keep, just to hold in trust.)

6. *Get professional assistance.* Have a good attorney on your side (not the family's attorney; someone to represent just you). And also have a respected CPA. You'll need both these people, at a minimum, in order to interpret trust documents and analyze trust practices. If you have an investment advisor or money manager, they can also help review the investments. But a note of caution: Be sure the particular individual is qualified in this very specialized investment area where so many legal and accounting technicalities are intertwined. Often standard investment advice is not correct in a trust context because of the tension between the needs of current and future beneficiaries.

7. *Review discretionary language.* If the irrevocable trust was set up by a parent still living, involve them in the bank's interpretation of terms such as "in the style to which she is accustomed." Bank officers usually do not live as well as wealthy people. Sometimes they are reluctant to authorize funds for lifestyles that they do not understand.

TRUSTEE DISCRETION

Whether or not trustees have discretionary control over distributing all of the income creates many issues for beneficiaries. In trusts where the income must all be paid out annually, trustee conflict with the beneficiary is usually limited. But where trustees are given discretion to judge a beneficiary's lifestyle and determine when and whether to distribute income, beneficiaries are at the mercy of these trustees. Trustees often impose their own middle-class standards on beneficiaries who have been raised in families used to upper-class lifestyles.

Even with trusts providing for the annual distribution of income, trustees often have discretion as to whether the payments are made once a year or in quarterly or monthly amounts. Recipients usually prefer to receive more frequent distributions than to wait an entire year to receive income.

DEFINING TRUST INCOME

The property in a trust can be designated for the benefit of both income beneficiaries (often the children) and remaindermen (often the grandchildren). The *income beneficiaries* are limited to the income produced by trust property during their lifetimes. The *remaindermen* receive the property in the trust itself at some future date, typically on the date of death of the income beneficiaries. When a trust is so divided, the definition and accounting of trust income becomes extremely important to the parties involved. Two concepts apply here:

First, the "sixty-five-day rule" allows income to be distributed sixty-five days after the end of the year and still count toward the previous year's distribution. If the income is not distributed by that date in early March, it returns to corpus. If the trustee does not provide information until after the close of the trust year, the beneficiary loses the opportunity to have an impact on when the income is accounted for and distributed. If the beneficiary does not have an interest in the corpus, then that beneficiary will forever lose the trust income not timely accounted for within the first sixty-five days of the new year.

Second, "trust income" is an accounting concept, and like any other, is subject to definition. If the trust language states "all of the annual income from the trust must be distributed to Janie," the language doesn't define what "all of the income" means. In general, trust income can be divided into two categories: income generated from the sale of assets that have appreciated, whether of stocks, bonds, and land (capital gains); and income that derives from earned interest, dividends, and rents on these assets.

Unless the trust provides otherwise, the appreciation or capital gain stays in the corpus or body of the trust; the earnings, to the extent that the trust provides them, are paid to the beneficiary. Capital gains taxes on the appreciated assets and property taxes must be paid from the trust, which files its own tax return. In addition, if the trust does not distribute all the non–capital gain income, then it must also pay income tax on these amounts.

These internal obligations must be met from the gross or total income before the "income" that belongs to the beneficiary, Janie here, can be calculated. These deductions from the amount that is available include trust income taxes that must be paid on capital gains; amounts that must be held back for wasting or depleting trust assets such as mineral interests; cash reserves; money for operating expenses for land and other capital intensive investments; and income tax reserves.

The amounts left for distribution are called "distributable net income" or "D.N.I." You may also hear the term "trust accounting income" or "T.A.I." The income that is then distributed to Janie will be taxed as Janie's income, rather than as part of the trust. Janie reports this income on her own Form 1040 Schedule E as trust income.

TO WHOSE BENEFIT?

The question of who ultimately receives the trust corpus places current beneficiaries at odds with the remainderman, the final beneficiary of the trust assets. For example, if you are the income beneficiary but have no claim on the corpus, then you want the trust invested for income production now. (Remember, all capital gains will revert to corpus. Except for guarding against inflation by keeping the corpus base large enough to produce adequate income, there's no incentive to the life beneficiary to encourage trust officers to retain any income or to engage in growth investments that produce no income.)

The exact opposite holds true if you are the future recipient of a trust now being managed for your ultimate benefit. Your goal will be to see the trust grow as rapidly as possible. Heavy burdens are placed on trustees not to lose the money, but there is no legal requirement that they grow trusts to keep up with inflation. Consequently, bank trust departments and other trustees are notoriously conservative in their investment strategies. If you can, you'll want to encourage investments that take more than average bank-type risk. Some beneficiaries have even offered to prepare letters for the bank files to protect officers. Problems occur when two or more current or potential beneficiaries have sharply contrasting goals. For example, if one sibling wants to preserve cash during his lifetime while his sister wants to preserve their substantial trusts for her own children, conflicts over the investment direction of the trust will ensue. Legally, the brother is entitled to force the trustee to invest in a reasonable amount of income producing assets, but sibling rivalry will invariably complicate matters.

While, strictly speaking, trust officers must act independently of beneficiaries, in point of fact, wealthy families often hold great sway over their banks. One example comes to mind of a woman whose family name was the same as the major national bank that held her money. She brought the head of the trust department to an investors' meeting so that she could suggest types of investments being offered. In these and other ways, even heirs from more modest families can informally influence the bank or trustee's directions by letting their preferences be clearly known.

CONTROLLING TRUSTS

With trusts, benefactors can control both wealth and behavior. If a father fears that his daughter will marry out of the faith, he can, to some extent, prevent income from being distributed. If a mother wishes to encourage her son's future advanced education, she can provide for additional educational distributions. With the trust, the benefactor can make full use of the bundle of rights and benefits that amount to "property." As we have seen, a trust's income can benefit one person during his or her lifetime, while the principal goes to another individual or to an educational institution or charity.

Spendthrift Trusts

Spendthrift trusts, or spendthrift clauses in trusts, prevent a beneficiary's creditors from attaching the trust for debts that the beneficiary incurs. Most often, parents are likely to create trusts with these provisions when children have had difficulty in managing their money. The parents' purpose is usually not punitive but preventive, the goal being to ensure that the child has adequate resources in the future when the parents are no longer around to help. Some states, including New York, even impose automatic spendthrift protection for life, income-only beneficiaries.

If, as a trust recipient, you find such a clause in your trust, don't be surprised.

Trust-Busting

Often heirs find themselves at the mercy of trust officers, especially with discretionary trusts that provide the trustees wide latitude in what income they can distribute. This dilemma has given rise to a set of attorneys specializing in "trust-busting," or finding ways either to end the trust, change trustees, or persuade existing trustees to loosen the purse strings. Good trust attorneys can comb the trust documents, the trust financial statements, the case law, and the trustee's performance records to find ways to make life more tolerable under the thumb of trust officers.

ROBERT NASH: A TRUST FUND BABY

At first, Robert Nash's free-flowing, curly hair and casual clothes hide what will soon become exceedingly obvious— Robert is the current beneficiary of a family fortune. Although Robert's usual explanation of his circumstances is long on his father's hard work and short on details about how he makes a living, do not be misled. The Nashes made their fortune in an investment most Americans only dream about: California real estate.

Robert's family's interest derived from owning the land for generations. The risk of development had fallen to the companies who leased the family land in the 1940s, 1950s, and 1960s, first as aircraft factories moved in, later as populations followed. Robert's family had reaped the rewards in the form of rents, which provided a steady income stream of cash to the family. Even today, with many of the real estate developments in decline, Robert's income stands at the top 1 percent of all Americans. The reason is that the developer has to carry the cost of the building and the underlying land isn't mortgaged. Although his income is atypical, many of his problems square with those of less fortunate heirs.

When Robert came to us in his new special edition Ford Explorer, he had been living his entire life off of his trust distributions. He had faced a constant struggle for control of his trust income, fighting with the bank trust department over the direction of his investments and for disbursements of the income. Although he enjoyed traveling, Robert rarely felt able to escape. Often, whether at his home in Newport Beach, California, or in his Boston brownstone, he found himself in conference calls about his income and investments.

Robert had been averaging about $650,000 per year in income from his $8,000,000 trust. He had steered clear of incurring any major debts and had learned to live quite comfortably within his admittedly generous budget.

As a "trust fund baby," Robert is the lifetime income beneficiary of an irrevocable trust created by his great-grandparents. After Robert's death, the benefits of the trust were to pass to Robert's children. At forty-five and still single and childless, Robert had no incentive to grow the trust. Rather, for him, the size of the income was all that mattered.

If he never had any children, Robert's benefits would pass to his brother Sam's children, Brian and Debbie. Only if Robert adopted a child or had one late in life would the remainder of the trust concern him directly. The provisions would allow his own natural or adopted children to inherit the trust corpus or bulk of the capital outright upon his death.

All of these essentially unchangeable terms had been determined by Robert's great-grandfather, the grantor of the trust, at its creation many years before the generation-skipping tax took effect.

LIFE INCOME BENEFICIARY

As an income beneficiary, Robert was only entitled to the income produced by the $8,000,000 in trust assets. In this way, his great-grandfather ensured that the capital base of the trust would be preserved to provide for his great-great-grandchildren as well as his great-grandchildren. (This type of trust no longer confers tax benefits because of the generation-skipping tax so it is not generally being created today.)

In trusts, capital gains (the money earned from the appreciation or growth of assets rather than from an income or interest stream) are excluded from the calculation of trust income. Instead, any gains are treated as part of the original trust principal, and increase the main trust corpus. Although inflation lowers the real value of a trust when the corpus, or property inside the trust, does not grow, many life beneficiaries, like Robert, prefer to take their annual income and reinvest it outside of the trust. Otherwise, the gains only indirectly benefit the income-only beneficiary by increasing the capital base from which the trust income is produced. By contrast, for beneficiaries entitled to invade corpus, capital gains are more favorable as an investment choice.

For Robert, as an income-only beneficiary, the asset allocation of the trust was crucial. Since he was not entitled to capital gains, growth of assets such as stocks would not directly benefit him. Even if the stocks held by the trust appreciated in value by ten times, such capital gains would become corpus and would be preserved for the next generation. (Of course, they would increase his earnings base, critical in inflationary periods.)

After years of contending with conservative bank officers who saw their prime duty as the preservation and growth of the capital of the trust rather than the increase of Robert's income, Robert had finally wrested day-to-day investment control from the bank. By bringing in outside advisors, he had redirected the trust investments to provide the income he desired.

When his father died, Robert was heartbroken. Robert's father loomed large in Robert's life. In addition, his father's death meant increased responsibility at a difficult time. For Robert, professional help was absolutely crucial to deal with the transition. His father's will provided $5.65 million outright in after-tax assets. (All of the inheritance over $600,000 had been heavily taxed because his father's estate far exceeded the amounts that could escape taxes, even with careful planning.)

ALLOCATING HIS ASSETS

Robert had enough income from his trusts to meet current needs; therefore, he would not use any significant portion of his outright inheritance to supplement his income. We asked Robert to share his personal objectives and his preferred use of the capital so that we could help him plan an investment strategy that would match his goals. Details were not important at this stage, but his objectives needed to be understood to determine the best strategy for managing his $5.65 million in additional wealth.

Robert wanted to maintain his current lifestyle. In addition to his support of the Democratic party, Robert now could realize another dream—to make a difference by helping children in poverty. Because he had no children (and because the trust would provide for them if he did), Robert was less concerned about growing the $5.65 million than with helping deserving organizations.

Before making sophisticated choices about Robert's investment strategy, we needed to analyze his current asset allocation. Given the mixture of assets between trust and nontrust holdings, planning required consolidating all the assets in one overview chart, divided by type. In Robert's case, preparing this overview required persistence and detective work. After combing through tax returns, accountants' statements, deeds, and bank trust documents, we determined that his pre-inheritance asset allocation included his two homes valued at $3,000,000; two cars worth $225,000; jewelry worth $275,000; rent interests in trust valued at $2,000,000; corporate and Treasury bonds, worth $600,000 and $400,000 respectively, and a $100,000 savings account (see Figure 4-1). With real property, personal property, real estate, bonds, and cash, Robert's funds did not appear to be especially liquid. One question we asked ourselves was what did the inheritance do to change the mix?

We used his father's estate tax return to determine the initial

Figure 4-1. Robert Nash Current Asset Allocation

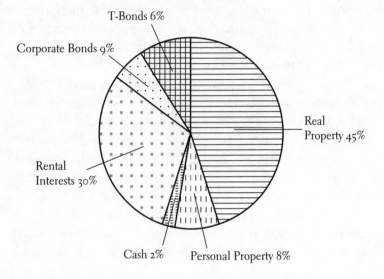

T-Bonds 6%

Corporate Bonds 9%

Real Property 45%

Rental Interests 30%

Cash 2%   Personal Property 8%

Figure 4-2. Robert Nash Allocation of Inherited Trust

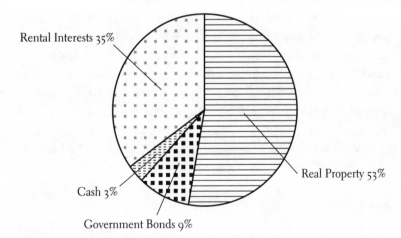

Rental Interests 35%

Real Property 53%

Cash 3%

Government Bonds 9%

Figure 4-3. Robert Nash
Initial Diversified Asset Allocation

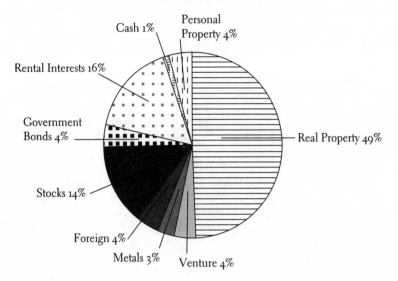

asset allocation of the inheritance. The inheritance included primarily land with a market value of $3,000,000; $500,000 in government bonds; $2,000,000 worth of rental interests; and $150,000 in cash (see Figure 4-2). A review of the estate tax return matched Robert's understanding of his father's holdings.

Taken together, Robert's asset allocation was not well-diversified given the multimillion-dollar size of his portfolio. Prior to getting the inheritance, Robert's own portfolio was already fairly illiquid. With the addition of more real property and long-term bonds, the portfolio would be even less liquid and less diversified given its increased size.

To remedy the situation, we reallocated Robert's personal funds to improve his combined (including the trust) asset allocation. Initially, Robert did not want to sell either of his homes, but that resulted in an allocation overly weighted in real property as is seen in Figure 4-3. Using the funds from the proceeds from sale

Figure 4-4. Robert Nash
Diversified Asset Allocation

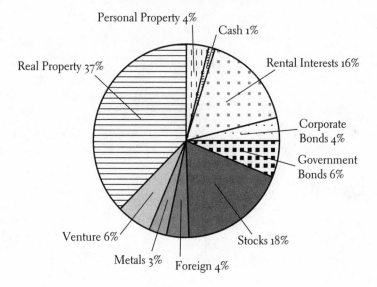

Personal Property 4%

Cash 1%

Real Property 37%

Rental Interests 16%

Corporate Bonds 4%

Government Bonds 6%

Venture 6%

Stocks 18%

Metals 3%   Foreign 4%

of his second home, his bonds, the inherited rental interests, and reinvesting his cash, Robert was able to develop the much more diversified portfolio shown in Figure 4-4. The new asset allocation provided more opportunities for growth with stock and venture investments while improving diversification with $500,000 in an international investment fund and $350,000 invested in precious metals.

As for charitable contributions, even without the keeping-up-with-the-Joneses motivation, Robert sincerely wished to help others. But Robert's social circle gave publicly and generously and he wanted to be a "player." Despite some fears that by "going public" he might be prey to less well-intentioned persons, image was important to Robert.

In order to make contributions systematically, Robert set up a contribution budget. One third of his income would be used for donations since the inheritance from his father would provide additional income to supplement that of Robert's trust. (Up to 50 percent of his total income, including that from the trust, could be given away and deducted for income tax purposes.) We also discussed the possibility of Robert's setting up a foundation. Although the foundation possibly represented a better long-term approach, setting up a foundation would place additional financial and administrative burdens on Robert. Like any new heir, he was better served by taking small steps, especially in the first year following his father's death, given the emotional and personal strains he was facing.

AMT CONCERNS

In the initial tax-planning review, tax projections showed that Robert was likely to fall into the alternative minimum tax. The AMT was designed to prevent high-income people from escaping taxation. As currently provided for by the Internal Revenue Code, the AMT removes certain deductions and imposes a different rate. Although at 26 percent the AMT flat rate is lower than the top income tax bracket of 39.6 percent, the net effect is that these individuals do pay taxes because of the loss of allowable deductions.

Without as many deductions to offset income, Robert would be better off with tax-free income. By taking advantage of investments from municipal and state bonds and bond funds, Robert could avoid adding new income to be taxed.

The AMT also affected Robert's decision not to go along with his plan to deed a conservation easement for his inherited land. The easement preserves the land from further development by granting it to a land trust. The owner, in this way, retains the right to possess the property during his or her lifetime. Normally, the grantor of the land is given a tax credit over a number of years for the appreciated value of the land which has now been donated. No such deduction or credit is allowed under the AMT.

Instead, Robert decided to retain the land. He would carry out his charitable and tax obligations by investing in a socially responsible mutual fund and donate to his local children's charities. Robert also became an investor in a recycling venture designed to make pavement from old tires. Robert has not lost sight of setting up his own foundation for the promotion of educational opportunities for underprivileged children, which he expects to accomplish in his ten-year charity-giving plan.

Whether or not you ever expect to benefit from or create a trust, this section provides a glimpse of a different world. The privileges of wealth extend beyond having money; even the tax structure rewards wealth and serves to maintain the status quo. In other words, the rich get richer.

MRS. AVERY: A WIDOW'S STORY

While family practices and psychology vary, the typical picture in the generation now passing was of a woman who stayed at home, with mothering and housewifery a full-time occupation. In that role, she often knew little or nothing of the family's finances. In extreme cases, she didn't even know how to write a check, much less have a checkbook. A great-aunt bragged, "I have never had to write a check in my life and I hope I will never have to learn how to. I left that to Ralph Senior, and now Ralph Junior handles all that for me."

Like the great-aunt, Mrs. Avery's case was typical, with the added twist that several million dollars were involved. The more money involved, the more family tensions rise.

Mrs. Avery's story was almost biblical in its proportions. Her autocratic Southern husband, Jonathan, inheritor of Mississippi Delta land, left the running of the house to his wife for which she had an allowance. All other matters of money were his and his alone. Jonathan Avery saw to the modernization of his 10,000-acre ancestral farmland. His older son, Perry, stayed home and worked through the years with his father. The younger son, Lewis, roamed the world on the family money, returning from time to time for family holidays, but never staying long.

When his father lay dying, Lewis returned in true prodigal fashion. He stayed through the funeral and shortly after his father was buried, began to attack the financial arrangements, which left management of the family lands in Perry's hands.

Mrs. Avery felt torn between her two sons. Her love for the son who had stayed and her longing to satisfy the restless Lewis brought her to her own sickbed. She had no knowledge of the business issues over which the brothers wrangled, and her husband's long-time attorney told her "not to worry her pretty little head."

Lewis had done a fair amount of reading about modern agriculture, and he wanted to mortgage the farm in order to purchase state-of-the-art equipment to turn the farm from low, but steady, profit margins to higher but riskier returns. In theory, this change of income could be accomplished through quicker crop rotation and bringing into farming service currently timbered lands.

Perry, for his part, felt the pain of the "good child" who had stayed with the family business year after year, only to see his brother upset his mother on the heels of their father's death. Perry felt he knew the business, and he feared that Lewis's interference would lead to the loss of the family land.

As the brothers vied for control, they also angled for their mother's disposition of her own estate. Because of past experience with Lewis's spendthrift ways, Mrs. Avery felt she should protect his future in a trust that creditors couldn't reach. Lewis lobbied hard to be treated as an adult, arguing that because he had been kept on a short string by his father his whole life, he had never learned to act responsibly or take the consequences, come what may.

Nothing in Mrs. Avery's experience had prepared her to deal

with her children in the context of her considerable estate. While as a mother, she was used to the two boys' different personalities and needs, as an adult she had never had control over money and she simply could not cope with the two brothers' demands.

Mrs. Avery is not alone. An equally difficult task arises when parents, all too aware of the costs of wealth, decide to let their children learn to live by their own wits. A story in *Fortune* magazine discussed this trend, citing several high-profile American families that had reached the decision to bequeath their fortunes to charitable foundations, leaving little or nothing to their children. The feeling in these families is that inheritance dilutes youthful motivation, creating more problems than it solves.

MAXIMIZE YOUR TRUST

While in the past many trusts were created to protect widows who did not know about finances or to control children's behavior from the grave, today's trust recipient is likely either to come from a family long familiar with the sheltering of wealth or a family that has used trusts as part of an entire estate plan. If you are the beneficiary of a trust, be sure you've taken advantage of the moves in the trust checklist.

Remember, as a trust beneficiary, you are in a position to enjoy the freedom that comes with additional income. Use the time you have to become knowledgeable about your affairs, but don't obsess about your lack of control—you will only have limited success in changing a trust set-up because of possible tax implications. And, if you don't like the control that trusts impose, you can take care of the next generation differently when you do your own estate plan.

PART II

MAXIMIZING THE PRESENT

He that wants money, means, and content, is
without three good friends.

Shakespeare, *As You Like It*

5

—◦—

MONEY MANAGEMENT

MOST PERSONAL FINANCE BOOKS start with a quote that sounds something like this: "The starting point for financial growth, in the absence of inheritance or windfall . . ."

Guess what? You are that exception. As a new heir, you need to look at personal savings, retirement planning, and asset management from a perspective different than the conventional norm.

For starters, new heirs can often avoid the slow process of accumulating savings for retirement. Rather, by following the steps below, the inheritance can be used as a capital base from which to plan for the future.

Step 1: *Budget your expenditures within your income.* In this way, you can prevent dipping into your new capital base at the expense of the future. Aside from the personal advantages of saving for your future, properly allocating your capital base also has a secondary indirect benefit: You will be providing important investment capital to maintain a healthy national economy.

Step 2: *Understand and maximize your tax position.* Your tax strategy for any significantly sized estate should be developed with the help of a professional advisor. But by understanding the basics of the tax code and your position in it, you'll be able to maintain control over your finances as well as interact with your advisors with confidence.

Step 3: *Plan for your retirement and your future.* By planning ahead for your retirement and allocating your assets, including the inheritance, you can avoid anxiety about your family's future while simultaneously taking advantage of the tax benefits afforded to retirement funds.

Set Your Financial Goals

Although most of us would clearly like to have *more* money, the *what for* is important in terms of your cash flow timing and growth needs. Consider the following:

1. Do you want to save money for your children's education?
2. Do you want to increase savings for your retirement?
3. Do you want to return to school yourself?
4. Do you want to change careers?
5. Do you want a second home?
6. Do you have a dream to travel the world?
7. Is buying a home for your parents a long-cherished hope?
8. Do you simply want to have more money in the bank?

Before taking a look at cash flow and taxes you must set financial goals. Financial objectives will enable you to put this information into a meaningful context. Think about your personal financial objectives that can be accomplished with your money: Are you more focused on your children's education, a comfortable retirement, fulfilling a lifelong dream, or charitable giving? These long-term goals will help you to plan now for your future, to budget your cash flow, and to understand your tax position. These goals will also help you to allocate your assets according to your personal liquidity, growth, and diversification needs.

MAINTAINING YOUR FINANCIAL HEALTH

Just as standard wisdom calls for a visit to the dentist and physician every year, finances need an annual checkup as well. But many people experience as much fear of reviewing their budget, taxes, and net worth as they do sitting in the dentist's chair. As a new heir you have more motivation than most to get that HP calculator smokin': Your financial position has changed. You have more to budget.

Your budget should be based on your cash flow, which is comprised of the money you bring in each year (inflows) and the money you spend (outflows). Before you consider the effect your inheritance will have on your cash flow, be sure to look at your pre-inheritance income and spending patterns. Determine whether you are meeting your expenses from income or going into debt. If you're not staying even, then you'll need to either cut spending or generate investment income from your inheritance. If you don't make a change, you'll face the constant temptation to invade your capital base.

YOU NEED TO BUDGET

Some new heirs think that because of their inheritance, savings and spending habits don't matter anymore. If you are one of the *Forbes* 400 heirs to a multimillion-dollar fortune, you may not need to worry. But unless you are one of the fortunate ones who don't need to consider your spending habits or your cash flow— and really even the richest do—the following discussion applies to you.

Budgeting now is important to ensure that your inheritance is properly managed for the future. Although you may face great temptation to use the money to enrich your lifestyle, by properly managing your current cash flow and your inheritance, you can take control. You can supplement your income, plan for your retirement, save for your family's future, and use your capital to achieve socially responsible goals, all the while growing your asset base and minimizing your taxes.

The importance of saving, even when a lump-sum inheritance stands before you, cannot be understated. The savings rate of the baby-boomers has been only one-third that of their parents' savings at the same age (although recent studies indicate that their parents are now spending as well). The savings rate now hovers around 3 percent. By limiting your spending to what you earn, you can break this pattern and help allay the economists' fear that the inheritance bonanza will be frittered away at the cost of the future.

ANALYZING YOUR CASH FLOW

Reviewing your past expenditures helps budgeting for the future. By completing Table 5-1, you will be able to estimate your monthly cash flow which will serve as a basis for your future budgets. If appropriate, you should use total family figures for income and expenses. For most items, think of what you spend monthly (such as your rent or mortgage payments) and multiply by twelve, or think of what you spend weekly (such as on food) and multiply by fifty-two. Such estimates often add up to more than what you may think you spend. For example, if you multiply food expense by fifty-two, you will be double-counting for the two weeks that you are on vacation. Like all good accounting, these estimates are conservative, erring on the side of overstating expenses and understating income. In this way, you can create a realistic budget with a built-in cushion.

TABLE 5-1: ANNUAL CASH FLOW

Annual Expenditures (Cash Outflows)	Amount
1. Housing	
Mortgage or rent	$_____
Property taxes	_____
Homeowner's/renter's insurance	_____
Utilities (oil, gas, water, electric, cable)	_____
Maintenance costs	_____
Homeowner's association fees	_____
Home improvements	_____
Other housing costs	_____
Subtotal, housing	_____
2. Food	
Home (groceries)	_____
Restaurant	_____
Take-out/delivery	_____
Subtotal, food	_____
3. Clothing (clothes, shoes, jewelry, etc.)	
You	_____
Spouse	_____
Children	_____
Laundry and dry cleaning	_____
Subtotal, clothing	
4. Transportation	
Loan/lease payments	_____
Auto insurance	_____
Fuel	
Parking	_____
Maintenance	_____
Other transportation (tolls, fares, etc.)	_____
Subtotal, transportation	_____

5. Medical
    Medical and dental, health and
    disability insurance and expenses   _____
    Medicine   _____
    Therapy   _____
Subtotal, medical   _____
6. Advisors
    Accountant   _____
    Lawyer   _____
    Financial   _____
Subtotal, advisors   _____
7. Phone   _____
8. Household purchases and supplies   _____
9. House cleaning and household help   _____
10. Education (tuition, books, supplies)   _____
11. Recreation/club memberships   _____
12. Personal care and improvements   _____
13. Fitness club/trainer   _____
14. Cosmetics   _____
15. Life insurance   _____
16. Contributions   _____
17. Entertainment and nightlife   _____
18. Vacation/travel   _____
19. Hobbies   _____
20. Pets   _____
21. Gifts   _____
22. Support of relatives/others   _____
23. Retirement plans (IRA, Keogh)   _____
24. Debt reduction (credit cards, student loans)   _____
25. Other   _____
Subtotal, other expenditures   _____
26. Taxes
    Federal income tax   _____

State and local income tax   _____

Social Security/FICA   _____

State disability/unemployment   _____

Subtotal, taxes   _____

27. Savings   _____

Total Expenditures   _____

If your cash flow is positive, you have been managing to save on your prior income. As a new heir with good money management skills, you are already on the right track toward maximizing your inheritance.

If you show a positive cash flow but you have not been consciously saving, then go back and adjust your cash flow entries to include a definite savings amount. One good budgeting trick is to do an "audit" of yourself. Watch your spending in a particular category or keep a journal of all your expenses for a week. See if your reality matches your recorded cash flow. Remember that people have a tendency to underestimate their expenditures.

If your cash flow is negative, your first temptation may be to think, "Who cares? I just got a nice, fat inheritance!" But stop right there. Budgeting is not just cash flow. Budgeting involves projecting future income and expenses in order to monitor the use of current cash flow. If you have a major inheritance and your inheritance is going to be used to supplement your income, then it should be used only to improve the future growth of your capital base. Otherwise, the benefits of your inheritance will quickly diminish over time. If you've never had a career, but have relied on family money, losing it would put you in approximately the same position as a long-term homemaker who suddenly divorces without any spousal support or financial settlement.

Remember to keep the size of your inheritance in context

Annual Income (Cash Inflows)	You	Spouse	Total
1. Employment income			
Salary	____	____	____
Commissions	____	____	____
Other	____	____	____
Subtotal, employment	____	____	____
2. Business income			
Self-employment	____	____	____
Partnership distribution	____	____	____
Royalty income	____	____	____
Other	____	____	____
Subtotal, business income	____	____	____
3. Investment income (be conservative in your estimations)			
Taxable interest	____	____	____
Nontaxable interest	____	____	____
Dividends	____	____	____
Realized gains	____	____	____
Rental income	____	____	____
Investment partnerships	____	____	____
Subtotal, investment income	____	____	____
4. Trust income			
Trust disbursements	____	____	____
Other	____	____	____
Subtotal, trust income	____	____	____
5. Retirement income			
Social security	____	____	____
Pension receipts	____	____	____
Other	____	____	____
Subtotal, retirement income	____	____	____
Total Income	____	____	____
Total Cash Flow (Income Less Expenditures)			____

when budgeting. If you inherited a modest or moderate amount, limit dipping into your funds to supplement your cash flow. Rather, reduce debt (especially where you are paying high levels of interest, such as credit card debt) or fund your retirement plan. Once your assets are allocated to increase the level of your investment income (discussed in the next chapter), your cash inflows will increase. Then you may be able to adjust your expenditures without decreasing your capital base.

By contrast, if you did inherit a substantial amount, you can realistically consider using the inheritance to balance your personal budget. Most likely, if you've received a major inheritance, you have been enjoying some level of family support all along. But now, if you overspend—or more likely, if you invest unwisely—you will bear the responsibility for, and the impact of, your mistakes.

BUDGETING FOR CONTROL

As one new heir warned, "The benefit of family fortune comes from controlling the flow of capital. But when you lose sight of that and your money takes control, you unhappily lose control of your life." By budgeting, planning, and taking control of your finances, you remain in the driver's seat. Simply put, budgeting is the process of thinking through your projected income and expenses to ensure that you do not overspend. With your new inheritance, it may seem unlikely you can overspend since any expenses in excess of your income can be made up by your inheritance. But if you continually cover your personal budget deficit with your inheritance, the inheritance will quickly disappear and your spending habits will be difficult to control in the future.

Unless the income from your inheritance alone provides you with enough to live on, by limiting your spending to your income, and allocating your inheritance for future growth, you will simul-

THE 4M FORMULA FOR BUDGETING

Budgeting should be done as a family exercise, if you are married, or individually, if you are single. Although the process of budgeting is essentially the same for everyone, your focus may vary depending on the size of your inheritance. Here are some tips:

———o———

MODEST

Make a reasonable budget based on your past income and expenses. Do not plan to use your inheritance to make up any deficit in current spending. Rather, the inheritance should show up on your budget only under current savings and future needs, such as retirement savings and your children's college funds.

———o———

MODERATE

Create a reasonable budget that balances income and expenses without using your inheritance. You can then allocate the inheritance between annual savings and future needs.

———o———

MAJOR

You can consider your inheritance in creating your budget. Best: Add a conservative projection of the income earned from your inheritance to a projection of the income you earn from work to determine your cash inflow, then budget your expenses accordingly.

———o———

MILLIONS

Although budgeting may now seem a worthless exercise, remember, *you can still overspend and squander your family's wealth.* A budget will ensure that your personal and investment expenses are reasonable, even for you.

taneously maintain a comfortable lifestyle, invest in growth, and save for the future. If your inheritance is large enough to provide significant investment income, you may be able to simultaneously grow your capital base and supplement your old income.

Let's look at an example. Say you put 40 percent of a $225,000 inheritance, or $90,000, into Treasury bonds, tax-free municipal bonds, and other dividend-producing assets. If they pay an average 7 percent annual interest, you will have an additional $6,300 to supplement your income each year.

In order to create a budget, you need to complete Table 5-2, which corresponds to the personal cash flow analysis that you developed in Table 5-1. The key component of any working budget is an analysis of the *variance*, the difference between amounts budgeted and amounts actually spent or received. You can calculate your variance each month, each quarter, or at minimum, each year.

Using this pattern, you or your advisors can budget your income and expenditures by month, by year, or both. Of course, the most important column is the one least used—the last. Checking the variances is the only way to measure whether you've really achieved your budgeted goals. If you have high negative variances in your expenditure categories, you are outspending your own budget. You must lower your spending in that area to stay within your budget and stay in control. If you find that you repeatedly have high variances (either positive or negative) in certain areas, you should adjust your budget to reflect reality.

Remember, your budget is a tool that is not written in stone. If your budget does not reflect your own financial situation, it is worthless. Also remember that it is a personal tool, helping you to remain in control of your financial affairs. Cheating on your budget with false information serves no purpose but to cheat yourself.

Computer programs can help you through the budgeting process and are especially useful if you want to test several different potential budgets or scenarios. But the reality is, you can achieve the same results by completing Table 5-2 using a pencil, a calculator, your receipts, and your memory.

TABLE 5-2: YOUR PERSONAL BUDGET

Item	Budgeted	Spent	Variance
Annual Expenditures			
1. Housing	____	____	____
2. Food	____	____	____
3. Clothing (clothes, shoes, jewelry,etc.)	____	____	____
4. Transportation	____	____	____
5. Medical	____	____	____
6. Advisors	____	____	____
7. Phone	____	____	____
8. Household purchases and supplies	____	____	____
9. House cleaning and household help	____	____	____
10. Education (tuition, books, supplies)	____	____	____
11. Recreation/club memberships	____	____	____
12. Personal care and improvements	____	____	____
13. Fitness club/trainer	____	____	____
14. Cosmetics	____	____	____
15. Life insurance	____	____	____
16. Contributions	____	____	____
17. Entertainment and nightlife	____	____	____
18. Vacation/travel	____	____	____
19. Hobbies	____	____	____
20. Pets	____	____	____

21. Gifts	____	____	____
22. Support of relatives/others	____	____	____
23. Retirement plans (IRA, Keogh)	____	____	____
24. Debt reduction	____	____	____
25. Other	____	____	____
26. Taxes	____	____	____
27. Savings	____	____	____
Total Expenses	____	____	____

Item	Budgeted	Spent	Variance
Annual Income			
1. Employment income	____	____	____
2. Business income	____	____	____
3. Investment income	____	____	____
4. Trust income	____	____	____
5. Retirement income	____	____	____
Total Income	____	____	____
Balance (Income Less Expenses)	____	____	____

If accountants and business managers normally keep track of your money, ask for their help in budgeting as well. Even moderate heirs may find seeking professional advice on a onetime basis helpful, since others can usually see what we cannot see for ourselves.

Nonlinear Managerial Accounting: Zero-based Budgeting

In this period of corporate downsizing and cost control, some managerial accountants and controllers, who are responsible for developing budgets in large, multidivisional corporations, have found creative ways to budget. Accountants realized that you cannot always assume that the past use of resources is the correct one. For example, just because you spent 15 percent of your income on clothes last year does not mean that you should do it again. To solve this problem, accountants have begun to use *zero-based budgeting* and *scenario planning* to develop budgets and projections for their corporations. (The federal government tried this approach under Carter's administration but failed.)

Zero-based budgeting is exactly what it sounds like: For each item in your budget, you start with a base of zero and determine the amount you should spend for each item. This process is repeated each year. Every dollar spent must be justified. As you can imagine, some division supervisors were not pleased when they found out they had to justify every dollar their corporate division received. Similarly, you may not be too pleased to justify your own phone budget when you start from scratch.

To make this process less painful, many accountants now use *modified zero-based budgeting*, which, as you might have guessed, is a combination of traditional and zero-based budgeting. This approach may best suit your needs. Rather than starting each line at zero, start each line at a minimum or base amount. Then you only need to justify to yourself any discretionary spending you plan to make in an area. For example, you might need to spend 5 percent of your income on clothes, so before budgeting or spending more, think twice.

Scenario planning is the process of thinking creatively about different potential outcomes affecting your financial position. For a corporation like Xerox, this includes thinking about other potential industries to enter or the effect of a company such as Kodak becoming a direct competitor. For you as a new heir, this means thinking about what would happen to your financial position if interest rates double (bond values would drop), if tax rates increase (tax-advantaged investments become more attractive), or if the stock market crashes (aggressive equity portfolios could be wiped out).

UNDERSTANDING YOUR INCOME TAXES

The only thing certain about taxes, aside from their inevitability, is their incomprehensibility. Even lawmakers themselves admit the difficulty of the tax system.

The Internal Revenue Code does not simply define a system for raising government revenues. It also serves to encourage certain types of activities and discourage others. Consequently, lawmakers have created extremely complex rules relating to permissible exclusions, deductions, credits, and deferrals. The intertwined economic and policy aspects of the tax structure form a constant debate as the government struggles to allocate values among competing groups while simultaneously battling the deficit.

Almost as soon as one set of tax code revisions is finished, a new round of "reform" commences. But certain issues and terms in the tax system remain constant. Our purpose here is to provide you with a tax primer, a "Tax 101" for understanding our tax system. With this base of tax knowledge, you can understand the advice of your advisors, the nature of tax policy disputes, and the basic effect of investment decisions or tax law changes on your overall tax position. For specific advice, you should check with your tax accountant or stay current on Internal Revenue Code updates yourself. Of course, if you're already a tax whiz, this section will serve as a quick refresher.

The tax system is overrun by arcane terms of art or technical terms with particular meanings within the tax code. Congress currently intends the U.S. to have a *stepped, progressive tax system,* which raises *marginal tax rates* (the rate of tax on each additional dollar earned) with higher levels of income. Despite this intent, many wealthy individuals with shrewd accountants aware of the numerous *loopholes* and *deductions* in the tax code actually have *effective tax rates* (the percentage of total income actually paid in taxes) that fall below that of individuals with lower incomes.

In addition, the code is written to provide more opportunities for saving for those with higher incomes. The wealthy are far more able to take advantage of the medical deduction for elective surgery, personal trainers, and therapists than are others.

In essence, we have created a "professionally regressive" tax system which rewards tax wizards and those who hire professionals. The uninitiated or uninformed are effectively penalized by not being able to take full advantage of the complexities of the tax code.

Tax Terms

IRC:	The Internal Revenue Code.
IRS:	The Internal Revenue Service.
Income tax:	Tax paid on all taxable income earned.
Estate tax:	Tax paid on the net value of a deceased person's total assets. Currently, $600,000 of this amount is excluded from estate taxes.
Tax rate:	The percentage of each taxable dollar earned that goes to the government. For example, for every taxable dollar earned at a 15 percent tax rate, 15 cents goes to the government. Under a stepped system, different tax rates apply to different levels of income. Under 1995 rates, if you are a single filer with $30,000 in taxable income, the first $22,750 will be taxed at 15 percent and the remaining $7,250 will be taxed at 28 percent.

Progressive tax:	Higher levels of income are taxed at higher rates than are lower levels of income.
Regressive tax:	Higher levels of income are taxed at lower rates.
Marginal tax rate:	The tax rate for an additional dollar of taxable income earned.
Exclusions:	Income that is not included as part of your taxable income (i.e., it is not taxed).
Deductions:	Expenses that can be subtracted from your income to determine your taxable income.
Credits:	Dollar for dollar reductions of your tax liability.
Deferrals:	The portion of your tax liability that does not have to be paid until a future period. The term can refer to exclusions, deductions, credits, and/or deferrals.
Loopholes:	Legal, but often sophisticated, means of reducing your tax liability. The term covers exclusions, deductions, credits, and deferrals.
Gross income:	Income earned in any form from any source.
Adjusted gross income (AGI):	Income after subtracting excluded income and certain "for AGI" deductions, such as self-employment taxes paid, some moving expenses, alimony paid, and business expenses. It appears on the bottom line of the first page of the U.S. Individual Income Tax Return (federal tax form 1040).
Taxable income:	Adjusted gross income less other deductions and personal exemptions.
Standard deduction:	An annually fixed deduction, based on your filing status, that may be subtracted

	from your adjusted gross income instead of subtracting itemized deductions.
Itemized deductions:	Expenses that may be subtracted from your adjusted gross income to determine your taxable income. These deductions, which require you to keep records of your expenses, would be taken if they exceed your standard deduction (which is usually the case when you own your own home).
Personal exemption:	An annually fixed per-person deduction that is subtracted from your adjusted gross income for yourself and each of your qualifying dependents to determine your taxable income.
Filing status:	Married, filing jointly; married, filing separately; single; or head of household (unmarried person with one or more dependents).
Capital gains:	Appreciation realized from investments that had increased in value when they were sold (e.g., stocks or real estate). Net capital gains are usually taxed at a rate more favorable than ordinary income because, it is argued, this tax break encourages investment.
Passive losses:	Losses realized from investments in which you are not actively engaged (e.g., losses from an investment in a real estate limited partnership).

As a new heir, you'll come into contact with both income and estate taxes. Your inheritance comes tax free to you. Any estate taxes are paid out of your donor's estate. We will discuss estate taxation later when we turn to the planning of your own estate. Here we will focus exclusively on income taxes.

Regardless of the number of sections and loopholes in the tax code at any given time, the tax structure essentially allows only five ways to lower current tax payments:

    1. Obtaining *exclusions* of income, which are not taxed (gifts received and most fringe benefits are excluded from tax);

    2. Taking *deductions* of expenses, which reduce taxable income (the first $100,000 of your home equity loan or second mortgage interest is deductible but credit card interest is not);

    3. Lowering *tax rates* (by grouping your deductions together in one year, you may lower your tax rate);

    4. Using *credits* to reduce the tax liability itself (the child care tax credit directly reduces the tax dollars you owe); and

    5. Utilizing *deferrals* to delay the tax (income and interest earned in a qualified IRA is deferred).

Some of the best tax breaks combine one or more of these moves. For example, the over-fifty-five one-time-only $125,000 residential capital gains *exclusion* might include *deferred* taxes on houses previously bought and sold. An IRA takes advantage of a tax *deferral* until you fall into a lower *tax rate* when your earnings have decreased after retirement.

INCOME DEFINED

The first step to understanding income taxes is to comprehend the tax code definitions of income. In tax terms, "income" is not simply your cash inflow; "gross income means all income from whatever source derived." Certain fringe benefits, such as assigned parking, are taxed even though they aren't received in cash. Three distinct types of income are relevant in determining your income taxes: *gross income*, *adjusted gross income*, and *taxable income*.

Gross income includes all income from wages, salaries, interest, partnerships, and businesses.

Adjusted gross income (AGI) equals your gross income minus both certain favored *above-the-line deductions,* including alimony paid, and deferrals of voluntary retirement programs such as allowable IRA's and Keoghs. Above-the-line deductions are favored because you do not have to itemize to get them. The adjusted gross income becomes the basis for certain other deductions, discussed below, such as those for medical expenses (which are only deductible by the amount that they exceed 7.5 percent of your AGI). Your adjusted gross income theoretically represents the money you have for housing, food, and other costs of living.

Taxable income is your adjusted gross income minus itemized or standard deductions and personal exemptions. No matter how large your total income, you pay taxes only on your taxable income unless you are one of the unfortunate few subject to the alternative minimum tax (AMT). The AMT affects high-income earners with high levels of deductions.

EXCLUSIONS

Most people think of deductions as the easiest way to reduce their tax liability, but the first place to save money on taxes is to receive income excluded from taxes altogether. If you can increase your actual income without increasing your "income" for tax purposes, you are immediately saving on taxes.

Exclusions don't appear in any of the income definitions on your tax return at all. Excluded income could be cash you receive from insurance proceeds or noncash, nontaxable fringe benefits. Fringe benefits constitute a majority of the exclusions for salaried taxpayers. Within strict limits, many noncash benefits provided to employees, such as employer-provided life and health insurance, are excluded from income calculations for tax purposes.

Excluded income, such as that provided by educational scholarships for tuition, fringe benefits, and interest from tax-exempt municipal bonds, is actually worth more than other income. That is because excluded income is earned in nontaxed dollars, and the value of this income increases with your tax rate. For example, at a 28 percent marginal tax rate, if you earned an additional $1,000 in excluded income, you would gain $280 that would have otherwise been paid in taxes had there not been an exclusion for that $1,000 earned. If your marginal rate is 39.6 percent, then you would effectively gain $396 on the same $1,000.

Taxing Effects

Although given for different reasons, exclusions and deductions have the same effect on your income tax liability. They only provide a proportional reduction of your tax bill. Credits, on the other hand, provide dollar-for-dollar savings. Here is a quick example of how the three work, assuming you have a 31 percent marginal tax rate:

Deductions

Deduction for qualified moving expenses	$10,000
Marginal tax rate	.31
Federal income tax savings	3,100

Exclusions

Life insurance proceeds received	$10,000
Marginal tax rate	.31
Federal income tax savings	3,100

Credits

Foreign tax credit	$10,000
Federal income tax savings	10,000

DEDUCTIONS

Depending on the type of expense or loss, deductions lower your gross income or your adjusted gross income. As with exclusions, the value of deductions varies with your tax rate. At higher marginal tax rates, deductible expenses become cheaper. For example, if your marginal tax rate is 28 percent and your deductible business stationery costs $100, you will save $28 in tax expense. Put another way, the stationery is actually costing you $72 ($100 minus the deduction's actual value of $28 equals $72). If your marginal rate is 39.6 percent, the stationery only costs you $60.40.

The complexity of the tax code can most easily be seen by the rules surrounding deductions. Lawmakers have tried to curb abuse and limit the amount of deductions taken by taxpayers while enabling taxpayers to recognize valid expenses and losses.

Deductions are subtracted from your gross or adjusted gross income to determine your taxable income. See Table 5-3 on page 120 for an example of the effect of deductions on your tax obligation.

Taxpayers with large deductions *itemize*, or list, them. If you itemize, you file your taxes on a "long-form" 1040 and specify deductions on additional schedules. Personal expenses show up on Schedule A and business expenses on Schedule C. Different deductions have different "floors," based on your adjusted gross income, which must be exceeded to qualify.

For example, allowable miscellaneous deductions, such as tax preparation fees to your accountant, may be deducted if they, along with your other deductions in this category, exceed 2 percent of AGI. The hurdle for medical deductions is 7.5 percent of AGI. By contrast, business deductions taken on Schedule C have no floor requirement although their availability is affected by other rules on businesses such as the rules limiting home office deductions.

If you skip itemizing, as do two thirds of all taxpayers, you receive the standard deduction. This set amount, which may be subtracted from your adjusted gross income, is designed to ease the bookkeeping burden of itemized deductions for individuals who have minimal deductions. The standard deduction also serves to balance the benefits of deduction for low-income individuals—whose expenses are correspondingly lower than higher-income itemizers—by providing them with a minimal deduction to offset their income.

If you own a home, the traditional rule is you itemize. The mortgage interest expense for your primary (and secondary) residence, and your real estate taxes, together with your other itemized deductions, should exceed the amount of the standard deduction. If you don't own a home, you are likely to benefit from the standard deduction and may not need to itemize. In years with high medical expenses or catastrophic losses, such as with earthquakes or floods, you might itemize, while in other years you might take the standard deduction. The amount of the standard deduction varies according to whether you are married, single, or the head of a household.

If you think you may need to itemize, keep a file of your receipts from expenses throughout the year so that you can accurately perform the calculation at the end of the year. Of course, each individual case varies, so you, or your accountant, need to compare the total of your itemized deductions against the standard deduction and take whichever is higher at the end of the year.

Depreciation: The Noncash Deduction

To account for the deterioration in value arising from age and use of property and equipment, *depreciation* is an allowable deduction. For tax purposes, depreciation expense is a deduction of the cost of a tangible asset, such as real property or machinery, over its estimated useful life. Depreciation becomes a confusing deduction for two reasons:

1. The useful life of an asset is based on policy requirements that do not necessarily reflect reality (for example, a computer may be obsolete in two years, but may have a useful life for depreciation tax purposes of five years); and

2. Sometimes taxpayers can choose which depreciation schedule to follow when determining the year's depreciation of a particular asset, while in other cases, depreciation methods are set by law. Two frequently used methods are *straight-line depreciation*, which deducts the same amount each year of the useful life of an asset, and the *Modified Accelerated Cost Recovery System (MACRS)*, which deducts more at the beginning of the asset's useful life and less at the end.

Depreciation provides an important deduction for companies and entrepreneurs, enabling a continuing stream of tax benefits for investments in machinery and equipment.

In addition to the standard deduction, all taxpayers are entitled to a *personal exemption*. This exemption is an annually adjusted, set deduction, indexed to inflation, that is allotted for each dependent of the taxpayer in a household as well as for the taxpayer. In theory, exemptions are intended to reflect the cost of food, lodging, shelter, and other elements of the cost of living. At less than $3,000 currently, it is clear that in reality the exemption is a politically negotiated amount. Like other deductions, the value of the personal exemption is contingent on your tax rate. As a result, large affluent families would save more money from the exemption than would a large poor family with a lower marginal tax rate. To offset this inequality, the personal exemption is phased out at high income levels. High income earners also lose a percentage of their itemized deductions through phase-outs. These examples illustrate several attempts by Congress to balance the benefits afforded to high- and low-income taxpayers in our "progressive" tax system. Any time you hear a tax debate, the underlying issue is the same: Who is the system to favor?

TAX RATES

In an attempt to place a larger tax burden on those with higher incomes, the U.S. has a *graduated, progressive tax system.* At rising, specified levels of taxable income, the government imposes increasingly higher tax rates. Your taxable income may be thousands of dollars less than your gross income, but the rate is still applied in incremental steps only to the taxable, not gross, income amount. The percentage of your taxable income that you pay in taxes is your *effective tax rate.*

The rate structure, along with deductions and exclusions, embodies the core of tax policy. The greater your taxable income, up to a certain point, the higher the percentage you pay in taxes.

This amount has shifted dramatically over the last two decades. In 1981, the highest marginal tax rate stood at 70 percent. This rate was lowered to 50 percent in 1984, and then down to 33 percent in 1988. In 1994, the highest rate moved again, up to 39.6 percent.

Tax rate tables are constructed according to your *filing status.* Filing charts are broken into four categories: "single," "married," "head of household," and "married filing separately." Except in the case of married persons who choose for various personal reasons to undertake the extra paperwork involved to file separately, filing status is not a matter of choice.

Just as the standard deduction varies to acknowledge that basic household maintenance costs depend on the size and type of family, the rate tables in theory recognize the differential costs attributable to running various households. For example, single people reach a higher tax bracket with less income than does a married couple filing jointly. The presumption by Congress is that married couples will earn and use more income for their basic needs than will a single person.

TABLE 5-3: CALCULATING YOUR TAXES

Given a variety of circumstances, a family's same gross income could lead to vastly divergent tax liability amounts due. Take the example of Andy and Jennifer who earn $100,000 as a couple and file jointly in each of two years. In Year 1, Andy and Jennifer both work in marketing, have no children, and take the standard deduction. In Year 3, the couple has a baby girl; Andy has his own consulting firm; they own a home; and they itemize. Jennifer is working two jobs in Year 3 and has a credit for excess FICA withheld at her second job. We assume no changes in exemption amounts or tax rates for the purposes of comparison.

	Year 1	Year 3
Gross income	$100,000	$100,000
Consulting business expenses	0	13,000
IRA contribution (deferred income)	0	2,000
Adjusted gross income	100,000	85,000
Personal exemptions (2 in Yr 1, 3 in Yr 3)	5,000	7,500
Standard deduction	6,550	0
$5,000 Interest on mortgage paid in Yr 3	n/a	5,000
$2,000 Tax planning fees (in excess of 2% AGI)	n/a	300
$2,000 Substantiated charitable contribution	n/a	2,000
Total itemized deductions	n/a	7,300
Current taxable income	88,450	70,200
$0–$39,000 × 15%	5,850	5,850
$39,000–$94,250 × 28%	13,846	8,736
Tax liability	19,696	14,586
Tax credit for excess FICA withheld in Yr 3	0	400
Federal income tax due	19,696	14,186

TABLE 5-4: THE EQUIVALENT YIELD CHART

This table shows the equivalent taxable yields on securities before federal income taxes, assuming a 30 percent effective federal tax rate, as compared with yields from tax-exempt state and municipal bonds. In the 30-percent tax bracket, a tax-exempt investment earning 4 percent is equal to a taxable investment earning 5.71 percent. To use the chart below, compare the particular tax-exempt investment return you're considering to the column on the right to see the effective yield.

Comparative Investment Yields*

Tax-Exempt	=	Taxable Yield of:
4.00%		5.71%
4.10		5.86
4.20		6.00
4.30		6.14
4.40		6.29
4.50		6.43
4.60		6.57
4.70		6.71
4.80		6.86
4.90		7.00
5.00		7.14

*Assuming a 30 percent tax rate.

The *marginal tax rate* is the amount of tax you would pay on the next dollar that you earned. For example, if your taxable income is at the limit of the lowest tax bracket (currently 15 percent), your next dollar of taxable income earned would be taxed at the rate of the next tax bracket (currently 28 percent). Only the new income would be taxed at the higher rate; the base amount is taxed at the old rate. That is why, unless you are in the lowest tax bracket, your effective tax rate will differ from your marginal tax rate. If we assume that some of your dollars ($22,750) are taxed at 15 percent and other dollars ($12,250) are taxed at 28 percent, then all your dollars are effectively being taxed at an average rate of less than 28 percent. In math terms, the amount is actually ($22,750 × 15% + $12,250 × 28%) ÷ $35,000 or 19.55 percent. Only income above the cutoff point is taxed at the next higher rate. Table 5-3 demonstrates how marginal tax rates are applied to taxable income.

Once you know your effective tax bracket and marginal tax rate, you can make quick calculations about the net value to you of additional deductions or additional income. You can also use your marginal rate to see whether a tax-free investment beats a taxable one with a higher total yield (see Table 5-4, The Equivalent Yield Chart). To figure the tax increase or decrease, multiply the applicable marginal tax rate by the amount of the increase or decrease in taxable income.

To be even more accurate, determine your combined federal-state rate. Because you can deduct your state tax payments on your federal returns, your effective state tax rate will be lower than your marginal state tax rate. Just as we combined your marginal tax rates at each level to determine your effective tax rate, we combine your local, state, and federal effective rates to determine your *effective combined rate*. Because local and state taxes vary greatly by municipality, it is often easiest to roughly estimate your rate by adding your state and local marginal rates to your effective federal rate. This will give you a conservative estimate. For your actual combined rate, which will be lower because of the deduction you receive for state taxes paid and because of the averaging effects of our stepped, progressive system, consult a local advisor.

CREDITS

In the constant attempt by Congress to use tax policy to encourage certain types of activities, no incentive is more powerful than the *tax credit.* A tax credit is the amount that is taken directly off the tax you owe. A credit reduces your tax bill dollar for dollar, whereas a deduction or exemption is only as valuable as your tax rate. Because of the effect tax credits have on reducing the total tax revenue received by the government, Congress is hesitant to allow them. Tax credits have been allowed for foreign taxes paid, certain investments, and dependent care expenses. Congress has also enacted an *earned income tax credit* to aid the "working poor." The earned income tax credit is the only type of credit where the taxpayer will actually receive a refund if the credit exceeds taxes owed.

In the past, many more credits were allowed to spur investment. If Congress in the future decides to promote business investment aggressively, tax credits could again appear prominently in the tax planning arsenal.

DEFERRALS

Accountants like to follow the "least and latest" rule. Pay the least amount at the latest date possible. Based on the simple financial rule of the time value of money, where a dollar today is worth more than a dollar tomorrow because of the interest that could be earned on that dollar today, this strategy makes sense. In tax planning there is an additional rationale: If you defer income while you are in a high income bracket, you may be able to recognize the income when you are in a lower bracket. For example, if you deferred $10,000 that would have been taxed at 39.6 percent during peak earning years, after retirement the identical $10,000 might be taxed at 28 percent, and you would save $1,160 (the

$3,960 tax that would be owed at 39.6 percent minus the $2,800 tax that would be owed at 28 percent).

THE ALTERNATIVE MINIMUM TAX

When Congress determined in 1986 that wealthy people, receiving their wealth in the form of trust distributions or other unearned income, should pay some tax, the Alternative Minimum Tax (AMT) was established. While at a lower flat rate (now 26 percent compared to the top income tax rate of 39.6 percent), the AMT removes many allowable deductions or "tax preferences" that are listed in the Internal Revenue Code. In addition, if a person's deductions exceed a certain percent of his or her income, they automatically shift into the AMT. Thus, if someone's trust income is high, say on the order of $500,000 to $1 million a year, the recipient might have professional fees and other deductions that exceed the statutory amount, and thus would be "thrown into AMT," as the saying goes.

If your affairs are sufficiently complex to require an AMT calculation, you should have a tax professional prepare your tax return. You would need to understand the AMT in order to make decisions about such issues as the optimal way for you to make charitable contributions.

Here's how the AMT works. Tax "preference" items are disallowed as deductions. These consist of certain types of depreciation (an accountant's version of decline in property value which may or may not match reality—property can be appreciating in value and still provide deductible depreciation); expenses on mineral drilling costs; charitable contributions of appreciated property; and others too obscure to apply to any but the most sophisticated beneficiary.

In addition, some itemized deductions must be subtracted from Schedule A, the place where personal deductions are taken.

These include charitable contributions; medical expenses in excess of 7.5 percent of adjusted gross income (the line on the bottom of the first page of the 1040 tax return for non-AMT taxpayers); casualty losses, such as fire or theft; home mortgage interest; and other interest expenses to the extent of investment income.

The AMT candidate then is tested to see whether the taxable income falls below $30,000 ($40,000 for a married couple); if so, the AMT does not apply and the regular filing rules apply. Any taxable income above these two figures is taxed at the flat rate of 26 percent. Your accountant should compare the AMT and regular tax liability. You'll be liable for the greater of the two taxes.

SPECIAL RULES

Aside from the basic rules surrounding the operation of the tax system, there are two special areas of the tax code that are essential to gaining a fuller understanding of the current tax system: capital gains and passive loss rules. The sweeping 1986 Tax Reform Act strengthened preferential tax treatment for capital gains while restricting tax shelter benefits through the implementation of passive loss rules. Both of these reforms were an attempt to provide an incentive for productive private investment and a disincentive for nonproductive, tax-motivated private investment.

Capital Gains

Capital gains are established when a capital asset is sold after being held for at least twelve months (or other requisite holding period) and the gain is not prohibited from receiving capital gain treatment by case law standards. Capital gains and losses are typically given special treatment by the tax code.

Capital gains and losses are divided into long-term and short-term gains and losses. The dividing line varies, but is usually a year.

Because net long-term capital gains are given special tax treatment, short-term capital gains and losses are netted with long-term gains and losses to determine the tax effects of your capital transactions. If the net capital gains are short-term, they are treated essentially as *ordinary* income. If the net capital gains are long-term, they receive favorable treatment and are currently taxed at a maximum of 28 percent (even if your ordinary marginal tax rate is higher). If there is an excess of capital losses over capital gains, the losses are currently deductible against your ordinary income up to $3,000. Additional capital losses beyond the $3,000 limit are *carried forward* into the future until exhausted.

For example, let's say you sell four stocks in one year. Two of the stocks were held short-term. Two of the stocks had been held for years. The sales of the long-term stocks combine for a net gain of $3,000. The sales of the short-term stocks net a loss of $5,000. As a result, you have a net short-term capital loss of $2,000. This short-term $2,000 net capital loss is considered "ordinary" and can be deducted against your regular income.

Now let's alter the performance of your stocks. The sales of the long-term stocks earn $5,000. The sales of the short-term stocks net a loss of $3,000. When combined, you have a net gain of $2,000. This net long-term $2,000 capital gain is taxed at the 28 percent capital gains rate, even if your marginal income tax rate is 39.6 percent.

New heirs get an extremely favorable tax break with the *new basis at death* rule. Heirs take their donor's property with a basis equal to its value at the donor's death (or an alternative valuation date six months later). As a result, heirs are not taxed on the capital gains that were earned on the inherited assets since the time the donor purchased it. If you inherit your parents' home, then as long as there is no appreciation on the property, you can sell it without paying any capital gains tax, even if the home they purchased for $50,000 is now worth $500,000.

Passive Loss Rules

Though once extremely popular, most of the tax benefits of limited partnerships have been lost by the passive loss rules in place since 1986. *Passive loss* rules impose a standard of involvement in activities that create tax-saving loss, and most salaried persons now have far fewer opportunities to shelter their incomes. Passive losses can now only be used to offset passive gains, not ordinary income, except in the year the passive investment is sold.

Wills, Estates, and Trusts

The rules surrounding the taxation of income received from trusts and property left to you are complex and convoluted. We will review trust and estate tax issues later in Part Three of the book.

Side Businesses

In addition to being a favorite component of the American Dream, entrepreneurship has become a favorable tax minimization alternative. With business, compared to the individual return, the "ordinary and necessary" costs of doing business, within some limits, remain fully deductible. Although business tax rates depend on the organizational form, such as a sole proprietorship, partnership, or corporation, even higher corporate rates are not as much a disadvantage as might be supposed because of the many deductions corporations can take.

If you start a legitimate income-producing business on the side and participate in that business regularly, continually, and substantially, and if the business does not show a profit, the taxpayer can use the losses to offset salaried income. But beware, reform has stiffened the performance rules for small businesses. To prove that you have a legitimate business and not a hobby, you may have to show a profit three out of every five years unless you are incorporated. Corporations face no such test. Although there is no hard-and-fast rule, once the business has passed the two-year mark with no profit, the burden of proof shifts to you to show it is a legitimate for-profit undertaking.

In addition, a special rule aimed particularly at side businesses, or businesses run by full-time employees after hours, applies. This rule limits the value of the home-office deduction, allowing you to deduct a "rental expense" for the portion of your house or apartment where you work. Usually the deduction can be taken only if a room is used exclusively as the principal work place of that business. You cannot use a home-office deduction to create a loss. The deduction can only be used to reduce your taxable income for an otherwise profitable business.

An advantage of being in business for yourself is that you can hire your spouse and children. You can deduct their wages as a business expense and your children's income is taxed in their lower individual tax brackets. The only caveat is that the wages must be reasonable compensation for actual services.

PUTTING IT ALL TOGETHER

Once your long-term investment objectives are established, your cash flow is under control, and you have a firm grasp on taxes, you are ready to learn how to manage your inheritance. With an understanding of these issues, as well as an awareness of the potential psychological effects of inheriting wealth, you have a foundation on which to allocate your assets, select advisors, and plan your estate.

6

ALLOCATING YOUR ASSETS

MOST OF US DEPEND on the postal system, even though we don't have a lot of faith in it. We send postcards, birthday cards, and all-important love letters every day. But if you were asked to send $2,000 you owed to someone, would you stick it in an envelope and send it in cash? Probably not. Most of us know better than to send large amounts of cash through the mail, instead taking care to send a check or money order. Taking such unnecessary risks is illogical. And yet, many of us will do little to protect our entire estates. Just as you learn to limit risk with cashier's checks, you must learn to allocate your assets. After combining your inheritance with your prior savings, you must develop a mix of assets which will meet your investment goals.

With asset allocation, you must consider the following factors, or what we call the Seven Investment Parameters:

1.   Cash Flow
2.   Taxes
3.   Liquidity
4.   Growth
5.   Risk
6.   Diversification
7.   Personal Preference

The multitude of relevant investment factors makes decision making complex. Each of these investment criteria lends itself to a slightly different allocation of investments that can range from land to cash. In fact, some of the factors taken individually, such as risk and growth, lead to conflicting conclusions. No "ideal" allocation of assets exists so don't waste your time looking for a magic formula. You must weigh the importance and level of each factor to you. Customize your asset mix.

To ease decision making, you should approach financial decisions in terms of the Seven Investment Parameters, each briefly described here and fully explained below:

- **Cash Flow**

    Cash flow involves the movement of your cash. You have cash inflows from investments in the form of dividends and income earned, including stock dividends, rental income, royalties, and bond interest payments.

    You also have cash outflows for an investment. These include the money spent acquiring the asset, whether it be the cash you pay to acquire stocks and bonds or the checks you write for your mortgage, and for some property investments, the payments you make to maintain or improve the property.

    The expected cash flow associated with a particular investment opportunity can be used to evaluate whether investing fits well with your budget.

- **Taxes**

    Each investment you make has potential tax consequences that can improve or hamper the expected return from the investment. Some stocks promising high annual dividends may be good for your cash flow needs but will increase your ordinary income and incur taxes at your marginal rate. On the other hand, growth stocks with no expected dividends offer the promise of capital gains, which will be taxed at the lower capital gains rate.

Some investments also offer tax savings benefits in a variety of forms, including deductions, such as the interest from mortgage payments for a second home; exclusions, for interest earned on tax-free municipal bonds; and rarely, credits, such as the credit for investments in low-income housing. These benefits can make some investments more attractive than they appear on their face.

- **Liquidity**

  Liquidity refers to the ease of transferring an investment to cash. Some assets, such as a savings account, are completely liquid. Other assets, such as real estate, are illiquid because it takes a long time to convert the full value of the assets to cash.

  It would be dangerous to have your entire asset base in illiquid assets. If your cash inflows did not provide a sufficient cushion, you would have difficulty quickly getting cash in an emergency situation. You may be able to call your stockbroker and sell your stocks within a few hours, but you would be hard pressed to do the same thing with your real estate broker.

- **Growth**

  Growth is the increase in the underlying size or original capital of an investment, as distinct from income or dividends from an investment. Some smart investments do not grow at all; rather, they offer steady long-term cash flows, such as blue chip stocks with high dividend yields.

  Whether an investment grows the capital base is sometimes linked to risk, but not invariably. When investing for growth, your primary focus is on the future value of the asset. In this sense, growth is a critical parameter when investing to finance future needs.

- **Risk**

  Simply put, risk is the potential for loss related to an investment. Although nobody wants to make unnecessarily risky investments, risk is typically thought to be positively correlated with growth or expected return.

No investment is risk-free; rather, risk is a matter of degree. As was shown by the crash of the Orange County, California, municipal bond market, even "low-risk" investments can be risky with changes in the marketplace or the intervention of outside events.

- **Diversification**

    The mix of assets in your investment portfolio determines how well you are diversified. Diversified investment portfolios are assumed to be safer than nondiversified ones. The problem is that while gains offset losses, losses offset gains. In this way expected portfolio returns may be lowered. Statisticians call this averaging effect regression to the mean.

    For example, standard theory suggests that an asset base consisting only of local real estate investments is poorly diversified because the entire base is subject to loss from a downturn in that particular real estate market.

    You should consider the effects of making a potential investment on the diversification of your portfolio, but keep in mind that diversifying may be costly. If you are heavily invested in highly appreciated residential property, selling it to better diversify (through the purchase of various types of assets with the money from the sale) would trigger a substantial tax bill for the capital gains.

- **Personal Preference**

    Investors should take their personal desires and preferences into account in making investment choices. Even experienced investors regret "rational" business decisions when they go against "the gut." High sentimental value can outweigh market value and should not be ignored.

INVESTING IN A CLIMATE OF CHANGE

The chief characteristic of today's global economy is constant change. While we sleep, Japan's markets start new days, often creating a roller-coaster effect across international markets that can change your financial position overnight.

Every day new financial products compete with economically significant news for attention. Even experts have difficulty staying current. So when financial advice is given in conventional formats—with topics such as insurance, purchasing a home, or understanding the stock market—you're usually left with dated information that lacks a common thread linking a particular decision to the wider economic picture. In this shifting climate, analytical tools, rather than memorized specifics, become critical. These tools are the focus of this chapter.

In order to determine your own best asset allocation, you must understand each of the Seven Investment Parameters and how they relate to one another. Of particular importance are the relations between liquidity and cash flow, risk and growth, and risk and diversification.

THE LINK BETWEEN LIQUIDITY AND CASH FLOW

If times are tough, the first thing on your mind will be cash. You may be rich on paper, but if you can't meet current costs from your income, you need to consider liquidity and cash flow as they relate to your investments.

LIQUIDITY

Some investments are more *liquid* than others. A house is not considered very liquid since it can take months or even years to convert the real estate to its full value in cash. Investments in a start-up venture may be even less liquid. Years could elapse before the investment can produce cash. There also may be legal restrictions on the resale of your interest.

On the other hand, savings accounts and publicly traded securities are highly liquid since a trip to the bank or a call to the broker can produce cash almost instantaneously. Of course, with stock you run the risk of needing your cash when the market is down.

High liquidity often involves tradeoffs. The most liquid asset, cash in your pocket, has the downside of no growth and potential loss or theft. In fact, because of inflation, cash that you hold for too long may actually lose value. A gumball machine took a penny 30 years ago; today it takes a quarter.

The actual measure of the liquidity of an asset is often unclear. For example, although it may take months to sell a house, there are many ways to generate cash for your ownership of the house. The ready availability of home equity loans, provided the borrower has a clean credit record, allows homeowners to get cash for their immediate needs by putting up their interest in the house as collateral. (Of course, there are risks here. You could lose your home if you can't meet the payments so we don't recommend home equity loans in general.)

Many other investments are best described as *semi-liquid*. These assets, such as short-term CDs, bonds, and Treasury notes, can be converted into cash fairly quickly. Many semi-liquid investments, such as one-year CDs, can be cashed in immediately, but you would face penalties for early withdrawal.

CASH FLOW

Unlike liquidity, the cash flow of an investment deals with the amount and timing of cash produced by the investment. For example, if you own ten shares of AT&T stock, your cash flow from the stock consists of your dividends. When you sell the stock, your cash flow will include the cash you receive from the sale.

Here's an important note to remember: Although both types

of proceeds are part of your cash flow, you are faced with a personal challenge when managing your assets. You must segregate the dividend cash flow (income) from the sale cash flow (capital). Even though they are both technically cash, when assets are sold, you must resist the temptation to take that cash into current income. Otherwise, you will never grow your asset base and build your personal net value.

Cash flow tends to be most important in long-term, less liquid investments because the longer funds are tied up, the more important current income becomes. For example, illiquid real estate investments producing no rent will tie up cash for years. If the investment has a negative cash flow (the rental income is less than the costs of the mortgage and maintenance) the property produces a long-term drag on your income.

Cash flow refers specifically to the cash, as opposed to the "revenue" or "net profits" (which are accounting fictions), that flows from an asset or investment during its life. Financial experts like UCLA's Professor Bill Cockrum argue that accounting book values are important but "cash is king."

THE RELATIONSHIP

In some cases, cash flow and liquidity are directly related. A house may continually appreciate in value without producing any cash directly until it is sold. Conversely, most savings accounts accrue interest and grow in cash value continually, provided the interest is reinvested. Yet cash flow is not necessarily tied to liquidity. An illiquid venture capital investment may produce a significant cash flow, possibly in the form of quarterly dividends, whereas highly liquid stocks may rise in value without producing any cash until sold.

To determine the appropriate asset allocation for yourself, you need to first determine your annual cash needs. Your cash flow can be determined by completing Table 5-1. If you cannot do a complete analysis, a general overview of your current income and expected expenses, using Table 5-2 on page 106 as a guide, is a good place to start. From these estimates, you can roughly determine the amount of cash you need to produce with your assets. Your required investment cash flow is the amount of current expenses that can't be met with other income.

OFFSETTING CASH FLOW UNCERTAINTY WITH LIQUIDITY

After you do your budget, you may realize that most of your planned expenses can be satisfied with your current income, but there is some uncertainty remaining. Perhaps you're not sure if your car will last another year, or you don't know how much your Christmas bonus at work will be. If you really do think that an additional expense will be required, or you cannot reasonably (and conservatively) estimate your income within a manageable range, adjust your budget and cash flow requirements accordingly. You must be honest with yourself about your income and your expenses when determining your cash needs.

Let's say that after some budgetary soul-searching, there is still some uncertainty about whether you will need more cash. Rather than keeping more of your wealth in cash to prepare for the unlikely, it may make more financial sense to keep these emergency funds in semi-liquid investments. For example, if you think you may need $15,000 to put toward a new car, rather than keeping the money in a savings account that only earns 3.5 percent, you can put that money in short-term certificates of deposit (CDs) or Treasury bills (T-bills) where you can earn up to twice the interest. When you do need the new car, you can withdraw the funds as soon as the investment matures (e.g., one year from the date of deposit). If you do not need the car at that time, you can revolve the account, putting the original funds plus interest back into a new short-term CD or T-bill.

As obvious as this point seems, many people keep far too much cash on hand instead of making sufficiently liquid investments. Consider a more exact case. Let's say you invested $15,000 in a one-year CD earning an annualized rate of 7 percent interest on January 1. On June 16 your car dies. You can't wait until next January to buy a new car, so you need to withdraw the funds before they mature. You can do this, but let's say the bank charges you a 7 percent penalty for early withdrawal. If you had known the car would die, it would have been wiser to place the $15,000 in a savings account earning 3.5 percent. But you did not know. In the absence of certainty, taking the higher interest makes sense.

How could you decide whether to take the risk? If there is a 20 percent chance that the old car will die, and we assume that this problem will last for a year (to make the interest rates and penalties in our hypothetical analysis easier to follow) then we must compare two calculations.

The first is the earnings we expect from putting money in the savings account, or $525 ($15,000 × 3.5%). The second is the expected earnings from the CD given the 100 percent penalty on earnings for early withdrawal and the probability of early withdrawal, or $840 ($15,000 × 7% × (100% − 20%)).

Even given the 20 percent chance of early withdrawal, the expected interest earned from the CD is higher than that of the savings account. As a result, it is financially rational for you to invest the emergency funds in the CD.

You also can see here why a semi-liquid investment is not normally a substitute for cash. If there were a 100 percent chance that a new car would be needed, the investment in a CD would make no sense since the money would clearly earn more in a savings account until spent.

THE TENSION BETWEEN RISK AND GROWTH

Risk and growth are usually considered to be directly related. The theory is "no risk, no profit." Increased growth is associated with increased risk and vice versa. Because of this relationship, specialists analyze risk in an attempt to maximize returns.

The reality can be different. Sometimes a low-risk investment can prove to be a gold mine while high-risk investments often go bust. The reality is, risk cannot be predicted with certainty. However, some investments, such as oil drilling, venture capital, starting your own business, and trading in commodities, are generally more risky than purchasing T-bills.

THE SUBJECTIVE NATURE OF RISK

If you are risk-averse and prefer to invest conservatively, you may not be willing to place a portion of your inheritance at risk in the hope of high returns. Diversification may provide you with a happy medium. As explained in the next section, diversification enables even the weak of heart to make some aggressive investment decisions without the worry that the entire inheritance is precariously at risk.

Risk itself is a highly personalized concept. Your preference for risk may differ greatly from your parents' or your spouse's.

Unfortunately, because risk preference is so personal, what appears to be a smart investment to you may be a horrifying possibility for your significant other or your family members.

Often disputes arise over conflicting views of the need to accept risk for growth. One side may argue that riskier investments are required to grow the asset base. They may argue that without growth, the real value of the asset base may be shrinking during inflationary periods. The other side could reason that the particular investment in question is too risky and jeopardizes the family's money, preferring instead a more conservative inflation hedge. Either side could be correct; the choices are subjective.

The Cost of Money Under the Mattress

While we're on the subject of risk and growth, it seems that the safest place to keep your cash might just be under your mattress. The truth is, it's not. Here's why:

1. **The Time Value of Money:** As you probably know, a dollar today is better than a dollar tomorrow. By tomorrow you will have lost the interest you could have earned had you invested the money today.

2. **Opportunity Cost:** Opportunity cost is the economic value given up by allocating resources for one use as compared to the best alternative use of that resource. The classic example is that the cost of going to business school includes not only the expenses of tuition and books, but also the money that could have been earned by a student working full-time rather than going to school. When managing your inheritance, the opportunity cost of making one investment is the cost of not making another investment with the same funds.

3. **Real v. Nominal Value:** One way that the government, banks, and finance teachers constantly fool people is with the *nominal value of money*.

The *nominal value* of a dollar today, tomorrow, or next year is a dollar. The nominal value, or the value normally referred to when someone talks about a "dollar," is not adjusted for inflation. It doesn't take into account what that dollar can buy.

Aside from considering opportunity cost when investing your inheritance, you must consider the real or inflation-adjusted value of savings or investment. In 1995, it took $1.50 to buy what you could get in 1983 for $1.00.

So remember, although every dollar under your mattress is still nominally a dollar when you take it out, in real terms each dollar will actually be worth less (since R(eal) = N(ominal) - I(nflation)).

If this concept is not confusing enough, consider its importance.

A lot of times people will sit around complaining that they remember the days when bread was 25 cents a loaf while today it runs more than $2.00 a loaf, $3.00 for gourmet varieties. They are talking about nominal value. Market effects and wheat prices aside, according to the Bureau of Labor Statistics, the real value of bread in inflation-adjusted dollars from 1941 is still about 20 cents.

Also, the government often shifts statistics between real and nominal dollar values. In some inflationary years, (nominal) wages are reported as increasing while real wages are actually falling.

When investing your inheritance, you must be aware of real values during sales pitches by money managers or financial advisors. Although your investment may earn $10,000 in twenty years, the present value of that $10,000 depends on inflation. If inflation grows at an equivalent amount as your return during the period of an investment, then in real terms, you will have gained nothing. You would not be able to buy any more than you could have before you made the investment. But at least your money will have kept pace with inflation. Such nominal growth is necessary during inflationary periods to prevent your capital base from shrinking in real terms; and, ideally, investment growth should exceed inflationary growth.

4. **Thieves:** If you thought you were the only one who hid your money under the mattress or in your sock drawer, guess again. Everyone does it, so if you ever get robbed, that's the first place they'll look!

Differences of opinion about investment risk may also manifest itself in the form of silver strings when conservative parents or grandparents leave money in a trust. Depending on who's tying the silver strings, your share of that trust may be limited to income, or a portion of the income limited by stringent or generous living standards.

While a recipient may interpret such limitations as a lack of faith in the beneficiary's management skills, these grantors are usually well-intentioned. Their creation of such a trust is meant to preserve the bulk of their intergenerational transfer for the future. By limiting you to the income of such a trust, your creditors are prevented from seizing the trust property and you are prevented from putting the entire asset base at risk (or spending the entire inheritance at once).

MEASURING RISK

Risk is an ever-changing reality. The returns associated with particular investments are often driven by a number of factors. Stock prices are sensitive to fiscal policy and market dynamics, as well as individual company performances. Real estate is typically a safe hedge against inflation, but temporary cyclical or permanent secular changes, like the decrease in demand for industrial property, may make such investments quite speculative. Even government bonds, normally low-risk, stable investments, are subject to move with changes in interest rates or Federal Reserve policy.

How do financial analysts measure risk? Because of the difficulty involved in accurately measuring risk, the ultimate estimates are subjective. The reason is largely because future interest rates must be predicted since most investments are interest rate sensitive. For example, generally when interest rates fall, stock prices fall and bond prices rise.

LIMITING RISK THROUGH DIVERSIFICATION

"Diversification is humility," said one manager of a major family fortune. Like the quarterback who calls the play with three eligible receivers or the gambler who spreads his chips around the roulette table, a sophisticated investor will hedge his or her risk through diversification. Unwilling to risk the entire estate on a singular asset or investment, a combination of different investments is chosen.

As the saying goes, "Don't put all your eggs in one basket," By spreading your combined personal savings and inherited wealth across several asset types, your potential risk can be minimized while your potential returns are maximized.

Technically speaking, risk can be divided into two types: *unique* risk related to the holding of a specific asset, such as AT&T stock; and *systematic* risk, relating to overall market performance, such as the entire stock market. Unique or unsystematic risk can be eliminated through diversification.

Diversification is also important when trying to minimize the tax consequences of investments. If your entire portfolio is represented by one highly appreciated piece of commercial real estate, then you will face a huge capital gains tax liability. By contrast, if you had a diversified portfolio, then you would be paying your income and capital gains taxes over a longer, more flexible period of time.

The advantages to even minimal diversification are outstanding. Finance experts have demonstrated that investing in fifteen to twenty stocks can reduce the variability of portfolio returns by almost 50 percent. In other words, the loss in value of some stocks in the portfolio can be offset by the gain in value of other stocks.

This risk reduction through diversification has limits—after about twenty or thirty stocks, there are no significant reductions in risk from further diversification, but even a few stocks reduce variability by as much as 25 percent (see Figure 6-1).

Money managers suggest investment in about twenty different stocks to gain the benefits of diversification. If you are unable to manage that many stocks simultaneously, you can still achieve a diversified stock portfolio by investing in a mutual fund.

These lessons about diversification from the equity market are applicable to asset allocations in the aggregate. Your inheritance can be divided among a number of assets representing a variety of investment vehicles.

Figure 6-1. Risk Reduction

Nonmarket (Unsystematic) Risk Reduction and Naive Portfolio Diversification

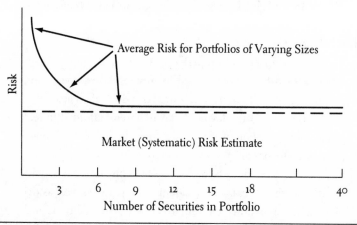

Source: J.L. Evans and S.H. Archer, "Diversification and the Reduction of Dispersion: An Empirical Analysis," *Journal of Finance*, December 1988.

ASSET TYPES

Let's review the most popular investments relative to cash flow, taxes, liquidity, growth, risk, diversification, and personal preference.

• **Cash**

Used by everyone, everyday, cash will represent at least a portion of your asset mix. As an asset type, cash includes more than just loose change; it includes savings accounts, checking accounts, short-term certificates of deposit, and money market funds.

Not surprisingly, one of the most common mistakes investors make is leaving too much of their capital base in cash. Just as it doesn't make sense to leave your cash under the mattress, cash in a savings account does not offer sufficient returns compared to other liquid assets. Often, new heirs end up with too much cash in their allocations because the inheritance adds cash to an already sufficient checking, savings, or money market account.

• Real Property

Ownership of real property (a house, land, buildings, or other real estate), whether used for residential or investment purposes, is an important component of a diversified asset allocation. Because of the favorable tax treatment afforded to real property and the potential for leveraging the investment, owning real estate has always been favored.

Real estate enjoys favorable tax benefits for interest payments and capital gains on residential property, as well as depreciation deductions for rental property. In addition, real estate tends to be a good hedge, or offset of risk, against inflation. Property values tend to appreciate during inflationary periods, which helps to preserve the real value of your capital base in inflationary times.

Oftentimes, an inheritance will involve the transfer of real estate. Although your personal preference for keeping the family's land may be an important factor in customizing your personal ideal asset allocation, you want to make sure that any inherited real property does not completely imbalance your total asset mix. If it does, sell some of the property to allow yourself to diversify your investment vehicles.

Real estate has historically appreciated over time, but the example of the California real estate market demonstrates that real estate can decline in value. Temporary cyclical changes, such as a recession and an earthquake, depressed the California market. In addition, permanent secular changes, including changing demographics, a shift away from industrial property use, and tax law changes, were brought to bear on California

THE 4M FORMULA FOR ASSET ALLOCATION

The size of your inheritance will often determine the degree of flexibility you have to consider in the interplay between risk, diversity, and growth. Since you will want to manage your inheritance in a single pool with your other funds (unless your marital circumstances suggest otherwise), the extent of flexibility you have in allocating your assets is determined by both your inheritance and your prior accumulation of assets. The following chart shows the probable state of the investment parameters for your combined asset portfolio. (Note: In this case, do not limit yourself to the size of your inheritance alone.)

	CASH FLOW	TAXES	LIQUIDITY	GROWTH	RISK	DIVERSIFICATION
Modest	low	some exclusions	high	low	low	limited
Moderate	medium	some exclusions	high	medium	low	limited
Major	high	exclusions deductions	low	fairly high	high or low	medium to high
Millions	high	exclusions deductions	low	high potential	high or low	high

As the chart suggests, the greater the size of the asset pool available for unified management, the greater the opportunities for flexibility and growth.

real estate demand. These cyclical and secular changes combined to bring a swift end to the fifty-year California real estate boom, reminding unfortunate investors that *all* investment vehicles are subject to the risk of loss.

- **Personal Property**

    Although we like to think of our cars, toys, and clothes as investments, they usually are not. In fact, based on most of the investment factors, personal property is a poor choice: no liquidity, no tax benefits, negative cash flow, and zero or negative growth. But don't forget about personal preference. If you really want something for yourself or your family, the value to you may greatly outweigh its theoretical cost.

- **Stocks (Public Equity)**

    The stock market affords you an opportunity to partake in the success of a publicly traded company. The risk involved in the stock market varies greatly from stock to stock, issue to issue, and market to market. Aside from the risks inherent in the market's volatility, as was apparent during the October 1987 stock market crash, there are also risks associated with the performance of individual stocks, known as *beta* risk.

    Blue-chip stocks, like AT&T, tend to be issues of large, mature, well-capitalized companies that appreciate slowly over time. These stocks tend to be fairly safe investments with only moderate expected returns, due primarily to the stability of the company. But as was shown in the case of IBM, these investments do not come without risk.

    Small cap stocks, such as Noven Pharmaceutical, start out as issues of smaller, less capitalized companies, often with strong growth potential.

    Penny stocks are low-cost stocks of small and midsized companies that tend to be risky, speculative investment opportunities, often with an equivalent chance of rapid capital gain or loss.

    Because of the advantages of diversification within stock market investing, you should strongly consider *mutual funds*, especially if you only have a modest or moderate amount to invest. Mutual funds place your investment in a pool of investors' funds. The fund's money manager invests in a number of stocks or bonds, depending upon the type of fund.

Because of their recent popularity, many mutual funds have been created to target specific industries, such as banking, or specific areas, such as socially responsible investments. Niche funds enable you to maintain some control over your investments by choosing a fund that matches your investment criteria.

The downside of mutual funds is the commissions and fees charged by the managers of the funds. If your equity investments are modest, the advantages of diversification and money management expertise probably outweigh the costs of most mutual funds. In addition, there are several *no-load funds* that do not charge up-front fees for the investment in the funds. Be aware that some funds also charge deferred "back-end" sales charges, often for any funds withdrawn within the first five years.

If your equity investments are significant, you may want to avoid such fees by diversifying your portfolio of stocks yourself, or with the help of a personal advisor or money manager.

• Venture (Private Equity)

Venture capital is more than simply a type of investment; it is a high-pressure, high-stakes world unto its own.

The enticement of venture capital is the potential for tremendous return on your investment.

The risks are many. It could be years before you see a dime, even if the venture proves successful. Your investments are typically limited by both legal restrictions on the resale of stock and the practical difficulty of finding buyers of such stock. Worse still, three out of four ventures fail.

Because of the high level of risk involved, venture capital investments should be limited to the discretionary portion, if any, of a large investment portfolio and only after thorough "due diligence" is conducted. (Due diligence is the process of verifying the legal and financial representations of the business.)

Despite the dangers of venture capital investing, the potential returns are not just pecuniary. Venture enables an investor to have a direct impact on the world through the flow of capital. But the personal satisfaction afforded by venture capital investments is offset by the high risk and lengthy terms of the investments. Consequently, venture should only be considered for aggressive investment strategies when a sufficient discretionary portion of the inheritance remains available for such risky investments. Never invest more in venture than you are willing to lose.

Funds for Everyone

The marketplace of mutual funds includes varieties suitable for every investor's palate. Mutual funds are not limited to stocks. There are bond funds, currency funds, commodities funds, and international hedge funds. Funds may be general or targeted to such areas as health care, high-tech, or socially responsible investments. Funds may be focused on aggressive growth, balance, or income production. In essence, even though you do not have direct control of your money in the fund, you can choose a fund that most appropriately suits your investment needs. Among your choices are:

Aggressive Growth Funds
These funds forgo income and conservatism in the hopes of speculative gains. Aggressive growth funds are riskier than their long-term growth fund counterparts. Both types attempt to buy stock in undervalued and fast-growing companies as investments.

Income Funds
Rather than focusing on the appreciation of capital, income funds seek to maximize current income through investments in dividend producing stocks as well as corporate and government bonds. Income funds tend to be more interest-rate sensitive.

Balanced Funds

These funds seek to preserve capital by investing in a diversified mix of stocks and bonds. The mix of investments provides both income and growth.

Keep in mind that there are endless combinations of these types of funds, with differing investment strategies and goals. If the options seem overwhelming, one alternative is to choose a family of funds from a money management firm with which you feel comfortable. With a family of funds, you can easily design a portfolio of funds customized for your financial needs and modify that portfolio as necessary.

• Debt (Bonds, T-bills, and Notes)

When you buy a bond or other debt instrument, you are essentially lending money to the issuer. Debt can be issued by companies in the form of *corporate bonds*; local governments in the form of tax-free *municipal bonds*; states in the form of *tax-exempt bonds*; and the federal government in the form of **U.S. bonds,** short-term *Treasury bills* (under six months), *Treasury notes* (under five years), and long-term *Treasury bonds* (over five years).

Because creditors are paid before shareholders, bonds are less risky than stocks. In addition, government bonds tend to be even safer than corporate bonds, but the crash of some regional municipal bond markets has shown that even municipal bonds are far from risk free.

High-yield or "junk" bonds are risky investments, usually in highly leveraged companies (i.e., companies bought with borrowed money secured by assets of the bought company), potentially offering high returns. Because of the level of risk involved, investment in these instruments should be limited to sophisticated investors.

Bonds are an important component of a diversified invest-

ment portfolio because they tend to be a safe hedge against inflation. In addition, unlike stocks, bonds tend to decrease in
value with increases in interest rates.

• IRA's, 401(k) Plans, and Keoghs

Strictly speaking, retirement accounts are not an asset type
but rather a way of holding assets. Your IRA can contain cash,
stocks, and bonds. Retirement accounts provide two benefits:
They enjoy favorable tax deferments and charge stiff penalties
for early withdrawal (which help force you to save for the future). You cannot directly shelter inherited money in these tax-
deferred investments which have been designed for salaried
employees and business owners. Nonetheless, if you work and
have failed to fund your retirement account because of budgetary pressures, you can allocate some of your inheritance to
pay for expenses and thereby free your job-related income for
retirement account contributions. You will shelter funds from
both the IRS and yourself and ensure a comfortable retirement
while simultaneously pursuing other, possibly more aggressive,
investment objectives.

• International Investments

For the same reasons that investments in U.S. stock markets and assets should be diversified, your asset mix may benefit from some international diversification. In this way, the
domestic portfolio risk is hedged, or somewhat offset, by international investments. For example, because a sudden downturn in the U.S. economy could simultaneously affect all
domestic investments, foreign investments may offset this risk.
You might ask, if international diversification makes sense,
where does this end? Good question. The best solution seems
to be *international funds,* including equity, currency, and
higher-risk hedge funds that invest a pool of funds in a variety
of international investments. Although there are costs associated with such funds, the ease of investment and the level of diversification available offset the expense as compared to direct

investment abroad. Other investors prefer instead to purchase foreign government bonds directly.

- **Minerals and Commodities**

Because of the high level of risk involved, investments in minerals and commodities, as well as investments in precious metals, normally should be limited to a small percentage of large portfolios.

Investments in gas and oil, if successful, provide steady, if variably priced, streams of royalties that could provide a handsome lifestyle. However, direct ownership of mineral rights is typically the result of significant luck or expense. In addition, mineral investments typically involve a language of their own so they should be limited to investors with an understanding of this area.

Commodities, on the other hand, can be purchased indirectly through investments on the futures exchange. These investments, which can be made on the Chicago exchange, are typically made by people or corporations with an interest in the particular commodity, such as Ford's interest in the price of steel.

- **Precious Metals**

Investments in gold, platinum, silver, and other metals can be made directly or indirectly by purchasing shares of mining companies or mutual funds specializing in precious metals. Although some people have personal preferences attracting them to precious metals, all metals share the risk of volatile prices sensitive to international demand.

If you enjoy the glitter of gold, you might consider buying one-ounce U.S. gold coins. They are not bulky and do not require reassaying (or revaluing) each time they're sold, as do gold and silver bullion. If you do buy precious metals, hold them personally unless you've bought into a fund.

Although it is not necessary for you to have assets in each of the above categories, limiting your investments to one or two categories creates unnecessary risk. Just as the athlete must be humble enough to recognize the contributions of teammates, you must have enough humility to realize that even the ideal investment has inherent risks that can be reduced through diversification.

THE MAGNIFICENT SEVEN IN ACTION

You may have already faced the investment parameters when allocating your personal assets, but when added together with your inheritance, you may find the challenge intimidating.

Take the example of Wendy, who inherited a house and Motorola stock from her parents' estate. Because she is already self-sufficient with her $55,000 advertising salary, she doesn't immediately need a more positive cash flow.

Because she already owns a house, the addition of the inherited family home would mean that real property would comprise 75 percent of her asset mix. Although real estate, over time, is a strong *growth* investment, real estate presents low *liquidity*. Ideally, for better *diversification*, Wendy should sell the inherited house. Since she does not have a *personal preference* for keeping this property, she may choose to sell.

With the funds from the house, Wendy could choose to invest in tax-free bonds, a socially responsible mutual fund, an international currency fund, and a tax-free money market account. While these choices both improve her portfolio's *diversification* and lower the portfolio's overall *risk*, this allocation will lose *tax* deductions that could have been taken with the real estate. Nonetheless, Wendy's mix of real estate, stocks, and funds will accelerate the *growth* of her asset base through *diversification* of an otherwise long-term real estate investment portfolio.

Wendy's moves matched the asset allocation goals she had charted out using the Seven Investment Parameters. You should create a chart when defining your investment objectives similar to the one Wendy used below:

Parameter	Current Status	Goal
1. Cash flow	Sufficient ($55,000)	Maintain
2. Taxes	Deductions available	Exclusions
3. Liquidity	Low (due to real estate)	Increase
4. Growth	Moderate (long-term)	Raise short-term
5. Risk	Moderate (not diversified)	Decrease
6. Diversification	Low (75% real estate)	Increase
7. Personal preference	None	None

The asset allocation will also enable Wendy to supplement her current income with investment income while simultaneously growing her capital base for the future. By understanding these and other investment concepts as they apply in the context of inheritance, Wendy is able to manage her inheritance responsibly.

Why the Market Won't Allow an Optimal Asset Allocation

It seems logical that with all of the financial experts and business schools out there, someone would have come up with the ideal asset allocation so that you don't have to worry about all of these technical financial considerations when managing your money. In reality either *subjective* factors intervene, or the *market* adjusts to level the playing field.

Subjectively, measures of risk vary. While trying out a new restaurant may seem risky to you, someone else dives out of airplanes for fun.

As for the market adjusting, market forces of supply and demand work against predicting pricing outcomes. Thus, if you allocate your assets based on today's supply and demand, tomorrow your portfolio may be out of balance.

How does the market adjust? Let's imagine that objectively ideal levels of risk, diversification, and liquidity exist. Now, if we make the even more fantastic assumption that risk and returns for a specific asset or financial instrument can be perfectly predicted (e.g., you *know* that G.T.E. stock will appreciate 10 percent next month), then everyone could know exactly where to invest, right?

Wrong, because the market would not allow it. Simply put, if you knew and we knew and everyone else knew for certain that G.T.E. stock would be worth 10 percent more next month, then we would all take all of our short-term investments effectively earning less than 10 percent this month and buy G.T.E. stock.

The problem is, if we all did this, then the demand for the stock would immediately drive up its price, which would in turn lower its returns. In this way, the market prevents what financiers call *arbitrage*, or money machines. It is these market restraints, combined with the subjectivity of the investment factors and the uncertainty of returns, that make ideal asset allocations personal, complex, and always uncertain.

CUSTOMIZING YOUR PORTFOLIO

Your asset allocation will be determined in large part by the size of your investment pool. The allocation will also be directed by the level of risk with which you feel comfortable.

This risk preference should take your age into account. If you have a strong, stable income derived from your job that will continue for some time in the future, you may want to take a more aggressive position than if you have retired or you are starting out in a new career.

MODEST INVESTMENT PORTFOLIO
(UP TO $50,000)

Your primary investment focus with a modest inheritance should be to provide for your retirement and your children's education. You should create a conservative portfolio that will protect against inflation.

Figure 6-2 shows both a conservative and an aggressive asset allocation for a modest investment pool exclusive of real estate. If you don't know the market, your investments in stocks should be made in no-load mutual funds to maximize the diversification of the portfolio. If you invest in stocks directly, try to spread your funds around a number of stocks, investing in firms you understand.

Investments in bonds should be limited to tax-exempt bonds to enable some tax benefits with the portfolio or a fund of such bonds. To the extent possible, hold cash in short-term CDs or T-bills; money markets typically earn two to three points less. You should usually not keep more than two to three months' salary in your checking or savings account.

MODERATE INVESTMENT PORTFOLIO
($50,000–$250,000)

With a moderate investment pool, you should seriously consider buying a home if you have not done so already. Our legal system has always favored property owners, and substantial tax benefits are limited to homeowners.

Figure 6-3 shows a typical portfolio for a homeowner with a conservative outlook on cash. This young career woman feels comfortable with over 20 percent of her funds in cash. Even though she is earning less than she would if the cash were in other investment vehicles, to her, the feeling of sitting on this much

Figure 6-2.
Modest Investment Guidelines

Conservative

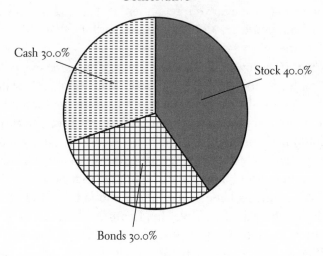

Cash 30.0%

Stock 40.0%

Bonds 30.0%

Aggressive

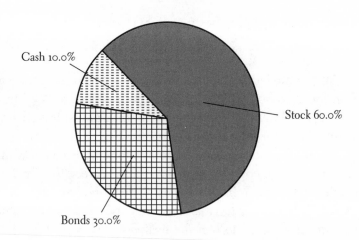

Cash 10.0%

Stock 60.0%

Bonds 30.0%

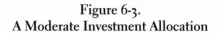

Figure 6-3.
A Moderate Investment Allocation

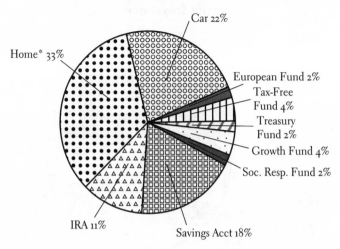

*Home estimated at $15,000, net of mortgage.

cash is comforting. She has molded her portfolio to suit her personal preferences.

MAJOR INVESTMENT PORTFOLIO
($250,000–$1,000,000)

With a major investment portfolio, you can do more with your money. You may want to consider purchasing real estate outright or putting funds into a second home. Consider a mix of both growth small-cap stocks and dividend-producing large-cap stocks. To ease this process, you could invest in a family of mutual funds providing both growth- and income-oriented equity funds. Figure 6-4 shows how the real estate investments could affect your asset mix. If you are at the high end of the investment scale, you may consider approaching the more diversified asset allocations shown in Figure 6-5.

Figure 6-4.
Major Investment Guidelines

Conservative

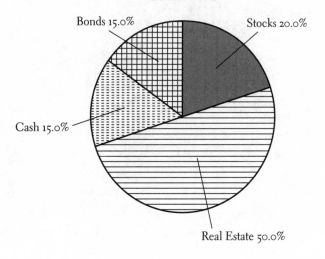

Bonds 15.0% Stocks 20.0%

Cash 15.0%

Real Estate 50.0%

Aggressive

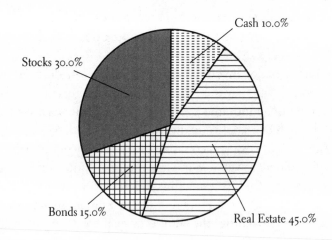

Cash 10.0%

Stocks 30.0%

Real Estate 45.0%

Bonds 15.0%

MULTIMILLION-DOLLAR INVESTMENT PORTFOLIO
(OVER $1,000,000)

Figure 6-5 shows more diversified asset allocations that are typical for conservative and aggressive investors with enough money to play different parts of the investment universe. With such a large investment pool, even the conservative investor can add metals, minerals, and international investments to the portfolio. Aggressive investors may also want to invest in an interesting and viable new business venture.

Although these charts provide a framework for thinking about your own asset allocations, remember that *every allocation must be customized for the individual.* You also need to consider your own investment objectives and investment criteria. By diversifying, you can more comfortably place a portion of your assets in higher-risk investments, satisfy your liquidity needs, and maximize your returns while minimizing the total risk of your investments.

USING YOUR FINANCIAL KNOWLEDGE

The importance of diversifying your assets cannot be overstated, especially in light of the risk, growth, and liquidity concepts discussed above. By being overly conservative and holding too large a proportion of your wealth in cash (much like the pioneers who hid their family fortunes under their mattresses), your asset base will stagnate, and potentially even decline in real terms, and socially responsible investment opportunities may be missed. By staying too attached to your grantor's past, you may place your family's future at the mercy of an unpredictable market that offers low returns or demands the absorption of too much risk. By over-relying on an "unbeatable" real estate opportunity, you could dangerously limit liquidity in investments that could suddenly become extremely risky, as was the case for many family fortunes in

Figure 6-5.
More Diversified Investment Guidelines

Conservative

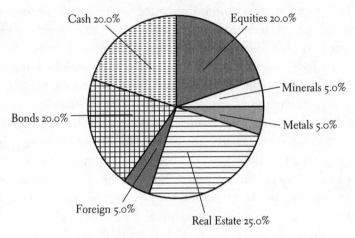

Cash 20.0%

Equities 20.0%

Minerals 5.0%

Metals 5.0%

Bonds 20.0%

Foreign 5.0%

Real Estate 25.0%

Aggressive

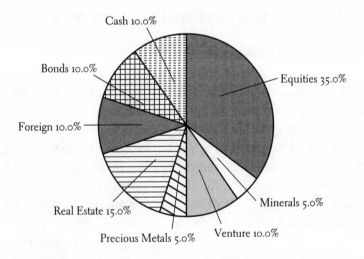

Cash 10.0%

Bonds 10.0%

Equities 35.0%

Foreign 10.0%

Real Estate 15.0%

Minerals 5.0%

Precious Metals 5.0%

Venture 10.0%

Note: This guide is fact dependent, subject to your individual needs and market conditions.

Texas in the 1980s and in California in the early 1990s. Each of these potentially damaging investment biases are exhibited by the stories of Sarah Hendon, Michele Greene, James Joseph, and George Alexander whom we will meet in the next chapter.

Everyone is susceptible to making poor investments. Even the top Wall Street analysts have lost as the market or the economy takes unexpected turns. Avoid the risks, costs, and dangers that you can control because there is no sure safe and quick way to grow your assets and produce income. As illustrated by the cases in the following chapter, proper planning and asset allocation can go far in properly managing your inheritance for yourself and the future.

7

---○---

CASE STUDIES IN ASSET ALLOCATION

EACH INHERITANCE SITUATION requires particular advice, but the general lessons of managing an inheritance apply to all heirs, no matter what their family background may be. In each of the four cases that follow, we focus on distinctive issues that may arise when combining the lump-sum receipt of an inheritance with your own portfolio accumulated over a period of years.

Sarah Hendon, Michele Greene, James Joseph, and George Alexander illustrate that inheriting money requires an active approach. Conserving the new assets while merging them into existing financial holdings requires careful attention and finesse.

Sarah Hendon, a major heir, typifies the danger of new heirs being overly sentimental about family investments. Sarah's refusal to diversify placed her inheritance at risk, and she used the fear of paying additional taxes as a shield to hide from the facts— she was unable to let go of her father's hard-earned stocks.

New York bookstore owner Michele Greene, a moderate heir, faces a different challenge. Her share of a co-owned Upper West Side bookstore netted her $60,000 a year, but produced few growth prospects due to the increased competition from national bookstore chains. When her mother's estate was settled, Michele's $100,000 share produced her first real opportunity to invest in a growth-oriented portfolio for future security. But like many small-business owners, Michele had concentrated her attention on her business. She had never enjoyed the luxury of exploring investment strategies. The inheritance afforded her the opportunity to build a balanced portfolio from scratch, but Michele didn't know where to start.

James Joseph, a modest heir, stands as a warning to the uninformed: The temptations of a lump-sum inheritance are great. He and his wife had squandered most of their inheritance, one that could have provided for his lifestyle and children for years to come, in just a couple of months. Now the potential value of the inheritance is essentially lost because his yearly income is not able to replace it, and his story remains as a lesson in responsibility.

George Alexander, a millionaire heir, reveals the complications facing even sophisticated inheritors. George inherited both personal and business assets, all of which require his attention. The complexity of his business hid an unbalanced overall asset allocation. The redistribution of his wealth enabled him to meet his cash flow and liquidity requirements while achieving both higher growth and returns.

Typical problems and biases facing new heirs loom large in these cases. By looking at their actions, you can begin to recognize your own challenges and work toward a more balanced approach.

SARAH HENDON: TIED TO THE PAST

Like many of her contemporaries, Dr. Sarah Hendon gained her position through persistence and hard work. Sarah's success began in 1961, when she received a scholarship to Cornell University to study biology. Nine years later, after changing her major twice, Sarah graduated with a Ph.D. in child psychology. All this while her father worked at General Mills, with his employee stock options constantly rising.

Even though she faced the dual challenges of being a single mother and a professional, Sarah had been self-sufficient for several years now. She had filed for divorce after eighteen years of marriage to Denzel and had retained custody of her sixteen-year-old daughter, Caryn. From her $75,000 annual take-home from her practice, Sarah had built a $65,000 asset base. Her treasure chest included her town house with $30,000 in equity; a Jeep Cherokee 4×4 and assorted furniture worth about $12,000; $15,000 in money market accounts (including Caryn's college fund); and an $8,000 Keogh.

Despite the coolness of her beige suit against her dark skin, the tension inside was apparent when she entered our office. When her father had passed away several months earlier, he had willed Sarah his General Mills holdings. When she received them, the stocks had a market value of $225,000, representing the majority of her inheritance of $275,000. She was proud to be the recipient of the stock of the company that had been so good to her family. Yet, when Wall Street trading became volatile and her nights sleepless, Sarah sought our advice. Once we generated a chart of Sarah's asset allocation, her lopsided investment portfolio was thrown into bold relief (see Figure 7-1).

Her stock at 77.6 percent ran far too high; real estate, 10.3 percent; money market, 5.2 percent; personal property, 4.1 percent; and an IRA, 2.8 percent. Just glancing at the chart shows how poorly diversified the investments were.

Regardless of Sarah's other assets, the addition of the inherited stock gave her an extremely undiversified total asset allocation. With over three quarters (77 percent) of Sarah's total assets in a single stock and the remainder of her more diversified holdings representing less than one fourth of the pie, Sarah placed her financial health at unnecessary risk. If the stock market fell by a substantial amount, as it did in October 1987, her inheritance could be reduced by as much as a third. This kind of risk is known as systematic risk, or risk from changes in the market as a whole.

Although converting some of the stock into other assets obviously made financial sense, Sarah hesitated. She admitted her sentimental attachment to the stock.

Figure 7-1. Sarah Hendon
Initial Asset Allocation

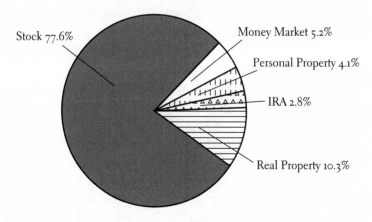

Stock 77.6%

Money Market 5.2%

Personal Property 4.1%

IRA 2.8%

Real Property 10.3%

Inheritance: $275,000

As a rationale for not selling, Sarah cited her concern about capital gains taxes. But, as we showed Sarah, this point was irrelevant. Heirs receive a *stepped-up basis* in stocks they inherit. The estate values the stock at its market value on the date of death (or six months from that date if it reduces the estate's tax liability). The estate then theoretically pays estate taxes on the stock at this appreciated value. In reality, the estate tax affects only estates valued at over $600,000. And the inheritor receives the stock with a new, stepped-up basis (at the appreciated value on the date of death).

So even though the stock may have appreciated since it was originally purchased, taxable capital gains would include only increases in the value of the stock since the date of her father's death, not from the time her father acquired the stock. In other words, if Sarah's father had purchased the stock at $4, the stock had a market value of $9 on the date of his death, and Sarah sold the stock at $10, the tax would be on the capital gain of $1 (the difference between the $10 sales price and Sarah's $9 stepped-up basis, as compared to the $6 in capital gains that she would have been taxed on had her father given her the stock during his lifetime). The capital gains tax liability that Sarah faced was consequently much lower than she had feared.

Sarah needed diversification. The balanced mix of different types of assets or investments is especially important in properly managing an inheritance because the addition of someone else's portfolio to your own often results in an unbalanced combined investment portfolio.

If her assets were a banana cream pie, and the huge stock slice were accidentally knocked on the floor, Sarah would never get to enjoy most of the pie. Sarah saw that it would be better to face the possibility of losing one or two small slices than one big chunk.

Similarly, financial analysts have learned that the increase in the number of stocks held in an equity portfolio from one to ten will reduce systematic risk by more than 25 percent. By holding more than one stock, the risk associated with the holding of any one stock is reduced. This same logic is followed by anyone who keeps more than one set of keys to reduce the consequences of losing any one set.

After our explanation, Sarah agreed to a staged conversion of the stock, selling a total of half of her General Mills stock. That portion would then be converted to achieve the more diversified asset allocation shown in Figure 7-2. At 38 percent, the proportion of equities was still quite high; but Sarah's personal preference for the General Mills stock, rooted in sentimentality about her father's lifework, put the exception within tolerable limits.

In addition, as seen in Figure 7-2, Sarah added to her real property by making a down payment on a piece of land next to her house, bringing the real estate total to 20 percent. She also entered other new markets in a modest way, allocating 6 percent to government bonds, 6 percent to municipal bonds, 4 percent to a foreign bond fund, and 4 percent to precious metals, in her case, in one-ounce gold Canadian maple-leaf coins.

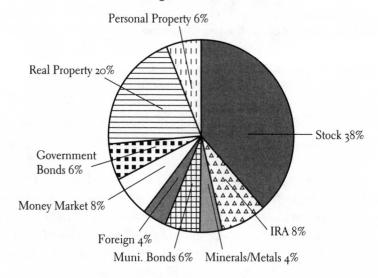

Figure 7-2. Sarah Hendon
Managed Asset Allocation

Personal Property 6%

Real Property 20%

Government
Bonds 6%

Money Market 8%

Stock 38%

Foreign 4%

Muni. Bonds 6%   Minerals/Metals 4%

IRA 8%

**Moderate Inheritance: $275,000
Aggressive Long-Term Growth Portfolio**

Once her capital base has grown, Sarah intends to set a small portion aside for socially responsible venture opportunities. Her dream: to provide capital for an African-American specialty shop selling crafts and children's toys. This riskier venture investment was not yet practical for Sarah with her limited assets. Later, when she could afford to be aggressive with a portion of her capital base (and stand the risk of loss), such an investment opportunity would empower Sarah to have a direct social impact through the flow of her capital.

In a more typical, conservative asset allocation, only about 20 to 30 percent of her assets would be held in equities, but as Sarah's case illustrates, new heirs should not completely discount their personal preferences. The satisfaction, or as economists call it, "utility," derived from following personal preferences does have actual value although it is often difficult to measure. If you try to deny your preferences, you'll cause yourself emotional turmoil that may not outweigh the risk in question.

MICHELE GREENE: INVESTING WITHOUT EXPERIENCE

Michele Greene has learned to live comfortably in her one-bedroom apartment at Eighty-fifth Street and Broadway in New York City. She spends most of her day at her Upper West Side bookstore with her partner Lauren. Over the last ten years, Michele has been designing jewelry in her free time. Four years ago, she began to display the jewelry in the store and has continued to sell a small but steady amount. Her long bookstore hours combined with her jewelry sales together netted her about $60,000 per year. Since she managed to take over her sister's rent-controlled apartment from her days at Columbia University, Michele's income was adequate to keep her enjoying life in the expensive city.

Most of Michele's income has been consumed on food, clothes, and satisfying her love for dance. At forty-two, she has long since learned to live happily as a single, curling up alone with a book or attending dance performances at Lincoln Center. She had always loved the pace of urban life. But the last four months have been difficult for Michele. She lost one of her best friends in the world, her mother.

When her father passed away three years earlier, Michele became even closer to her mother than before. Michele had handled the closing of his estate, so she knew that at her mother's death, the remainder of her parents' assets would be divided between herself and her sister. Her mother's executor, their family attorney, confirmed the arrangements. When the sale of her parents' house was complete and the taxes paid by the estate,

Michele and her sister would each receive about $100,000 in cash. At the time, the inheritance seemed little comfort to the emotional loss of her mom, but as the months passed, Michele realized that she needed to prepare for managing her inheritance.

When we first met Michele, she leaned toward putting most of the money into her bookstore. She felt it would provide a good cushion for the operation and would enable her to "relieve some stress" by taking the edge off of the operation's carefully managed cash flow.

Although the store provided Michele with a comfortable, steady income, there was little opportunity for growth given the proliferation of large, corporate bookstores throughout the city. Even if the store were sold, a financial windfall for Michele seemed unlikely, given the competition, the store's modest revenue stream, and her partnership with Lauren. Infusing additional working capital would do little to change this picture. Lauren had no equivalent amount to invest, so for minimum gains in operational cash flow, Michele would lose the chance to grow her inheritance.

Instead, if she pursued a medium-growth, long-term investment strategy, Michele could grow her inherited capital base while maintaining her current lifestyle on her current income. If she later desired to pursue a different lifestyle, she would be able to use the investment income from the future, larger capital base. Given her current needs and interests, as well as the enjoyment she receives from her work, there was no reason for Michele to attempt a new lifestyle or to risk her inheritance on the bookstore.

Turning to the issue of investments, Michele argued for keeping the inheritance in her savings account. But while this strategy made some sense for her, given her modest savings account, a significant portion of Michele's wealth would be underinvested if the inheritance were not better allocated.

Michele's chief concern turned on the issue of safety. She wanted to bolster her savings account and have cash on hand in case of a problem with the bookstore. To her, preserving the $100,000 intact in a savings account was more important than growth. However Michele was forgetting about inflation. Earning 2.5 percent compared to inflation of 3.5 percent, money in her savings account would actually decline in real value. By selecting virtually risk-free Treasury bonds, her earnings could double the yield of her savings account without significantly increasing her risk. Of course, Michele would want to diversify her portfolio because if inflation really heated up, even the government bonds would not be that safe. Remember, in an inflationary climate, the income from the bonds is fixed, but the real value of that interest income declines because of inflation. As a result, the prices of the bonds you hold drop.

With our help, Michele developed a diversified portfolio of moderately risky assets (see Figure 7-3) which emphasized moderate long-term growth and minimal total risk. Michele allocated $10,000 in U.S. large cap stocks which are mostly safe, blue-chip stocks from Fortune 500 companies. She placed another $10,000 in an aggressive growth equity fund. The fund's investments were in more aggressive small cap stocks from small and midsized companies. (Usually with the smaller capitalizations there is greater risk, but the potential of greater growth, than with larger, more heavily capitalized companies.) These equity investments, with varying risks and returns, offer the potential for growth of the capital base. Also, some of the stocks provide dividend income that could be reinvested or could supplement Michele's income.

Corporate bonds were purchased for $10,000; U.S. Treasury bonds and other government debt instruments accounted for another $25,000; and $15,000 was invested in a double tax-exempt, New York municipal bond fund. Such "muni" bond funds provide modest yields and safely diversify income while qualifying for federal and/or state income-tax breaks. Typically such funds, although they earn one to two percentage points less than similar corporate bond funds, have higher effective yields because they

Figure 7-3. Michele Greene
Planned Asset Allocation

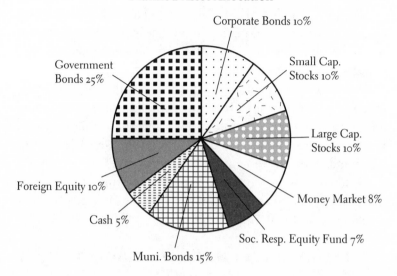

Corporate Bonds 10%

Government
Bonds 25%

Small Cap.
Stocks 10%

Large Cap.
Stocks 10%

Foreign Equity 10%

Money Market 8%

Cash 5%

Soc. Resp. Equity Fund 7%

Muni. Bonds 15%

Moderate Inheritance: $100,000
Long-Term, Growth-Oriented Portfolio

are exempt from any income taxes. (Look at Table 5-4 on page 119 to see the earnings equivalents for different tax brackets.)

In Michele's case, filing as a single person, her effective federal tax bracket is 30 percent. Following the first column of Table 5-4, we see that if the fund is earning 4.9 percent, the earnings are equivalent to a taxable fund at 7 percent in her 30 percent effective tax bracket.

Financial analysts have recently broadened the concept of diversification to the global scale. Not only should assets be diversified between national markets, but national markets should be somewhat balanced with international markets. In this way, risks related to the U.S. economy can be partially offset by the performance of international markets, such as the European Common Market. To complete the diversification process and add international components, another $10,000 went to a European Growth Fund.

Michele decided to use the remainder of the inheritance, outside of $13,000 held in cash and money-market accounts, for socially responsible investing. Although the term was new, the concept was not. Michele wanted to invest in funds that had been created to consider a company's qualitative contributions to society along with its quantitative returns. She also considered joining an investment group set up to invest capital in socially responsible ventures. As a starter, $7,000 went into the Calvert Social Equity Fund, a socially responsible growth fund.

With this asset allocation plan, Michele met her goals of maintaining her current comfortable lifestyle while growing her capital base for the future.

JAMES JOSEPH: LOSING FOR THE MOMENT

At thirty-four, James Joseph received an unexpected letter from the executor of his uncle's estate, notifying him that he was his uncle's sole heir.

James worked as a senior manager in the marketing department of General Insurance. With his $54,000 salary he had been hard-pressed to provide for his daughters Randy, three, and Ashton, six, even given the help of his wife Kim's $10,000 earnings as a part-time decorator.

In April, James received the unanticipated inheritance from his uncle's estate, a check for $125,000. While he knew that his uncle had always worked long hours as a business manager, James thought his uncle's earnings went to sustain his life in the fast lane, traveling around the country with no family to support. James had no inkling he would be the lucky beneficiary of his uncle's unsuspected generosity.

James remembers thinking that the inheritance could not have arrived at a better time. His accounts were running on empty. Large credit card bills haunted him, but using plastic to pay plastic had become a habit. With his frantic efforts to make ends meet, James needed a break.

James's first thought when the letter came was "vacation!" Upon return from their two-week Caribbean cruise, Kim convinced him that they should redecorate the kitchen and living room. The couple then upgraded the furniture to match the upgraded lifestyle they planned with the new inheritance.

For three months James and Kim hit the best restaurants, went on weekend getaways, bought new clothes for everyone, and purchased a high-end home entertainment system. They had paid the outstanding balances on all their debts, including Kim's Honda Civic and their many credit cards. James arrived at our office with only $35,000 left in his savings account.

Although he had paid off his debt, it was too late for us to help James save the majority of his inheritance. Now the challenge would be to conserve what remained and to help him budget to avoid overextending himself again. One key problem: The habit of overextending credit cards is hard to break. For this reason, rushing out to pay all bills never makes sense. First, a new plan and new habits must be set in place.

At our suggestion, James agreed to use a portion of the remaining balance to set up an educational trust for Randy and Ashton. We advised him to leave $5,000 in liquid savings and money-market accounts to meet any emergency cash requirements. The remaining $15,000 was spread among a mutual fund, municipal bonds, and Treasury notes to position James for the growth of the remaining asset base.

We also worked through a budget with James to ensure that Kim and James would stick to a spending plan that fit their resources. The couple agreed to limit future travel to local road trips until James or Kim earned more. Restaurant bills were slashed in half. Kim went on a clothes budget, and James agreed to limit the upgrades of his multimedia entertainment system.

James's experience was a primary reason for this book. Had James properly managed his inheritance, he could have supplemented his family's income to make them more comfortable; provided for his children's education; and grown an asset base for his, Kim's, and his children's future.

Table 7-1 compares the growth of James and Kim's $35,000 remaining to the potential position had the couple chosen to preserve their capital. Assuming an investment at 8 percent, with all the earnings reinvested, after five years the $35,000 will have grown to $51,426 compared to the potential of $183,666 for the full inheritance. But after thirty years, the $35,000 would amount to only $352,193 compared to $1,257,832, a handsome sum that could have been grown from a modest inheritance. Now their challenge will be to hang on to what's left so they can grow the remainder.

Obviously, earning a steady 8 percent over 30 years requires intelligent investing as well as self-discipline. By leaving principal untouched and reinvesting earnings, these returns can be produced with a balanced, medium-growth portfolio as illustrated with Michele Greene (Figure 7-3).

TABLE 7-1. COMPARISON OF INVESTMENT GROWTH

| Years Invested | Amount Invested* | |
	Original Inheritance	Amount Remaining
0	$125,000	$35,000
5	183,666	51,426
10	396,521	111,025
30	1,257,832	352,193

*At 8 percent annual return, all earnings reinvested.

Instead, like too many unsophisticated new heirs, James attempted to create a new lifestyle instead of managing his inherited wealth.

GEORGE ALEXANDER: INHERITING MORE THAN MONEY

The son of a successful business owner, George Alexander faces transition at the helm of several family-owned and -run businesses in the clothing industry. After growing up in the business, George's turn to accept control of the companies finally arrived. He had prepared for that day all his life, yet he felt the weight of responsibility for his family, his employees, and the memory of his exceptional parents.

His personal life was also in transition. Just as he took over as chair of the board, George was preparing to marry. His own new family would have to be considered along with his sister and brother in any financial plan he made.

George's financial situation is extraordinarily complex, but the issues he faces provide lessons for us all. His inheritance involved not just one, but three, companies. Although similar in operation, each of the three entities had their own finances and records, and each entity was separately taxed. His parents had also set up a charitable foundation, with its own assets, which he now had to oversee as chair of the board. Over the years, George also had amassed a significant amount of his own personal assets, as well as a growing IRA account. To complicate matters even further, George had cross-collateralized, or shared, the risks among all of his personal and business interests (with the exception of the foundation). In other words, George readily transferred funds and assets between the many entities he managed. (To avoid tax problems, his accountant had made sure that proper paperwork reflecting these exchanges was prepared. For example, if one business needed cash, another would advance the cash as a corporate loan with written documentation.)

Despite his view of the wealth as a single basket to be managed and grown, George had not considered the overall allocation of his assets. He had cross-collateralized the risk, but not the asset allocation, of his wealth. Because of the complexity of George's financial situation, we set an immediate task of providing a simpler overview of his position. Like a map with too much detail, a complex re-creation of George's asset allocation was difficult to navigate. By contrast, a summary of his combined personal and business assets proved much more helpful as a starting point for planning.

Even though his challenges were on a large scale, George shared with bookstore-owner Michele Greene a need for sufficient cash to cover potential business shortfalls. Each of George's businesses appeared to have sufficient working capital (funds for operations) to satisfy its own cash needs. But following his parents' lead, George operated from an extremely conservative stance in his estimations of liability and risk. This strategy protected the companies when the 1990s recession hit, but lower demand had sharply decreased growth in operations. The companies could survive the recession, but George felt stymied in his effort to grow his assets to provide for his family and for the future. George came to us seeking growth through investment while his operations were down. Our review revealed an opportunity for long-term growth, lower risk, and higher returns through the permanent reallocation of his assets.

First, we determined the asset allocation for each individual entity. This step was only preparatory since the result was too complex to provide a useful overview. We then combined the allocations of each business to determine a combined asset allocation. We chose to exclude the assets of the foundation from this combined total since the legal restrictions placed on the management of the foundation and the use of its assets make the foundation a completely separate entity with a life of its own.

With this combined analysis in hand, George saw his cash-rich position. Understanding that over 18 percent of his investments were in cash with an additional 13 percent in money market accounts (see Table 7-2), he could now achieve returns superior to those offered by the various money-market accounts in which each business left its working capital reserves. The combined allocation and the combined liabilities indicated that George could satisfy even the most conservative measures of liability with about 10 percent of his assets in cash, far less than the previous combined total of almost 32 percent in cash. This cash, as in Michele's case, could be moved to higher-yielding financial instruments, such as stocks, bonds, and commodities. To ease George's concern that he be positioned for even the worst-case scenario (e.g., a hurricane closing all three company sites simultaneously), he chose moderately liquid financial instruments, such as CDs, bonds, equities, and foreign securities. Although an emergency conversion of some of these holdings to cash prior to the maturity date could be costly if it ever became necessary, the slight risk of such costs would be more than offset by the likelihood of higher returns in the interim.

In addition to underinvested cash, the analysis revealed areas for reducing overhead. For example, transferring all of the accounts to one bank allowed for a significant reduction in banking fees, as well as enabling better overall coordination among the entities.

Although the assets were spread over several businesses, the combined asset allocation was inadequately diversified. Intuitively, George had thought that if his assets were spread among several different entities, his risk would be hedged through diversification. This belief, however, was only partially correct. Even though he held cash, bonds, and real estate in each of five differ-

Table 7-2. George Alexander

Liquid Assets	Personal	IRA	Business	Total	%Total
Cash	$720,000	$10,000	$1,475,000	$2,205,000	18.24%
CD's	20,000	0	0	20,000	0.16%
Money Market	90,000	450,000	1,010.000	1,550,000	12.82%
Tax-Free Money Market	0	10,000	40,000	60,000	0.49%
Gov/Agency Bonds	0	760,000	406,000	1,166,000	9.65%
Municipal Bonds	120,000	0	50,000	170,000	1.41%
Corporate Bonds	0	0	240,000	240,000	1.99%
Mutual Funds	250,000	0	0	250,000	2.07%
Stocks	0	16,000	0	16,000	0.13%
Foreign Securities	100,000	0	0	100,000	0.83%
Net Liquid Assets	1,300,000	1,246,000	3,221,000	5,777.000	47.79%

Non-Liquid Assets					
Ltd. Partnerships	50,000	50,000	0	100,000	0.83%
Personal Property	280,000	0	0	280,000	2.32%
Real Prop/Fixed Assets	1,570,000	0	1,900,000	3,470,000	28.71%
Notes Receivable	600,000	0	85,000	685,000	5.67%
Accounts Receivable	17,000	0	789,000	806,000	6.67%
Inventory	0	0	301,000	301,000	2.49%
Prepaids	0	0	127,000	127,000	1.05%
Cash Value Insurance	0	0	540,000	540,000	4.47%
Total Non-Liquid Assets	2,517,000	50,000	3,742,000	6,309,000	52.21%

Total Capitalization	$3,817,000	1,296,000	6,963,000	12,086,000	100.0%
% Total	31.58%	10.81%	57.61%	100.00%	

ent entities, he was still only holding cash, bonds, and real estate. George needed to diversify beyond these basic holdings.

While maintaining the independence of each of the entities, we used George's combined portfolio to determine the proper allocation of his assets. We sought to create a diversified total investment portfolio. To accomplish this, some of the cash from company A went into foreign securities and bonds; some of the cash from company B went into equities; and some of the cash from company C went into precious metals. Also, George bought a home for himself and his new wife from his personal funds, adding to the total amount of real estate.

In the end, George had diversified his family's entire estate and positioned it for long-term growth.

NEW HEIRS' CHALLENGES

Each of the families in this chapter faced challenges typically confronting new heirs. Although the size of Michele's inheritance vastly differed from that of Sarah's, both women were concerned about diversification. Sarah had an additional focus on taxes. In George's case, a simple overview was needed to allay his liquidity concerns and enable him to reinvest his cash for higher returns.

In each instance, a more sophisticated review of the situation enabled a more responsible use of the inheritance. While most apparent in the case of James Joseph, who had chosen to spend his inheritance on himself without seeking advice and without considering his options or the consequences, all the heirs improved their prospects by responsibly managing their inheritances.

8

ADVICE ON ADVISORS

WELL-CHOSEN ADVISORS can help you think through each of your financial decisions connected with the estate, as well as advise you on non-estate issues. Whether your choice involves buying a home or deciding to place your IRA in a self-managed account, your investment decisions are bolstered by personal, expert advice. Most important, your advisors can provide, with your input, an overall financial strategy that fits together all the pieces of your financial picture. Rather than a haphazard, piecemeal approach, a professional team can work together, with your guidance, to integrate your financial issues into a coherent plan. Even if you have yet to inherit, choosing advisors now will give you time to establish a relationship before you are faced with bigger challenges, such as tackling a trust department or dealing with the intricacies of estate planning.

Inheritors of smaller estates may first come into contact with advisors when receiving their inheritances, and the process can be intimidating for the uninitiated. Even for those used to dealing with legal, accounting, and other professionals, coordinating the myriad of estate details at such an emotional time can seem overwhelming.

To use your advisors well, the first requisite is trust. Advisors must have your own best interests in mind, not the ideas of your spouse, if you are a widow, or your deceased parents. No matter what your personal position, using advisors well is a part of personal financial empowerment, which is hard to achieve if you don't feel comfortable. Family advisors sometimes take a paternalistic approach, especially with older women, but you need advisors who will take time to explain basics you don't understand without making you feel intimidated or humiliated. So it is important to establish whether you need to select new advisors or work with those who are familiar with the estate because they prepared the will, trust, or tax returns.

Twenty Ways to Cut Costs and Effectively Use Your Professional Team

Here are twenty tips on using professionals effectively and efficiently. Each of these concepts on how to manage your professional team is discussed later in this chapter.

1. Hire and be willing to pay for competent professionals.
2. Delegate and don't second-guess.
3. Allow advisors to delegate.
4. Focus on the big picture.
5. Be consistent.
6. Moderate perfectionism.
7. Recognize that complex questions often do not have bottom-line answers.
8. Listen to advice and be decisive.
9. Don't push every rule to the limit.
10. Take care of as much of the administrative work of running your finances as possible yourself.
11. Recognize that life involves trade-offs and take responsibility for your choices.
12. Use advisors as gatekeepers to those seeking investments and contributions.

13. Plan and work in weeks, months, and years rather than in minutes, hours, and days.

14. Follow through in a timely fashion.

15. Give a limited power of attorney for specific projects if you will be on vacation or hard to locate; do not give a general power of attorney.

16. Be aware of a professional's time constraints and plan ahead.

17. Only use demanding deadlines when necessary.

18. Keep good professionals.

19. Encourage open, informal communication.

20. Courtesy and tact are free; use them even when you're footing the bill.

SELECTING THE RIGHT TEAM

Your choice of teams will depend upon the complexity of your affairs. If you are a person who has handled your own finances and even prepared your own tax returns, as many people without deductions do, the idea of adding both an accountant and a lawyer to your life may seem overly complicated and expensive. By contrast, if you have inherited a large estate, you may require several lawyers, accountants, private bankers, money managers, and others.

Even with a modest inheritance, you are well advised to consult the most competent attorney and accountant that you can. These two professionals represent the minimum advisory group a person with a middle income should have. Even if you only meet once or twice when you first receive your inheritance, seeking their advice is critical to avoid future costs that may far outweigh what you pay now.

Regardless of your exact needs, the question remains: What will these professionals do for you? Below is a discussion of the various advisors you may encounter or hire and the services you should expect from each of them.

ATTORNEYS

Receiving an inheritance calls for two activities that should be discussed and handled with an attorney:

- Reviewing the estate closing, including the will and/or the living trust and the estate tax return, to ensure that your benefactor's wishes were carried out; and,
- Preparing your own will and/or living trust so that your new assets will be protected for your family and/or for your chosen charity.

Estate planning doesn't happen just once. You need a general advisor to help you ensure that with each significant change in your life—marriage, birth or adoption of children, divorce, death of a spouse, receipt of an inheritance, or the move to another state—your estate documents are revised to reflect that change.

If you already use an attorney for general personal and business advice, find out if that attorney is familiar with estate planning. If not, ask her or him to refer you to a colleague who is. Keep your original attorney in the loop since that person will be familiar with future changes and can alert you to which changes in your assets or family affect the will or living trust you have prepared.

Selecting the right attorney for your needs may not be easy. An attorney is usually the most expensive member of the team. Both price and quality vary tremendously in this field. If you do not have an attorney now, talk to friends that do. Gather names of attorneys that receive positive reviews. You could also ask other professionals you know, such as your accountant, or check with the county or state bar for lists of lawyers by area of expertise.

One issue that arises in selecting attorneys (and other professionals) is the choice between big firms and small firms. Depending upon the sort of affairs you have, a big firm may be best able to serve the variety of your needs. Big firms generally assure quality control, but that assurance has two costs. On the one hand, your work will be handled by several people, meaning a loss of intimacy with your advisors. On the other, big firms tend to charge higher prices, which reflect the higher overhead costs of larger firms. And nuances may be lost as different attorneys deal with the same issue.

By contrast, small offices are flexible and usually less expensive. However, there is less review built into the system, so if an attorney (or other small-firm professional) makes a mistake, you may not realize it.

Paying Professionals: Fee Arrangements

All professionals are under time and money constraints, bounded on the one hand by the necessity to complete tasks according to the strictures of the profession and on the other by the need to keep costs within reason. But keep in mind that professional fees are negotiable, and considering creative fee arrangements may enable you to work most comfortably with your advisors.

One of the best ways to keep costs under control without undercutting necessary work that may not appear important to you (like an attorney's habit of documenting every step or an accountant's tax projections) is to set monthly or quarterly dollar *target amounts* for fees. Ask the professional to alert you when fees may exceed these preauthorized amounts.

Another approach is to place the professional on a *retainer basis*, which provides both parties the comfort of maintaining the relationship at a fairly constant cash-flow level. For people with continuous business activities that require constant professional interaction, retainers may be the most cost-effective fee basis.

Also consider *value-based billing*. Many professionals today will expect to be paid according to the value of their work and their engagement letters will state that expectation. Professionals who bring special expertise to million-dollar deals expect to be compensated accordingly, not simply by the hour. The flip side is also true: Several hours spent on a matter that saves only a few hundred dollars should cost you less than the putative hourly bill. Explore your professional's willingness to work on other than a straight-time basis. But keep in mind, if professionals make concessions to you and cut costs on small matters, be willing to pay the upside when deserved.

Note the special case of *referral fees*: When attorneys (and some other professionals) refer business out, some states allow attorneys to take referral fees. Certain states require that if such fees are taken, they be revealed. But do ask. Many nonlitigating lawyers do not engage in this practice, preferring instead to exchange business. If the attorney does accept referral fees, you should not have to pay the referrer and the referee hourly fees for the same project unless the original attorney stays substantially involved. Although it is not necessarily illegal for a professional to take both referral and hourly fees, it smacks of double-dipping.

When shopping for an attorney, select at least two or three lawyers to interview, either in person or by phone. Take note of the responsiveness of the office. If you do not receive a prompt call-back (unless the attorney is in trial or out of town), you may assume the office is too busy to accept new business. Make sure that you have a good feeling about the professional and her or his staff. If your personalities don't click, no matter how strong the reference, think twice. The advisor is there to serve *you*; you have to be the one who feels comfortable.

Different attorneys have different policies about initial free meetings and price quotations. Without seeing the nature of the matter you wish to have handled, it is difficult for an attorney to predict, much less quote, an exact fee. The more completely and succinctly you present yourself initially, the better the estimates of cost you will receive.

Attorney fees are negotiable. Often attorneys will give you a flat fee for a definite task, such as drawing a will. If the attorney does not operate this way, but hourly, try to obtain a range of time and cost beforehand.

Once you have shopped, expect to be asked to pay a retainer in advance that equals from one half to all of the initial amount of the work you are requesting. You will be asked to sign an *engagement letter*, outlining the attorney's responsibilities as well as your own. Some attorneys and accountants, especially in large firms, will even ask your permission to obtain a credit report.

To underscore, as with all professionals, the most critical question is: Do you feel comfortable enough with this person to reveal your innermost fears and needs? If you do, you have potentially found your personal attorney. If not, keep on shopping. In either case, the new reality of American life remains: Either you are a lawyer or you need one.

ACCOUNTANTS

If you don't have one already, find an accountant who is familiar with the complexities of estate planning or with any other tax issues that might arise in the receipt of your inheritance. Usually a certified public accountant (CPA) is preferable to a bookkeeper or other tax preparer who may not be capable of more complex work, but experience and personality should be the primary criteria in your choice. Be sure that the individual is familiar with estate planning concerns. Don't let certification per se be the decisive factor in your choice of advisor—many CPAs specialize, and estate planning may be outside the professional's area of practice. Make your decision on a combination of experience, recommendations, personal rapport, and fees. Even some IRS-admitted tax preparers make mistakes, as does the IRS itself. (A recent study found a 30 percent error rate in IRS information given to consumers—not a positive prospect when you think of the complications of estate tax planning.)

In making your selection, you'll have to choose an appropriate individual or small or large firm just as you needed to in selecting an attorney. As you consider accountants, be sure they can answer questions such as "What steps can I take to save taxes on income from my inherited assets?" or "Would I be better off incorporating my business?"

Once chosen, your accountant should be kept well-informed, even if you decide to prepare your own income tax returns. As your assets grow, new opportunities to arrange your affairs in accordance with the tax laws arise. You'll need someone who keeps up with these changes and has sufficient working knowledge of your personal financial affairs to help you think proactively.

Previously, many accountants were trained more with an eye to looking back at what had transpired in order to complete tax returns rather than focus on projecting ahead for tax planning. Today, emphasis within the profession is undergoing a shift: more accountants now provide the kind of proactive advice that keeps their clients ahead of the game.

Accountants often request a meeting with their clients in the fall to do year-end tax planning. At this point in the tax year, time remains to shift income and deductions in accordance with earnings and changes in the tax laws.

One difference between attorneys and accountants is the level of confidentiality required by the profession. Despite the sense that the information you are giving is confidential—and a good professional will keep it so—there is no legal protection in the form of accountant-client privilege. Quite the opposite: Stories have surfaced in recent years of accountants turning in clients for the handsome rewards offered by the IRS for tax cheats. Be on notice: If you have questions that you think need legal protection, ask them of a tax attorney, not an accountant. Further, if an accountant's work papers are summoned by the IRS, the accountant must turn them over; by contrast, an attorney is legally and professionally bound by *attorney-client privilege* not to turn over such privileged documents.

A word on accountant personalities: Yes, there is such a thing as typecasting. If there's ever been a straight-laced, conservative, HP-grinding, spreadsheet-number-crunching professional, an accountant's the one. Sometimes talking to these numerical whizzes makes one's head spin. But, as at least one of the authors likes to think, any stereotype is easily shattered.

With these two professionals—the attorney and the accountant—forming the core of your team, it's important to make sure that you have coordinated their information and strategy. Once these members of your team are chosen, hold either a conference call or planning meeting at least once to set your initial strategy.

MONEY MANAGERS

The money manager's job involves making your money grow by taking a fee (not a commission) for providing investment advice and then actually investing the money. These professionals come in as many varieties as there are investment vehicles, because most money managers, no matter their attempts to balance your portfolio, come with built-in biases in one investment direction or another. The key: Make sure their biases match your own.

Money managers generally exercise fiduciary control over the money they manage, meaning they obtain the right to engage in trades and transfers once you have placed your money with them. Commercial bank money management divisions keep the funds within their institutions, investing them directly from there. Smaller managers work with *custodian* institutions or banks with whom they have established ongoing business relationships; therefore, the manager doesn't literally keep your money but depending upon the type of contract you sign, can exercise limited or very broad powers over your funds.

Horror stories in the news warn of the possibility for abuse of this power. Once you click with the manager's style and investment leanings, check client references directly. Ensure that you only give as much power over your funds as feels comfortable to you. You may decide to start with limited trading powers and then gradually add more general powers once you feel secure about trusting your money manager.

The size of your investment portfolio will determine whether you should or could employ the help of a personal money manager. For moderate portfolios over $100,000, a money manager should be considered unless you are comfortable investing by yourself and you have a solid investment track record. Major estates over $250,000 should be professionally managed, or at minimum, professionally advised. Recognize when shopping for advisors that some money managers limit their work to millionaire clients with huge investment portfolios.

Portfolios under $100,000 are usually too small for professionals to manage individually because the potential fees do not sufficiently compensate for the manager's work. Smaller portfolios can best benefit from money managers by investing in professionally managed money-market and mutual funds.

Money managers' fee structures are based upon a percentage of the money "under management," as they say in the business. Fees usually run from 1 to 2 percent of money managed, although like most fees, these too are negotiable. The more money you have under management, the lower the percentage fee. Most managers operate with a graduated fee structure: The first monies invested are charged the highest percentage and as the funds increase the percentage lowers proportionally. For example, the first $500,000 may command a fee of 2 percent; the next $500,000, 1.5 percent; the next million, 1 percent. If you place a large amount under management, such as two or three million dollars, you can negotiate a lower flat fee for the entire sum.

You will have to provide guidelines and goals for the manager. A manager probably cannot deliver both high income and rapid growth simultaneously. If your primary need is a steady stream of cash, the money will be invested differently than if your focus is on long-term growth.

Money managers are regulated by the Securities and Exchange Commission (SEC), where they must be listed as "Registered Investment Advisors" and are theoretically subject to voluminous securities codes. In practice, regulation by the SEC is not always consistent. So when entrusting your hard-earned and inherited resources, the watchword is: Buyer beware.

STOCKBROKERS

A stockbroker's job is to sell stock. Most stockbrokers are paid on commission—no sale, no commission. While the industry is surrounded by research and financial advice, whenever you take "free" information from a stockbroker, or any other commission-based consultant, you're paying a price. No matter how well-intentioned and honest the person, stockbrokers need to sell stocks to eat.

Does this mean you should avoid stockbrokers? No. Just be clear about their mission. Stockbrokers can be great resources, once you have understood their area of expertise and use it correctly. Stockbrokers should not be your financial strategists. Your stockbroker can be a good source of information about stocks *once you have decided independently of the broker what portion of your assets belong in stocks and what growth profile you need.*

Stockbrokers often offer other services that do not depend upon commissions. At a full-service brokerage house, you can also obtain *cash management accounts* (with checking and debit card features); pension plans, whether IRA, 401(k) (for a business), or Keogh's (for the self-employed); and interests in mutual funds and other types of investments that have built-in fees rather than commissions.

Whether it's preferable to use a full-service broker or a discount house will depend upon your level of sophistication and your volume of trades. Discount houses charge commissions that are about half those of full-service brokers, and most houses have a minimum commission for trades, no matter what the size, from $25 to $75. The commission structure is based upon the number of transactions, the number of shares involved, and the price of each share.

In general, commission structures are set by the houses at 1 to 2 percent. Big institutions like banks pay less than a half percent to engage in *block trades,* or trading of large amounts of the same stock, usually over 10,000 shares. If you have a money manager who in turn uses a house to trade at a discount, negotiate having the manager's savings passed along to you.

Minimum fees can make small trades comparatively expensive. Nonetheless, transaction fees should *not* affect your decision to buy or sell a stock.

Two avoidable problems face unwary brokerage clients. *Churning,* or unnecessarily trading to generate commissions, represents a potential trap for small and large investors alike. Repeated transactions are made even when a longer-term strategy would have been more financially productive.

The other potential problem with both large and discount brokerage houses alike is the tendency toward stock exposure that is riskier than you wish. Stockbrokers are influenced by corporate marketing efforts and incentive commission structures to push certain riskier stocks, so make your personal risk tolerance clear.

With stockbrokers, as with money managers, you'll need to determine how much trading leeway to authorize. When a stockbroker wishes you to consider a particular investment opportunity, it's wise to talk it over specifically rather than authorize the broker to trade your account within general guidelines. If you want to delegate trading authority, in general, granting this discretion to a money manager represents a wiser choice since the money manager's fee will be paid irrespective of trades made.

Although the standard wisdom is that if you are a small trader you should consider a discount house, recognize that the higher commissions charged by larger houses include access to a wealth of research data. Therefore, if you want to educate yourself about stocks and the market, the $50 to $75 minimum at larger houses may be worth the price of the ticket.

FINANCIAL PLANNERS

During the past several years, the proliferation of investment opportunities, including life insurance, mutual funds, annuities, and hedge funds, has resulted in an increased number of professional financial planners. Unlike accounting or law, this profession is almost entirely unregulated by government agencies. In many states, virtually anyone can adopt the label of financial planner, regardless of his or her qualifications.

A hidden concern with financial planners is that many of them work on a commission basis, rendering any advice potentially biased toward a particular financial product or product line. In fact, several industries have set up financial planning services as part of their marketing efforts.

For example, an insurance industry financial planner once demonstrated the new dedicated computer he had purchased from his large national insurance company as part of his arsenal of sales tools. The computer walked the salesman and the customer through a series of questions. No matter what the response, the program invariably recommended life insurance along with other financial advice. Trying to trick the program by claiming adequate or even excessive insurance was in vain. The computer marched through to its preprogrammed conclusion: Buy more insurance.

No matter what their designation, planners either work for commissions, fees, or a combination of the two. The CFP (Certified Financial Planner) and ChFC (Chartered Financial Consultant) have been increasingly visible in recent years, while financial advisors who have earned older professional designations, such as the Chartered Life Underwriter (CLU), continue to play an active role in the field.

The question remains: How to find an unbiased planner who is also competent? A CPA must complete an undergraduate degree or equivalent, sometimes must do postgraduate work, must gain experience in the field, and must also take a battery of qualifying exams. A lawyer must graduate from both college and an accredited law school (fourteen semesters) and pass a state bar exam. By contrast, the CFP designation is equivalent to about eighteen college semester hours (about one semester).

Nevertheless, planners can provide an overview that is sometimes missing from other professionals' advice. If you are tempted to try a financial planner, look for a member of the National Association of Personal Financial Advisors (NAPFA). This organization works primarily with middle-income clients. The NAPFA members only take fees—no commissions—a step in the right direction for the trillion-dollar industry.

Be aware, however, that financial planners' training usually equips them to deal with questions from a more general, less specific, perspective than that of either an accountant or an attorney. If you assemble the right teams, one of these other two professionals can serve as your generalist. If not, be sure to choose a fee-only planner.

INSURANCE AGENTS

Your insurance agent should help you tie all of your insurance together, making sure, for example, that your homeowner's policy contains a general liability *umbrella* clause to protect you in case of lawsuits that arise from accidents on your property.

A good agent with whom you have developed a long-standing relationship can be worth her weight in gold. If you buy a new car, she can issue a binder by phone. If you live in an area prone to natural disasters, she can make sure you are adequately covered.

Just remember, the agent's fees come from sales, so check with your team before adding substantial or expensive products to your portfolio.

REAL ESTATE AGENTS

While some people don't think of a real estate agent as part of the financial team, a long-term relationship with the same agent can keep you in good stead, whether you're buying or selling a property. When selling, even in a city some miles distant from the agent, you can always have your agent place the sale with a local agent. Your agent will earn some part of the fee (practices vary from state to state) and will look after your best interests.

If buying, likewise, use the agent to negotiate for you independent of the selling agent. (Technically, both agents are paid by the seller from the commission on the sale of the house.) Your agent should be familiar with your needs and know how far you would want to take a negotiation. Even if you are an attorney (and if you're not, an attorney should always check all real estate documents), like any other buyer you are better off negotiating at arm's length. Having an agent enables you to think while in the midst of a rapid exchange of offers and counteroffers, whereas if you are on the front lines negotiating for yourself, you might get carried away. If you don't know an agent or broker you can trust, use your attorney instead to represent you.

USING FAMILY ADVISORS OR SELECTING YOUR OWN: YOUR CHOICE

When dealing with large estates, family ties often include a set of advisors to be inherited along with the money. Lawyers, accountants, trust officers, and money managers have psychological investments in past decisions, which may not fit your needs.

If your inheritance comes with professionals attached, remember that their loyalties may lie elsewhere, with other family members or even with the past. To gain a sense of whether these advisors can serve your needs, meet with each one separately and elicit his or her point of view about topics that matter to you. Establish whether you feel comfortable around each individual. You will want the feeling that you could call at four in the morning and that advisor would stand ready to help.

If you are comfortable with the existing advisors, establish your own priorities by communicating with them clearly. Ask the advisor to confirm your understanding of his or her role and professional fees with a new engagement letter, even if the professional has served the family for a long period of time.

If you don't feel comfortable, you'll need to shop for other advisors. Once you make up your mind to change, avoid too much explanation so as to avoid alienating your family and former advisors. You do not need to overexplain—you have an absolute right to choose the professionals you wish.

MANAGING YOUR TEAM

Inheritances come in many sizes, from a $25,000 parents' savings account to a multimillion-dollar fortune grown several gen-

THE 4M FORMULA FOR ADVISORS

———•———

MODEST

One meeting with a lawyer or an accountant is necessary to put your inheritance in order, assuming that the executor is competent.

———•———

MODERATE

At least one meeting with both a lawyer and an accountant plus some time with someone regarding your investment direction should do the trick.

———•———

MAJOR

You will want to build a professional team including, at minimum, a lawyer and an accountant. You should also consider adding other professionals discussed, such as a money manager, to your team. Plan to meet once a year to fit your inheritance into your existing income, tax, and investment picture and to continue implementation. You also need professional advice to revise your estate plan. Remember, if your inheritance increases your personal net worth to more than $600,000, *your own estate* will include more than the threshold taxable amount. Estate planning is a must.

———•———

MILLIONS

You should build a professional team that you can grow with as you preserve and grow your inheritance. Work with your advisors to coordinate an overall estate, tax, and investment plan.

erations back. Team sizes need to match inheritance sizes. For more modest inheritances, a small team, composed primarily of a lawyer and/or an accountant, will do.

For larger inheritances, a more sophisticated approach is desirable. You will want to build a solid professional team, which may include many of the different types of advisors described above, to maximize the growth and use of your inheritance.

Whether you have one lawyer or many advisors, you are the leader of a team that includes you as a member. Some argue that great leaders are born; others argue that great leaders are made. In either case, using proven management techniques will help you to enhance the performance of your personal professional team. Effective *supervision, communication,* and use of *information* stand at the core of a good management style.

With proper supervision, you coordinate the efforts of your team in the most efficient manner. Delegate or assign tasks in accordance with the abilities of team members since certain tasks, such as tax planning, could be accomplished by more than one team member. Also recognize that some tasks, such as overall planning, should be handled by team members together. Delegate tasks using general objectives mutually established by you and your advisors. For example, "By September 15th, I would like to have a new strategy for my growth-oriented investments. Be sure to explain my options and any legal or tax implications as well."

Communication can be achieved through both formal and informal lines. Facilitate the communication among your advisors by copying them on key documents, calling regularly, and meeting occasionally. You will be able to supervise their activities, delegate tasks efficiently, and increase the flow of information.

The point of having these advisors is to gain information. This information forms the basis for decision making about legal and financial positions. Up-to-date news also allows you to shift tactics to meet legislative changes or economic movements, and to respond to crises.

ACT AS A LEADER

Most great leaders exhibit the ability to inspire through personality or example. Commanding respect often requires more than charisma. Sensitivity to the needs and strengths of individuals on the team can inspire the kind of loyalty and productivity you want. While many captains are aware of the needs of the team as a whole, powerful leaders also recognize the individuality of each member of the team.

Exhibiting your own dedication clearly inspires others. When you are committed to doing something and you are willing to go to any lengths to achieve the goals you have set, people respond in kind. In the corporate world, a company president who is willing and able to take any job in a manufacturing plant gains an enormous response in employee productivity. (The Japanese actually require most of their executives to be able to do any job in the company.) For a new heir, showing the willingness to conquer technical financial matters provides this kind of leadership.

Don't confuse respect with *positional power*. As an heir, especially to substantial wealth, you may experience immediate deference, but you'll have to earn respect.

The more effective form of authority is *personal power*, which is derived from working *with*, not simply directing, team members. People with personal power are able to have others respond to their wishes because *they* asked and not because "they're the boss and they said so."

If nothing else, a simple policy common to many strong leaders should be followed: *acknowledge and empower each person with whom you come into contact to be her or his own best.* For example, if your accountant also has an investment bent, allow that person to share ideas for portfolio growth. If your lawyer's lifework includes an interest in international investments, embrace the information she or he can bring to the table. In both individual and group settings, underscore strengths. When team members sense this consideration coming from you, they respond in kind.

MAINTAIN LONG-TERM PROFESSIONAL RELATIONSHIPS

By developing a long-term relationship with your advisors you will establish mutual trust and improve the level and quality of service you receive. You'll better understand the abilities of your advisors, which will improve your ability to delegate, and they will better understand your wants and needs, which will improve their ability to service you.

Most professionals will go the extra mile for clients they care about. In the busy world of professional life, no amount of money can command attention for a client who is perceived as difficult to serve or who constantly changes advisors. So once you are comfortable with your informed selections, stick with the people who have invested time and energy in getting to know you, not just your affairs as they appear on paper. Long-term relationships will save you money too, because like a new mate, new professionals (and clients) must be courted.

HOLD REGULAR PLANNING MEETINGS

Whether you have a modest inheritance and meet only once with your sole advisor or you inherit a large estate and hold quarterly meetings with your professional team, any budget for professional services, large or small, should include regular planning meetings, even if only once every two or three years. Aside from the initial meeting, when your team will obtain a complete overview of your situation, these meetings enable you to develop your relationship, allow open communication, and enable brain-storming with the team. Even if your inheritance is very small and doesn't warrant this kind of attention, if at all feasible, use the experience to enrich your regular income and investment activities. One heir complained about the cost of meetings, feeling they were a "waste of time" and nothing was accomplished. She cancelled all advisory meetings for a year. At the end of the year, her professional costs had risen because none of the professionals were clearly aware of what the others were doing. In addition, no one was responsible for reinvesting her dividends. At the end of the year, the result was that 25 percent of her assets were cash — a lack of coordination that cost her several hundred thousand dollars in lost income. All for want of a $1,000 meeting. While this example may seem extreme, it happens on smaller scales whenever a team doesn't have a chance to communicate.

To run a meeting effectively, create an agenda and save new business for the end of the meeting. Don't follow the example of one heir, who came late to each meeting. While his advisors waited in a conference room, their fee clocks ticking, the client spent the next fifteen minutes making telephone calls about lunch appointments and basketball tickets.

Instead, come prepared. Read all the materials your professionals have prepared for you in advance and write down questions about specifics. Allow some time for dialogue on each issue — don't always demand a bottom line, for, many times, no bottom line exists. Rather, a series of decision-trees branch in several directions, and a set of choices must be made to reach one or more viable alternatives, each with different ramifications. For example, if you ask, "What's the bottom line, should I invest in this property or not?", at best you'll get a partial answer. If you ask instead, "How does this investment affect my asset allocation? How does it affect my growth? How does it affect my taxes?", you'll receive perspectives that will aid you in making the decision. Also remember to ask: "What would be a better choice?"

How to Complain and Get the Results You Want

In the world of commercial transactions, things will sometimes go wrong for the consumer. If you find yourself in the position of having to complain about services, tried and true techniques will increase the likelihood of your getting what you want. Here are seven pointers for systematically achieving the best results.

1. *As a preventive measure, establish yourself as a preferred customer.*

By becoming a regular and familiar client, you will receive good service in the first place. This practice will usually save you the trouble of having a reason to complain.

2. *Before you complain, outline the problem for yourself and clarify how you would like it resolved.*

Put down on paper exactly what you perceive is wrong, as best as you can, including when the "symptoms" began, what they are, and what the "diagnosis" is. Once you can state the problem and preferred solution precisely, you are closer to resolution. Simply griping without specifics can turn any situation sour.

3. *Be organized: as a routine habit, keep copies of all correspondence and bills.*

If you have a legitimate concern about a professional bill, check your own notes from each conversation with that professional. Check to see what you have authorized, how much time was spent talking about it on the phone, and what your price expectations were.

If the complaint is instead about the quality of the service rendered, your correspondence with the professional will assist you in deciding how to tackle the problem. In addition, review your file and notes about the issue at hand and see what obvious issues arise in your own review. Trust your ability to engage in such a review.

4. *Decide on the best person to complain to and the best means of reaching that person, whether by letter, telephone, or personal visit.*

In most cases, you should first bring up the problem, whatever it is, directly with the professional and try to resolve it. But in some instances, another approach will be necessary. If you are dealing with an attorney or an accountant in a large firm, then you may need to speak with a higher-up if your concern is not resolved.

5. *If you can't get satisfactory resolution dealing directly with the firm in question, it's time to turn to a professional or government organization.*

If approaches within the establishment do not work, remember that every professional, whether fee- or commission-based, is governed by some outside authority. For attorneys, it is the state bar; for accountants, the state board of accountancy; for money managers, the SEC; and for the commission-based professionals, the state departments regulating the particular field. In addition, if you feel the matter extends beyond professional performance and into the problems of malfeasance or fraud, your local or state district attorney can become involved.

In general, when dealing with professionals or with any other situation requiring complaint satisfaction, if in doubt, start at the top. Whether you have a problem involving a large amount of money, a policy variation, or a waiver, avoid getting a "no" lower down the authority ladder. Once people have dug into their positions, it's harder for higher-ups to intervene, whereas one of the prime functions of bosses is to decide when to make exceptions to rules.

6. *Keep your cool at all costs.*

Remember that angry accusations will very likely elicit an angry or defensive response and give the person with whom you are dealing the excuse to decide that the problem is your personality and not a legitimate complaint. In legal circles, the professional complainer is known as a "litigious" person, and being tagged with this label is the kiss of death.

Do start out with a strong, clear statement of your case: "This is what happened, and this is what I want done." Don't be tentative, as in, "This is what happened . . . I think . . . but I don't know if you can do anything." You are risking, not engaging, the full attention and real effort from the individual you are approaching.

Whatever you do, don't begin with the threat of legal action. Court is the appeal of last resort, not the first option in a complaint process.

7. *Figure out the "opportunity cost" of making and resolving your complaint before you pursue it to the fullest extent.*

Spending $300 to solve a $100 complaint doesn't make economic sense, and you may lose a valuable professional relationship in the process. Unless "being in the right" is really worth the psychic and economic hassle, you may prefer to temper your complaint with considered action. Remember that powerful people choose their battles carefully.

SPECIAL PROBLEMS WHEN YOU CAN'T FIRE TEAM MEMBERS

There are two times when you may have no choice over the professionals on your team: during the estate settlement stage when you are working with an executor chosen by your benefactor and throughout the life of a trust if you are the beneficiary.

Your relationship with the executor, unless a family member, can normally end within nine months (the date when the federal estate tax return is due) unless the estate is terribly complex or the will is subject to court challenge.

With trustees, however, your challenge may be to get along for years with people whose ideas and objectives are diametrically opposed to your own. With these people, as in any situation that involves give and take, good negotiating techniques are a must. While a full-scale negotiation course is beyond the scope here, some key negotiating techniques are:

- Try to see the other side's point of view.
- Work from a nonconfrontational stance, using facts and logic, rather than emotion, to make your points.
- Empathize with the other side's entire position, not just stated goals, including the personal and institutional imperatives that drive the people with whom you are negotiating.

- Be persistent. If you reach a stalemate, return again at a future date.

Keep in mind that even if you do not favor a professional that you must work with, the relationship will continue, at least for a limited duration. That means, where possible, treat these individuals with the same courtesy you do the other advisors on your team, and maintain a professional relationship at all times to ensure that you do not jeopardize your rights and privileges because of a personality conflict.

KEEPING PROFESSIONAL COSTS UNDER CONTROL

People with resources tend to use professionals more than the average person, and indeed they often need more advice as their finances become more complex. The following tips, which were summarized above, will help you to use your advisors in the most cost-effective manner. Some of these tips might seem obvious, but you would be surprised to find how often otherwise smart people fail to heed them.

1. *Hire and be willing to pay for competent professionals.* To use these rules, you have to work with, rely upon, and delegate to people you can trust. Good professional advice is expensive. Bad professional advice is even more expensive.

2. *Delegate and don't second-guess.* When you delegate matters to your professional advisors, outline your goals and then allow time for results to be achieved. Don't try to oversee *how* they are achieved. The habit of second-guessing is costly, especially when it creates an atmosphere of fear or animosity among those who work for you.

3. *Allow advisors to delegate.* Be aware that you can save money if professionals are able to delegate work efficiently among

themselves. Also, for matters that don't require the professional's direct attention, call the professional's assistant.

4. *Focus on the big picture.* Let others focus on the details and give them room to perform unless they ask for your help.

5. *Be consistent.* Don't give mixed signals about your intentions regarding delegation. If you want to manage more and delegate less, do so on a steady, ongoing basis.

6. *Moderate perfectionism.* Being a perfectionist costs money. If you are willing to put up with moderate standards of performance, less expensive personnel can do more tasks for you. Also, perfectionism causes professionals to overprepare, which can be costly. A corollary to this rule is: Don't nitpick.

7. *Recognize that complex questions often do not have bottom-line answers.* By foreshortening the process of discovery and discussion, you may lose valuable information that should be learned now, not later.

8. *Listen to advice and be decisive.* Once your team has offered its expert opinions, extending decisions and continuing to explore options is more costly and usually does not produce better results. This also means avoiding "cocktail-party wisdom." Every advisor has clients who routinely go to cocktail parties, meet other professionals seeking business, and come back with "new" information that they've been trying to explain for months.

9. *Don't push every rule to the limit,* although many rules have exceptions and there are endless gray areas in the law. Clients who attempt to find the limits of every rule, much like tired children pushing their parents, stress their advisors and run up unnecessarily high bills.

10. *Take care of as much of the administrative work of running your finances as possible yourself.* Do your own meeting scheduling, coordinate your own conference calls, and draft your own letters. Do your own footwork, getting the basic information, rather than pay professional rates to find out information that you

can get yourself. And keep track of documents. Every time you ask for duplicates, it costs the professional (and you) staff time.

11.   *Recognize that life involves trade-offs and take responsibility for your choices.* If your income is high, you may choose to pay others to fight life's financial, legal, and paperwork battles for you, freeing yourself to enjoy the money you have. If you choose to let others do the work for you and it costs money, even a lot of money, look at the costs of the alternatives. If money was saved or made because others kept track or if your time was well spent in enjoyable activities while your professional advisors "minded the store," don't begrudge the money you spent. Remember that time is money and even if a significant portion of your income goes to others for services, it may be worthwhile if it allows you to pursue your own interests.

12.   *Use advisors as gatekeepers to those seeking investments and contributions.* Remember that advisors may act as gatekeepers for you. Good advisors can screen out requests for investments and contributions, helping you limit your choices to the best opportunities. Recognize that gatekeeping also brings power. Many gatekeepers gain in power as a result of helping you to select ventures and charities to support. Remember, to many middle-income professional gatekeepers, having the opportunity to influence the course of events, even secondhand, is an important perk of the advisory position. If you enjoy the day-to-day power brokering, by all means require that all requests be routed to you directly and then use the advisor to render an opinion for you. Or, do as some donors do, and delegate the noes, saving the yeses for yourself. From your point of view, the salient issue is: "Do I need or want the extra hassle and exposure of dealing with all the requests; and, am I willing to pay the price of screening?"

13.   *Plan and work in weeks, months, and years rather than minutes, hours, and days.* The more planning you can build into your activities, the easier it is for professionals to service you cost-effectively.

14. *Follow through in a timely fashion.* Repeated attempts to finish the same project are costly. Information and momentum are lost. It costs time and therefore money for professionals to refresh themselves about an old project each time the subject is reraised.

15. *Give a limited power of attorney for specific projects if you will be on vacation or hard to locate; do not give a general power of attorney.* While a general power of attorney is unnecessary and inadvisable unless you will be on an extended trip (and even then you'd want to know the professional well since she or he could, in theory, do anything), a limited power of attorney can allow your professional to move ahead on deadlines within the parameters you have established.

16. *Be aware of a professional's time constraints and plan ahead.* Most professionals are busy (and you don't want a professional who isn't busy, do you?), so you need to consider their schedules with yours where possible. You should also try not to intrude on professionals' holidays. Professionals lead busy lives with many demands from their clients, colleagues, and communities. They need their holidays and vacations to recuperate. Lonely people with money, to the dismay of their advisors, often decide to engage in transactions during the holiday season. Unless you are dealing with an actual emergency, save it for January 2nd.

17. *Only use demanding deadlines when necessary.* Demanding immediate attention often requires professionals to inefficiently rearrange their schedules, which, if done unnecessarily or repeatedly, may both strain the relationship and cause the professional to treat such demands as crying wolf. Also, many clients will make time demands on their advisors but will not respond in kind on their own end. Because clients constantly violate this rule, the obvious should be reinforced: Do not demand a report tomorrow if you are not going to read it for a month.

18. *Keep good professionals.* Once you've made informed decisions and picked your team, create an atmosphere of trust. Set up mutually agreed-upon review times for renewing your commitments, then stick with your decisions about the professionals you have chosen.

19. *Encourage open, informal communication.* At more relaxed times, professionals may share observations that they may hold back in more formal office settings.

20. *Courtesy and tact are free; use them even when you're footing the bill.* Surprisingly, many otherwise astute people have not recognized that treating others with consideration produces better results. Often people will go out of their way for you (and it won't cost extra) if you go out of your way to acknowledge their efforts.

If you follow these tips, you can save money on professionals who will produce more effective work. But remember, if your goal is to free your time to enjoy your inheritance, you will have to pay for the privilege. Strike the balance between doing things for yourself and having them done in terms of a budget that works for you.

Keep in mind that being rich, or even a paying customer, doesn't automatically make you right. Assume that the professional's time is as important as yours, give respect to what professionals say (otherwise, why did you hire them?), and recognize that your team can only function as effectively as its leader.

PART III

PROVIDING FOR THE FUTURE

> Men must endure
> Their going hence, even as their coming hither:
> Ripeness is all.
>
> —Shakespeare, *King Lear*

9

—○—

PLANNING YOUR ESTATE

AMONG CIVILIZED HUMANITY, no two topics are more fearsome or inevitable than death and taxes. Estate planning combines both. Whether you are a new or expectant heir, the child who will inherit from parents, the parent who will be leaving an estate, or the beneficiary of a trust, you need to conquer the basics of estate planning. Because estate planning involves dealing with your own death or that of a family member or friend, it is a chore understandably approached with seriousness and difficulty.

The laws of inheritance regulate the disposition of private property after the owner's death. The will or trust sets out your property plans. If you do not prepare a will, trust, or a "will substitute," state intestacy laws will designate the beneficiaries of your estate for you. (See Chapter 3 regarding will substitutes such as joint tenancy.)

Dying intestate, without a will, trust, or will substitutes, can cause major problems for your relatives. The process of administering your estate can become burdensome and the state's choice of beneficiaries might not match your own. Failing to take care of your loved ones by not planning for their future is a poor way to say goodbye.

FOUR GOOD REASONS TO PLAN YOUR ESTATE

Even though death may seem remote, there are good reasons to create a will or trust:

1. To ensure that your spouse will inherit as much of the estate as you wish, consistent with the objective of minimizing taxes;

2. To specify who should take care of minor children if both parents die;

3. To choose an administrator for the estate; and

4. To specify special gifts to charities, friends, or relatives who would not inherit anything under the statutory provisions for those who die without a will or trust.

PLANNING THE FUTURE WITH TOOLS OF THE PAST

Like voting, the right to make disposition of your property developed over time from the purview of the privileged few to the right of the many. Nonetheless, the past still renders some of the twists and turns of estate planning virtually unintelligible to the average person.

For example, most states require that if children are to be omitted from a will, the will must specifically address the point and specifically name the children omitted. Otherwise, the estate will face the problem of the *pretermitted heir*, the heir that the will's maker forgot. While forgetting one's children sounds far-fetched today, in an earlier time, the recognition of legitimate and illegitimate heirs was a topic of great concern. Or, as the story goes:

A rich dying man called his lawyer to him for the purpose of disposing of his worldly goods. "How many children have you?" the lawyer asked.

"That, sir," said the old-timer, "will be decided by the courts when my will is contested."

As you approach the topic of estate planning, whether as the beneficiary or the benefactor, keep in mind that its complexities derive from two contrapuntal themes: the burden of the historical past and the necessity to project onto the future every possible or foreseeable outcome.

The contemplation of possible future outcomes and the provision for every contingency in the language of the will and in the overall estate plan is a topic that does not come easily to most people. The play *Daddy's Dying, Who's Got the Will?* successfully captures the Southern preoccupation with inheritance, a preoccupation linked to the South's more recent agrarian past and its own particular cultural mode. By contrast, the average non-Southerner thinks of inheritance only in terms of a single generation. Regardless of your upbringing, you need to imagine all possible scenarios when preparing your will. One or more of your potential heirs may die in non-sequential fashion, requiring contingent planning of your estate.

Signing a modern will derives from medieval relationships to property. In the Middle Ages, in order to convey property from one person to another, a clod of earth from the property was literally handed from one man to another. This rite, called *seisin*, required several witnesses to observe and validate the ceremony since it was conducted without the benefit of paper. Likewise, the signing of a completed will today, although considerably more relaxed, harkens back to this earlier time. Most states require formal will-signing ceremonies. In general, one or more disinterested persons must witness the signing of the will in order for it to be valid.

Unlike many contracts concluded without the benefit of a lawyer, few people prepare their own wills because of the complexity of this area of the law. Since such a large number of requirements derive from the mists of history, technical expertise is mandatory.

YOUR ESTATE

Much of estate planning is the flip side of closing the estate of another. You'll need to make choices about living wills, burial, and the beneficiaries to your will or trust. If you have minor children, you'll need to select guardians. The primary issue that you'll face as donor, however, wasn't even considered in your role as recipient of the estate—estate taxes.

Most estate planning involves tax issues, especially with larger estates. Under current federal tax law, estate tax rates start at 37 percent for taxable estates over $600,000 and top out at 55 percent for taxable estates over $3,000,000. In addition, for very wealthy individuals with taxable estates of more than $21 million, a flat 55 percent tax applies to the entire taxable estate, with no graduated rate on the smaller amounts.

Although most heirs of substantial estates make a formal estate plan, 60 percent of all estates in America transfer without a will or trust. So before we discuss formal estate planning, let's see what happens if you die without a valid will or trust.

WHAT HAPPENS IF YOU DIE INTESTATE?

If you fail to make an estate plan for yourself, the court will make one for you that includes disbursing the property, picking a guardian for your children, and selecting an administrator. Without a will, you will also not be able to leave a gift to your college or favorite charity since state intestacy laws do not provide for charitable gifts.

Whether you fail to make a will, or make one early on and don't update it when necessary, the state may step in. *Each state's property and intestacy laws determine who will receive what portion of your estate.* You must check your own state's laws to determine how the intestacy laws would specifically apply to you.

In general, spouses receive one third to one half of the estate and *issue,* or your children (who may or may not include adopted children), receive the rest of the estate to be divided among them.

If you do prepare a will but then remarry, and the current spouse is omitted, she either will get her intestate share, in community property states, or what is known as a *forced or elective share,* which may be smaller than the intestate share, in common-law states.

Likewise, pretermitted heir statutes in most states are predicated on the idea that failure to mention a child in a will was an oversight so the omitted child should get a share of the estate.

PLANNING WITH PROFESSIONALS

As a new heir, estate planning is part of your financial arsenal. And being well informed can make your use of the proper estate-planning professionals more effective.

On the other hand, while you can properly engage in a certain amount of self-help, preparing your own will from kits or even computer programs should be approached with caution. Any but the simplest asset base and family structure will require both an attorney and an accountant. Don't trust insurance salespersons posing as financial planners to put together your estate plan. And be forewarned: If you have a large estate and you create your estate plan yourself, any mistakes you make will probably cost your heirs much more in legal fees and taxes later than you could possibly save now by doing it yourself.

One estate-planning attorney tells the story of a client who didn't trust lawyers. Instead, he chose to use a will kit he bought from a stationery store. When filling in the blanks on the preprinted will form he wrote, "I give all my *personal* property to my wife." He did not make any residuary bequests or bequests covering anything else he did not specifically gift away. As a result, when he died, the house he owned—by far his largest asset—fell into intestacy. He had only devised his personal property, not his real property. Under the state intestacy laws, his children were entitled to half of the house and only reluctantly agreed, after a legal battle, to let their stepmother stay in her home.

In this case, because the client did not know the legal distinction between real and personal property, his estate plan was completely destroyed. Self-help in this case was much more costly than the legal fees for a properly prepared will.

In our examples, we will focus exclusively on federal tax law for the purpose of simplifying our illustrations. State estate and other death tax laws vary a great deal and some may be virtually irrelevant to the overall financial calculation. Many states do not even have such taxes although some impose an additional estate tax or levy an inheritance tax on the heirs' shares. If you have a large estate, you'll need to check with your local attorney or accountant.

If you or your spouse are not U.S. citizens or you have assets located abroad, you will need to consult a specialist to deal with international tax issues that may apply.

TAXING ESTATES

The single most decisive factor in your estate planning will be the amount of your assets that is subject to estate taxation. Under current law (and be on notice—tax laws are always subject to change), net estates over $600,000 for an individual and a total of $1,200,000 for a married couple should be planned differently than other estates. At those points estate taxes kick in, with tax rates as high as 55 percent. Estates under $600,000 pass virtually tax free at the federal level, and tax returns for these smaller estates are not required.

THE 4M FORMULA FOR ESTATE PLANNING

---o---

MODEST

Have a lawyer create a will or living trust to distribute your estate. If you have minor children, be sure to appoint proper guardians.

---o---

MODERATE

Retain a lawyer to draft a trust document and will to distribute your estate. Also consider the use of will substitutes such as life insurance, payable-on-death bank or stock accounts, and jointly held property. These assets automatically pass to the survivor or beneficiary upon death. Make sure the beneficiaries are designated properly.

---o---

MAJOR

Consult your attorney to create a living trust, or create an irrevocable or testamentary trust to minimize your estate tax liability. If you are married, make sure to preserve both of your estate tax credits so you are able to exempt your full $1,200,000 as a couple.

---o---

MILLIONS

Work with an estate-planning expert to develop a long-term strategy to minimize your estate tax liability and effectuate your plan for your estate. You should have a program in place to fund annual gifts to reduce the size of your taxable estate, perhaps through the use of an irrevocable trust. You should also consider the income and estate tax benefits of a charitable remainder trust.

The Internal Revenue Code defines the taxable estate as the *gross estate* minus allowable deductions. The gross estate is "the value at the time of [your] death of all [your] property, real or personal, tangible or intangible, wherever situated" (IRC Sect. 2031).

The estate actually subject to the tax will be the taxable estate plus lifetime gifts requiring the filing of gift tax returns.

To calculate the approximate value of your taxable estate, first you need to determine the aggregate net value of assets under your control. In other words, add the value of:

- Your home, less the mortgage on the property;
- Life insurance owned by you, payable for the benefit of your estate, or transferred within the last three years;
- Your bank accounts;
- Stocks, bonds, and certificates of deposit;
- Interests in partnerships, ventures, and money-market and mutual funds;
- Your car, jewelry, clothes, furniture, and artwork; and
- Any other assets owned by you or held by the trustee of any revocable trusts you created.

Then you can subtract the estimated allowable deductions including funeral and administrative expenses; claims against the estate; and unpaid mortgages, liens, taxes, and other indebtedness with respect to property included in the gross estate (IRC Sect. 2053). In addition, an unlimited deduction is allowed for charitable and religious transfers. Uninsured casualty or theft losses that arise during the settlement of the estate may also be deducted. Finally, the law provides an unlimited deduction for qualified bequests to a surviving spouse.

A rough calculation can approximate the value of your estate for the purposes of estate planning. The precise value of your taxable estate is difficult to determine because the Internal Revenue Code (IRC) sections are subject to multiple interpretations, from IRS Revenue Rulings to Supreme Court cases. Even the time of valuation of the estate is optional: either the date of death or an alternate valuation date (as late as six months after that date), depending on which date would minimize the estate tax liability. If your situation calls for an interpretation of the more specialized tax sections of the IRC, you should seek professional advice.

A TRUST, A WILL, OR BOTH?

The choice of document or documents to include in your estate plan is dependent primarily on two components: your individual characteristics and your estate tax position. To make the choice you will have to consider your objectives, the size of your estate, your marital status, your age, and the types of holdings in your estate. These nontax factors should always come first.

Whether you choose a *formal witnessed will*, a *holographic will* (from the Greek "wholly written," meaning a handwritten will, which is allowed in about half the states), a revocable living trust, an irrevocable trust, or a combination of these instruments, depends on the complex interplay between individual objectives and the rules of the tax system.

Remember that trusts themselves can be further divided into a number of types, each with a specific objective and tax treatment. Trusts have the practical effect of controlling the uses to which money can be put after the grantor's (donor's) death; therefore, trust variations are almost as complex and varied as human relationships themselves because they're the legal expressions of the grantor's desires and fears.

Testamentary trusts, created by will at the death of the grantor, cannot be modified except by the express modification provisions, if any, contained in the will. *Inter vivos trusts*, set up to take effect during the life of the trust grantor, include both revocable living trusts and irrevocable trusts (see Chapter 4, Trust Terms, pages 63–66). Revocable living trusts can be modified or cancelled so long as the grantor is alive. Once created, irrevocable trusts cannot be changed, except within some limited parameters that must be outlined in the original trust document.

While there's not a strict one-to-one correlation between trust type and tax rule, each major trust type is treated differently under the tax code. For example, revocable living trusts are used to avoid probate, for ease of administration, and for flexibility; but because the IRS treats the revocable trust property as part of the decedent's estate, they have no estate tax consequences.

If, like most people, your taxable estate is under $600,000 and your concern is mainly to see that your money passes hassle free to your immediate family, you can employ a living trust in combination with a will. The will would cover residual gifts (for property left outside of the trust) and guardianship appointments.

At the opposite extreme, the wealthy face estate taxes at rates of up to 55 percent on their estates. To minimize the impact of these taxes, a variety of tax moves is required. In addition, to meet other objectives, such as preserving wealth for several family generations and making significant donations to charity, these estate plans need to be carefully designed. The bigger the estate, the more complex the objectives are likely to be, prompted in part by tax avoidance and in part by the desire to leave a mark on the world.

Irrevocable trusts can be used to shelter assets from estate taxes in a number of ways. For example, through the use of a trust, up to $1 million can pass to grandchildren (or to anyone two generations down from the grantor) without any generation-skipping transfer tax. With *marital deduction trusts,* an unlimited amount can be passed tax free to a spouse and up to $600,000 can be passed tax free to other beneficiaries. These trusts can be created either by will or by an irrevocable inter vivos trust made during the grantor's lifetime.

There are many other types of trusts that you might encounter. Some of these are new legal creations while others, such as a *Clifford trust* or a *spousal remainder trust,* were eliminated by the 1986 Tax Reform Act. If you have run across these latter types of trusts as an heir, you will not be able to use them in planning your own estate.

In the next chapter, we will discuss alternatives to minimize your potential estate tax liability.

State Planning

State laws govern estate planning. Consequently, the *domicile at death* (the place where you lived when you died) will control the passage of most of the property owned by the deceased. A Uniform Probate Code has been adopted in seventeen states. Important differences remain among the others. Consult counsel in your state when creating your estate plan because correct advice can vary dramatically depending on where you live. Here are selected key differences between the laws in California and New York.

California	*New York*
Holographic wills are valid.	Most holographic wills are void.
You can cross out or amend gifts by hand if you sign your name by it.	Attempts partially to revoke a will by physical acts are ineffectual.
Surviving spouses own half of the community property.	Surviving spouses can opt to take an elective share of the estate.

WILL SUBSTITUTES

Wills and trusts are not the only ways to pass property; will substitutes have become an extremely popular estate planning tool. Certain property interests will pass at death in accordance with the manner in which the property has been titled, regardless of the existence of a will or trust. Included in this category are: (i) properties held in joint tenancy, (ii) Totten trusts or payable-on-death stock and bank accounts, and (iii) annuities, life insurance, and retirement accounts with named beneficiaries. The use of will substitutes may prove to be the most important component of your estate plan if all of your property can be conveniently entitled to pass directly to your desired beneficiaries and you have (a) no estate tax concerns and (b) no minor dependents who need a guardian designated.

ESTATES UNDER $600,000

For total estates under $600,000, no special tax concerns govern your choice of documents. Instead, the selection depends upon the type of assets and, to some extent, your age. A young person wouldn't ordinarily set up a living trust. A simple, less expensive will suffices. A will avoids the hassles involved in transferring title each time assets change as the young adult progresses through life. However, if the same young person has only a mother to concern himself with and he owns a condominium, a living trust would allow him to pass his home directly to her with no probate costs or delays.

On the other hand, a young businesswoman with a business partner would have to think twice about a living trust because placing the business assets in the trust could involve additional paperwork for every transaction, possibly inhibiting both business dealings and credit opportunities. For her, a will would work best.

Estate taxes have been abolished for transfers between spouses. But for couples with a combined estate exceeding $600,000, marital trusts (described in Chapter 10) are required to preserve each spouse's $600,000 estate tax exemption so that the couple can pass up to $1,200,000 to their children or other benficiaries free of estate taxes.

For couples whose combined net estate stands at $600,000 or less, your main concern will be providing for your spouse to inherit hassle free and for your children if they are minors. You won't need to set up spousal trusts; however, make sure that as your estate grows with your investments, you adjust your estate plan as necessary.

If you have no heirs and live with your long-time same-sex companion, estate planning may involve putting your entire holdings in joint tenancy. In this case, the surviving partner would automatically become the owner of any property so held, including real estate, automobiles, and even bank accounts.

If you have remarried but want to provide for your children from your first marriage, either a trust or a will could meet your planning needs. State law will dictate the minimum rights of the surviving spouse to your estate.

Steps to Create a Living Trust

1. Make a determination that a living trust fits your estate-planning needs by talking with your lawyer and accountant. (If you haven't yet chosen the professionals you need, see Chapter 8.)

2. Decide on who will be your trustees. Usually, you would be the first trustee with one or more persons chosen as successor trustees or co-trustees. Remember, the revocable trust means you can revoke or end it at any time. After you stop serving, your trustee will have significant powers over your assets, so be sure you have chosen people you trust absolutely. If you do not have such a person, choose a bank trust department.

3. Have the living trust document prepared by the attorney you have selected.

4. Work with the attorney to put your main assets in the trust. The deed to your home and other real estate will be signed over to the trust, e.g., "The Smith Family Trust." (Note: Placing your assets in a living trust should not trigger a mortgage lender's acceleration clause or any property tax consequences, but it's wise to double check.)

5. It may not be advisable to put your day-to-day personal checking account in the trust as the checks may be difficult to use in every-day transactions such as shopping. Also, it may not be advisable to put any other assets that are likely to be sold soon in the trust. Too much additional paperwork could be required to obtain co-trustee signatures for every transaction although state laws are changing to make living trusts easier to run.

6. If you intend for life insurance to be excluded from the estate, do not place your life insurance in a revocable trust or designate the trust as the beneficiary of the insurance. In order to qualify for special treatment, the life insurance must be placed in an irrevocable trust and meet the non-ownership requirements outlined below.

7. Retirement accounts can't be placed in the trust. Any transfer of the IRA, Keogh, company pensions, or 401(k)'s will trigger taxes plus a penalty if you're under fifty-nine and a half years old.

8. Children's trusts also must remain outside the living trust. They must be irrevocable to preserve their tax-free status.

9. Be sure the trust has a general provision to cover all property not specifically listed in the trust, but recognize that a general assignment may not fully cover all potential assets of your estate.

10. Be sure that you are clear in the trust document about the extent to which you wish the trust to cover expenses if you are ill, such as for life extension, medical care, nursing home, and in-home nurses.

11. Even with a trust, you must still leave a will, although it then becomes a simpler document. In addition to naming a guardian for minor children, the will disposes of any assets that do not fall under the trust. For example, if you were to neglect to transfer a particular asset to your trust, it would likely pass into the trust following your death under the terms of your will.

12. When the deeds are returned from the county recorder or clerk, be sure to place them in a safe location such as a safety-deposit box. However, unlike the days when a lost deed could mean lost property, under modern recording practices, if an originally recorded deed is lost, a replacement in the form of a certified copy can usually be obtained at a minimal cost.

13. Discuss the living trust provisions with those whom it will affect, your heirs and your successor trustees.

THE THORNY ISSUE OF ESTATE TAX PLANNING: ESTATES OVER $600,000

The complexity of your estate planning will partially depend on how much in excess of $600,000 your gross estate is valued. Currently, a taxable estate worth $700,000 has a federal estate tax liability on only $100,000 for which the tax at current rates would amount to $37,000. You would have to decide how much extra expense you're willing to incur to save what may be a relatively small amount. However, some are of the view that any amount of tax is too high and wish to plan accordingly.

If the taxable estate comes to $1 million or more for an individual, or $1.5 million or more for a couple, then strategy becomes critical if the goal is to preserve the estate rather than donate it to charity.

Unlike your experience as the recipient of an estate, where the income and estate taxes will have been paid prior to your seeing penny one, the starting point for planning a major estate is taxes. All of your plans for your loved ones will come to naught if your estate is consumed by taxes that could have been properly avoided.

Assuming that you have a spouse or dependents that you care about, the structure of your bequests starts with the question: "How much of my estate can I pass tax free?" The answer to this crucial question will determine the net or after-tax size of your estate. For example, if you want to provide for your ten-year-old child's education, you must first estimate the cost of the education and then adjust that amount for inflation to determine the after-tax amount needed.

To take the example a step further, assume for a moment that your bequest to this child is one of a number of specific bequests. You will need to ensure that there are enough after-tax resources in the estate, once liquidated or turned into cash, to cover all of your specific bequests. If you fail to take taxes into account, you could end up shortchanging someone you care about deeply.

The apportionment of the tax bite on your estate should be spelled out according to your desires. For example, if you wish to leave $25,000 to your sister and $50,000 to your aunt, with the remainder to go to your children, the amount left to your children may be diminished by the estate taxes for the $25,000 and $50,000 gifts in addition to the estate taxes on the assets that they receive.

On the other hand, if you state in your will how you want the taxes paid, your wishes will be met. If you do not address this issue, the state will determine where the ultimate burden will fall. Most states now require that estate tax be equitably apportioned among the persons benefiting from the estate in the absence of other specific provisions.

To summarize: the linchpin of the estate tax system is the amount that can be passed tax free. The estate tax reform measures passed in conjunction with the 1981 Economic Recovery Tax Act (ERTA) significantly raised the amounts that can be passed tax free.

In Chapter 10, we will detail estate planning techniques used to minimize the estate tax liability of major estates.

PROTECTING YOUR CHILDREN

Wills are about more than money and taxes; they also provide protection for your minor children and dependent parents.

If you have minor children, make guardianship arrangements and discuss them with your children. One client, Anne, remembers listening to a "Stella Dallas" radio episode that involved a mother's sudden death. Anne worried that her own mother would die, but she was too afraid to tell her mother. For weeks she tried to ask her parents about what would happen if they died. Her fear was that she'd have to live with an aunt she didn't like. Children often think much more about their parents' death than parents realize, so it is essential to both make plans and communicate them to your children.

You'll need to reach agreement on the choice of guardian with your spouse or former spouse, and both of your individual wills should reflect this agreement. The guardian of your children (for example, your sister) needn't be the same as the financial guardian (for example, your attorney). You might have a loving sister who would make a good parent, and a financially capable friend whom you would trust to protect your child's financial future by ensuring that your assets were kept intact for your child or children.

Take time to sit down with your children and discuss your plans. Express that while you expect to be around for a long time, the reality is that no one knows exactly how long their life will be. If possible, empower your children by allowing them to assist in the arrangements you make, especially for physical custody.

If you are a single parent with a living former spouse who is the natural or adoptive parent of your children, the law generally assumes that the other parent will become the children's guardian. If you have concerns that the finances would not be properly handled, you can still separate the financial arrangements and appoint a trustee for the money in your estate, leaving your former spouse with only physical custody. In marriages where money was an issue, this plan will provide you peace of mind regarding your children's future welfare.

Be sure to discuss your plans fully with any potential guardians. Don't appoint someone as a guardian unless they expressly agree. Then, to be sure your wishes are followed, include the details in your will or living trust document.

Failing to appoint a guardian can lead to protracted and costly litigation with various relatives and even friends laying claim to parenting your children. While possibly motivated by the best of intentions, the effect on the children can be devastating.

The same set of concerns holds true if you have aging parents who count on you for all or part of their support. In this instance, you might wish to leave the money in trust for them or arrange for a financial custodian to provide for them and preserve the funds.

A SPECIAL WORD ON ADOPTION

If you have adopted children, be sure to include them by name in the language of your will. Because of antiquated rules that trace back bloodlines for the purpose of selecting kings and earls, our own laws sometimes omit adopted children.

In one case, a childless beneficiary of a trust adopted a child. The trust language chosen ("issue of my body" rather than "natural and adopted children") caused the remainder of the trust to go not to the adopted child but to a distant cousin.

People have sometimes used this type of language to control or prevent alternative lifestyles. For example, some states allow homosexual couples to adopt one another as adults in order to circumvent inheritance laws that do not recognize nontraditional unions. But adult adoption is another matter. Be sure to protect your own adopted children and grandchildren. Nothing could be more devastating to these children than to learn that, after all, they are not full family members.

OMITTING GROWN CHILDREN FROM YOUR ESTATE

The sanctity of family is sufficiently strong that the law looks with disfavor on the disinheritance of children. Between generations, the reasonable expectation exists that family money, property, and personal mementos will be passed from one generation to the next. The law assumes that children will inherit equally from their parents.

But there are many real-world examples where that expectation is not met. Children may have their own resources. One child may be better off and not need the money. Children may have so disappointed their parents that the parents wish to see their hard-earned money kept from wasteful or spendthrift children. Or, parents may feel that inheriting too much wealth is not healthy for their children, preferring instead to put their estate to work for the benefit of the community and encourage their off-spring to make their own way in the world. Business publications recently have explored the topic of skipping all but modest inheritances for your children's own good.

If you decide to omit a child for any reason, you must discuss your thinking openly and completely with your family. Since love and money are often confused in many families, be sure that your reasons for the decision are clearly spelled out to your children.

GRANDCHILDREN

If you want to provide for grandchildren, consider the generation-skipping tax provisions discussed in Chapter 4.

PLANNING FOR SINGLES AND THOSE WITH ALTERNATIVE LIFESTYLES

Much of estate-planning advice centers on married couples. Estate tax law provides huge breaks for married persons. No such provisions exist for single persons or people who have chosen to live together without marrying. Particularly because no spousal forced share, community property, intestate share, nor spousal exemption is available, unmarried couples should ensure that their relationships are preserved in their estate plans.

Putting property in both names as joint tenants or in a living trust can protect this commitment by protecting the surviving partner. However, property passed through joint tenancy or placed in a revocable trust is still considered part of the gross estate for tax purposes, so estate taxes cannot be avoided through this arrangement if the estate of either partner exceeds $600,000.

Also, in the case of unmarried persons who have children together, these children are legally "illegitimate." In some states, their rights to their parents' property are nevertheless recognized (with the best protection in Louisiana). However, by preparing a will or trust that makes intentions clear, such children can be best protected.

With homosexual couples, additional problems of inheritance can occur if the couple suffers family disapproval. Parents may use silver strings to tie the passage of their estates to their own beliefs.

In the states that permit adult adoption between homosexual couples, the couple, after an official adoption, can gain some of the estate-planning protections offered to other legally recognized family members, such as an intestate share if the deceased partner's will is found invalid.

Finally, for single people who may not have close friends or relatives who can stand in for them (or who might not legally have the right to do so), a will and a *durable power of attorney* for health-care decisions are musts.

USING INSURANCE TO AUGMENT YOUR ESTATE

You may wonder whether you have sufficient resources to take care of your dependents were you to die tomorrow.

"Insurance is the universal estate builder," according to one estate-planning book. Maybe. Certainly a variety of messages from advertising and print media suggest that if we fail to buy insurance we will be remiss.

Let's look at the issue from the perspective of providing for dependents.

PROVIDING FOR DEPENDENTS

In a family where one or more breadwinners contribute to the income of the family, each of those breadwinners should be insured to replace their salaries. Insurance is the instant answer to a lifetime of savings for those with dependents. However, the price you pay for that peace of mind is exorbitant when compared with the earnings you could make on money similarly invested were you to live to your full actuarial life expectancy.

To figure the face amount of insurance, you'll need to establish certain parameters:

- The duration for which you want to provide funds.
- The amount of funds required annually.
- Other resources that can be used to meet this same need.

Since cash flow is always a concern, those with young children need to figure the number of years they have to cover until their children can take care of themselves. Sit down and carefully assess the impact of your death. Include the cost of the funeral (which averages $5,000 nationally), the cost of replacing your services (cooking, driving, child care), as well as the need to replace your annual income.

Next, decide how many years of income you want to replace. If you are a married breadwinner, provide enough time for your family to adjust and reorganize financially. The industry starting point is usually five years with the assumption that the surviving spouse's earnings will grow in time while budget adjustments are made. On the other hand, if you are a single parent, you'll need enough insurance to provide for your children, including their educational expenses, until they can become self-supporting.

Let's use the five-year example. There are two methods of determining how much insurance you need. One method assumes that the family would want to keep their inherited capital intact. Therefore, you project an annual interest rate, then figure the principal adequate to indefinitely generate interest earnings equal to the annual need. For example, to provide $30,000 a year, with the 10 percent yield assumption, you would need a combination of insurance and other liquid assets with a face amount of $300,000 (try not to count your family home—being forced to move on top of your death would be terribly traumatic). Assuming no other large liquid assets, that amount of insurance might be prohibitive for a young single parent.

The second method of calculating insurance needs may be more within reason. Assume that within a given period (e.g., five years), the fund would be exhausted. Work backwards, factoring in the real interest you would earn on the principal in the meanwhile and discount, or reduce, the face amount to reflect any interest earned. Thus, if you wanted to achieve $30,000 a year for a limited period, say five years at 10 percent interest, you'd need insurance and assets with a face amount totaling about $125,000.

Using Table 9-1, think about the projected needs for your family to arrive at a reasonable amount of insurance.

TABLE 9-1: ESTIMATING YOUR INSURANCE NEEDS

1. How many years do you want to provide for your family? _____
2. How much will they need per year? _____
3. Multiply line 1 by line 2. _____
4. How much will you set aside for burial costs? _____
5. What are your projected probate or trust expenses? _____
6. Add lines 3, 4, and 5. _____
7. What are your total current assets, not counting your home, less your liabilities? _____
8. Subtract line 7 from line 6. _____

The amount in line 8 is the face value of the life insurance policy you need now to provide for your dependents and keep your other assets intact. This chart assumes no inflation and that the insurance proceeds will be exhausted at the end of the term.

Then look at Table 9-2. This table will give you the amount you need if you assume diminishing capital.

TABLE 9-2: HOW MUCH INSURANCE
(By Income Amount)

Annual Income	For How Many Years			
	5 Yrs	10 Yrs	20 Yrs	30 Yrs
$50,000	231,500	421,750	706,750	899,250
75,000	347,250	632,750	1,060,000	1,348,750
100,000	463,000	843,500	1,413,500	1,798,500
150,000	694,500	1,265,300	2,120,000	2,697,500

Note: Assumes an average annual inflation rate of 4 percent and an annual interest rate of 8 percent. (All numbers are rounded.)

For a nominal fee, the Consumer Federation of America offers a rate of return analysis on current or prospective insurance policies. Send a self-addressed stamped envelope to the Consumer Federation of America, Insurance Group, 1424 16th Street, N.W. #600, Washington, D.C. 20036.

ESTATE TAX RETURNS

Income, estate, trust, and state tax returns must be filed for taxable estates over $600,000. In addition, partnership and corporate returns are due if any partnerships or closely held corporations are involved in the estate. Overseeing and filing these returns may be the job of the executor.

When you plan your own estate, your concerns involve primarily federal estate and state death taxes. By contrast, the inheritance you receive as an heir is not considered income and therefore will not be subject to income taxes.

OTHER CRITICAL DOCUMENTS AND ESTATE-PLANNING CONSIDERATIONS

Aside from typical tax and estate-planning considerations, related tasks should be completed. Durable powers of attorney, living wills, and burial instructions prepare you and your family should an unfortunate situation arise.

DURABLE POWER OF ATTORNEY

The durable power of attorney allows your loved ones or attorney to carry on for you when you are not in a position to help yourself. Whereas the living will deals with preserving or letting go of your physical self, the durable power of attorney for business purposes deals with your mental and physical capacity to cope with your financial and legal affairs.

Properly drawn, the durable power allows others to take over for you when you are temporarily or permanently incapacitated. Unlike *conservatorship*, which requires a court order for someone to step in and help you, the durable power of attorney has flexibility.

The durable power of attorney for health care (DPHC) enables you to delegate to anyone the power to make decisions about your medical treatment during your incapacity, including the decision to terminate life support. Because of the complexity of the legal, ethical, and medical issues involved in this area, it is important that your DPHC be made in strict accordance with your local laws. Medical professionals are usually willing to work with attorneys-in-fact, but want to protect themselves against potential litigation in this highly charged area.

These powers are set up in separate documents, typically apart from a will or trust, and are governed by state law.

THE LIVING WILL

Some states allow a living will that directs your doctors regarding the extension of your life by extraordinary measures. This enables you to leave clear written information on your views about preserving your own life in the face of lingering illness. Like the DPHC, the living will must strictly comply with state law. Unlike the DPHC, which grants powers to third parties, the living will serves as an instruction given by you directly to your physicians.

Be sure to indicate your wishes about artificial life support for extended periods, organ donations, and autopsies. Be as explicit as you can. These decisions often involve hefty hospital fees, so your loved ones could find themselves facing a "my money or your life" choice. Under life and death pressure, few of us would say regarding a loved one, "Don't spend the money." Your guidance, planned in advance, will help your significant others tremendously.

BURIAL INSTRUCTIONS

Because the funeral industry has come under serious criticism in recent years, the Federal Trade Commission (FTC) has promulgated regulations that attempt to protect unwary and vulnerable consumers. However, rather than rely on arm's-length federal assistance, provide your heirs with clear instructions as to your own preferences.

Know the burial costs and customs of your area, but don't assume that you'll die where you live now. For example, as an heir, you may have discovered that your parent purchased a "pre-need funeral arrangement" linked to the services of a particular funeral establishment. If a person dies away from the funeral home, these policies may prove expensive since the cost of flying the body back could exceed the seemingly inexpensive cost of the burial. More recent policies should include airfare for the coffin.

In planning your own funeral, remember to specify the following items:

1. The type of service you want.
2. The type of burial or cremation.
3. If burial, the type and general expense level of the casket.
4. The location where you wish to be buried.
5. Any other information that is important to you.

Obviously, in order to think these issues through you'll need to do some research. If getting caught up in plot purchasing turns you off—and why not?—then talk with your extended family. If you are an urban resident in a major city, plots can be prohibitively expensive, and if bought under burial pressure, difficult to choose. Better: See if members of your family are buried in locations outside the city where an extra grave can be added. The cost of flying a body and casket runs about the same as a coach fare, so this solution may be preferable to some than the cost of an urban plot.

Also be aware that while the Federal Trade Commission requires that funeral prices be quoted over the telephone and itemized separately, many people in the throes of grieving pick a funeral home and send their relative there. Once the body is at the funeral home, comparison shopping is emotionally draining. Unless you are willing to move the body to a less expensive home, you are at the mercy of the choice you have hastily made.

As a twenty-five-year-old, you might be able to ignore issues such as whether you have burial insurance and where you would wish to be buried. By middle age, especially after your parents are aging or deceased, it's incumbent upon you to make these decisions so that the burden does not fall on others. It's not easy to contemplate one's own death in such detail; however, the alternative is to leave the chore for others to deal with at a most difficult time.

Preserving Your Paper

Once having taken the time and effort to prepare an estate plan, people often stumble over the implementation practicalities. Details such as where to put each document can be critical, but sometimes professionals stop short of providing this all-important advice.

Will

You should have only one original will, but keep copies of your will in at least three locations: with your attorney, in your safety-deposit box, and with a close relative or at your home. If you don't want to leave an original outside of the safekeeping of a bank or law office, be sure to have a photocopy available. Opening a safety-deposit box may involve legal steps that can consume valuable time if your executor and others are not aware of your wishes. If you do choose to have your attorney safeguard the originals of your estate planning documents, be sure to notify the attorney of any change of address. Also, keep your safety-deposit box information up to date.

Living Trust
This document should be kept in the same locations as the will. You will also have deeds for property belonging to the trust that should be kept with the original trust document.

Living Will
Put this document on file at your family- or primary-care physician's office. Place another copy with other key documents and keep them together in a marked envelope in your home. Share a copy of this document with close family members as well. If you have verbally reinforced your desires, it will help them to implement your wishes if the need arises. In addition, file an original with your family attorney.

Durable Power of Attorney
An original of this document should be on file with your family attorney as well as with a key family member or the person who would exercise the power. Of course, you must trust the person you have selected not to be overreaching in choosing when to activate the power. However, if you only place the document in a safety-deposit box, a court order would probably be required to open the box, defeating the purpose of the durable power of attorney, which is to avoid going to court when and if you are incapacitated.

Burial Instructions
Leave your burial instructions somewhere that can be readily accessible to your survivors. Include information about the location of your will with these instructions. Remember, the funeral instructions will be needed first so that arrangements can be made immediately. It's best to locate a copy in your home and place backup copies with your minister or rabbi, a trusted friend, and even your doctor. A master copy should also be left with your attorney and in your safety-deposit box. But remember, a death certificate and/or a court order is ordi-

narily required to open the safety-deposit box, even if you have made an heir a signatory, because such boxes may be frozen upon the death of the box renter. (In areas where word of mouth doesn't routinely spread the news of the death, heirs can get into safety-deposit boxes if they are signatories, but this practice is not advisable.)

THE HUMAN SIDE OF ESTATE PLANNING

Estate planning is difficult. Even if there were no technicalities, the thought of planning for your own death is uncomfortable. Add to that the reality that the estate tax system is extremely difficult to comprehend, much less conquer.

Far too many people do not adequately plan their estates, partially as a result of the complexities. Instead, the burden falls upon their friends and family, who are already facing a difficult time, and who are not emotionally or legally able to optimize the handling of the estates. By reading and understanding this chapter, you have taken an important step in responsibly managing your own estate.

Before we leave this topic, we must remind you not to forget the human side of estate planning. For all the loopholes, contortions, and configurations available, the bottom line is that in dealing with your estate, you are attempting to place your affairs in order as a way to bring closure to the material aspects of your life. But do not neglect the importance of spiritual closure in the midst of all the money management. Despite the allure of tax savings and trust creation, your primary concerns should always be your family, your friends, and your soul.

10

Minimizing Estate Taxes

Given tax rates as high as 55 percent, once you cross the $600,000 line for the value of your taxable estate, your estate-planning focus shifts quickly to tax minimization. Without proper planning, the majority of your estate could go to the government instead of to your intended heirs. Even if you deem the U.S. a worthy beneficiary of your assets, your capital would have more effect if it's placed in a charitable trust with instructions on its productive use, rather than handed over to the IRS.

Many new heirs consider the prospect of passing a major estate valued at more than $600,000 unlikely. In fact, other assets aside, the appreciation of your home alone could put you over this amount. Combine the future value of your house (less mortgage payments still due) with the expected value of your stocks, IRA, life insurance, and other investments, and you may find yourself capable of passing the $600,000 mark sooner than you think.

The methods for minimizing your estate taxes involve four primary areas: marital trusts, annual and other gifts, irrevocable insurance trusts, and charitable trusts. In addition, one area of estate tax law addresses family businesses and family farms, both of which require special attention to remain intact after estate taxes. We will take each of these five areas in turn.

ESTATE PLANNING FOR MARRIED COUPLES

Beginning in 1948, Congress started inching toward a marital deduction for estate taxes. In 1981, taxes on estates passing between spouses were abolished completely.

An estate of absolutely any amount can be passed tax free between spouses. The snag occurs when the estate passes to the next generation of heirs. The "tax-free" transfer is in actuality a tax-deferred transfer.

If the entire estate is passed directly from one spouse to the other, there is no tax. Without proper planning, however, one spouse's $600,000 exemption is lost by leaving all the property to the surviving spouse. When the estate finally goes to the children, $600,000 that could have been passed tax free is taxed.

The marital estate tax problem is straightforward. The desire to use the full $1,200,000 exemption available to couples ($600,000 for each spouse) has led to a cottage industry of marital estate planning for couples with estates larger than $600,000. Lawyers found that trusts enabled one spouse to provide for the other and make provisions for his or her children without losing either of the spouse's $600,000 exemptions.

As discussed below, a basic trust arrangement used by married couples to preserve their combined $1,200,000 exemption involves a combination of a *bypass trust,* and either *the marital deduction trust* or a *Q-TIP trust (qualified terminable interest property trust).*

Keep in mind that you do not need to leave your money in trust. If your goal is to enable your spouse to fully control and enjoy your estate, you may be best advised to leave it outright to your spouse. Remember that the avoidance of estate taxes comes at the cost of control.

The exact disposition you can make of your property, if you

are married, depends upon the state in which you reside. (See the marital property box on page 248 for the distinction.) The federal tax laws, in general, are not concerned with this issue, the one exception being the basis treatment accorded to appreciated property in community property states.

BYPASS TRUST

You may have heard the term "A-B Trust." With this deceptively simple term comes a complex estate-planning maneuver involving a two-tiered transfer of assets meant to preserve both spouses' exemption amounts. The key element of this arrangement is the B trust, also know as a bypass trust, decedent's trust, exemption trust, or unified credit trust. Under the basic form of the bypass trust, the surviving spouse is given a lifetime interest in, or the income earned on, a trust valued at up to $600,000. [Note: In some cases, the surviving spouse may also be given limited access to the principal of a bypass trust (i.e., the actual trust property, not only the income earned on that trust property).]

The goal of this estate plan is to avoid inclusion of the bypass trust in the surviving spouse's estate. The trust is legally considered part of the deceased spouse's estate for tax purposes, but because the bypass trust falls under the $600,000 exemption amount, the trust is not taxed. Then, because the surviving spouse does not legally own the trust (hence the loss of control by the surviving spouse), the bypass trust does not get taxed as part of the surviving spouse's estate.

These legal fictions can be confusing, so let's consider a concrete example. Scott and Amy have a house, stocks, bonds, life insurance, and other assets netting them a $900,000 estate. Since they want the entire estate to eventually pass to their children free of estate taxes, they decide to employ a bypass trust. When Scott dies, he leaves $600,000 in a bypass trust and passes the other

$300,000 to Amy directly. The $300,000 is not taxed because all transfers between spouses are tax free. The other $600,000 is not taxed because Scott is entitled to exempt $600,000 from estate taxes. When Amy dies, the remainder of the bypass trust is left to their children. Although Amy lived off of the income from the trust, the $600,000 in bypass trust property is not taxed as part of Amy's estate because she never owned it. The remaining $300,000 (assuming Amy lived off of the interest income and never spent any of the original $900,000 in capital) is left in a trust she created for their children. This $300,000 is not taxed because up to $600,000 of Amy's estate is exempt from estate taxes. In other words, with planning the couple was able to pass their entire $900,000 estate to their children without paying any estate taxes.

An estate plan utilizing a bypass trust begins to make sense as the total estate of the spouses exceeds $600,000. Using a bypass trust in conjunction with a marital life estate trust or a Q-TIP trust (or an outright distribution to the surviving spouse) can expand to $1,200,000 the portion of the estate that will escape taxation by reason of the spouses' deaths.

Normally, the surviving spouse is named trustee of the bypass trust. If that appointment raises concerns because of his or her age or investment experience, a relative, friend, trusted advisor, or bank trust department can be named as trustee or as a co-trustee with the surviving spouse.

To avoid being taxed again at the death of the surviving spouse, the trustee of the bypass trust originally could not allow the surviving spouse to spend any of the principal. The IRS has since eased this rule to allow the surviving spouse to spend the principal in "limited" circumstances. The trust document must be precisely drafted to allow an "invasion of the corpus" (spending of the trust principal) for only the beneficiary's "health, education, maintenance, and support." The courts have narrowly interpreted this rule. Trusts providing for the beneficiary's "comfort" have failed, resulting in the loss of one of the two possible $600,000 exemption amounts.

Spousal Trust Options

The goal of each of the three primary spousal trusts is the same: to preserve the couple's entire $1,200,000 estate tax exclusion. Given the desire to minimize taxes, the choice of spousal trust is personal. Each one has advantages and disadvantages, so use the combination of spousal trusts that best suits your needs. Most planning for couples with estates of over $600,000 involves using the bypass trust for the decedent's first $600,000 of assets and either the marital deduction trust, the Q-TIP trust, or an outright gift to the surviving spouse for the balance of the decedent's assets.

The Bypass Trust
Advantage: You can impose any legal conditions you wish on the distribution of the property in the trust.
Disadvantage: The legal restrictions necessary to avoid taxation at the surviving spouse's death reduce that spouse's control over the use of the corpus.

The Marital Deduction Trust
Advantage: You can provide for your spouse for life and give your spouse control over the corpus.
Disadvantage: You lose some control over the distribution of your estate. Your spouse gets the income for life and can appoint future beneficiaries.

The Q-TIP Trust
Advantage: You can provide for a second spouse and still ensure that your children will receive the remainder.
Disadvantage: You must give your spouse the income for life. Q-TIP treatment must be elected by the executor at the death of the first spouse.

Bottom line: The bypass trust enables you to impose conditions on your spouse's receipt of your estate and to preserve the full exemption available to you and your spouse. The marital deduction trust gives your spouse broad power over your estate. The Q-TIP trust protects your children from a first marriage when you remarry. By combining a bypass trust with a marital deduction trust or a Q-TIP trust, the full $1,200,000 exemption available to married couples is preserved.

THE MARITAL DEDUCTION TRUST

The marital deduction trust imposes two requirements: First, all the income of the trust must go to your spouse for life. Second, that income must be reported on the spouse's income tax return.

Say you are married to Jimmy. Jimmy must be able to will the trust assets any way he pleases, even if he leaves them to your nemesis Jeannie. The right to make that disposal is called a *power of appointment*. Since Jimmy can choose whomever he pleases, he enjoys a *general power of appointment*, rather than the *special power of appointment* (which limits to whom Jimmy can give your money), that you wish the law allowed in this instance.

Don't despair. If Jimmy is lazy or forgetful and fails to exercise his power (i.e., to designate to whom he wishes the trust fund to go at his death), your will can specify it for him. But remember, Jimmy must have the right to exercise the power of appointment for the tax break to work. In this case, you would be better advised to use a Q-TIP trust, restricting Jimmy's power to appoint your property outside of your family.

THE Q-TIP TRUST

To avoid giving your spouse a general power of appointment, you can choose the other trust that achieves tax savings if you are the first to die, the Q-TIP trust. Members of Congress noticed that more marriages were ending in divorce (including their own). In their wisdom, they stepped in and provided another opportunity to claim the marital deduction, this time removing the requirement that the spouse has a general power of appointment over the trust.

The only two specifications are (1) your surviving spouse must have the right to the income from the trust for life; and (2) when your surviving spouse's estate tax return is filed, the executor must advise the IRS that assets in the trust were not taxed on your death because your executor claimed a deduction for them under the rules of the marital deduction.

The critical difference between the Q-TIP trust and the original marital deduction trust is the power of appointment. In cases of remarriage, the Q-TIP trust is advisable to ensure that children from a first marriage are not passed over by the surviving spouse of a second marriage.

OTHER MARITAL PLUSES

Before we leave the special rules of the marital estate behind, here are a few more pointers to keep in mind. Again, the more complex your estate, the more important it is that you seek professional help in making these complex plans yourself.

Gift Taxes

There is no gift tax between spouses if both are U.S. citizens, but the gifts from one spouse to the other will become part of the donee spouse's estate that is eventually taxed. Tax-free gifts to a spouse who is not a U.S. citizen are limited to $100,000 per year. Also note, if you are planning gifts to grandchildren, you'll need to coordinate these with the GST provisions. This area definitely requires professional advice.

Adjusted Basis

The *basis* of a capital asset is the value used to calculate gain or loss for income tax purposes. The basis is not necessarily equal to the purchase price of the asset. For example, if you buy a house for $100,000 and put in improvements of $15,000, your basis would be $115,000. If you sold the house for $215,000, your capital gain would be $100,000. This profit is taxed at the capital gains rate, currently not in excess of 28 percent for long-term capital gains.

In the estate context, when anyone passes appreciated or depreciated land or other real property through an estate, the basis for the property is adjusted, or *stepped-up* or *stepped-down*, to the current market value. So if appreciated land is eventually sold, the beneficiary only has to pay gains on the difference between the stepped-up basis, or market value at the death of the donor or at the alternative valuation date six months later, and the current market value, no matter how much the land had appreciated before the donor's death (see Steppin' Up, page 256, for an example). But the assets are taxed at the stepped-up value in the estate. Of course, if the property has depreciated in value, the gain or loss to the beneficiary upon a sale will be measured by reference to the stepped-down basis. In today's financial environment, assets that would receive a step-down in basis should be sold pre-death to take the tax loss.

For estates over $600,000, married couples encounter a special twist. If one spouse inherits appreciated property from the other, the cost basis of the property steps up to the market value at the time of death, as explained above. But since couples can arrange their estates so that no estate tax is paid on the death of one of them, the income tax on the gain is eliminated even though no estate taxes are paid on the capital gain. This is one of the all-time great tax loopholes. The only difficulty is that you can't predict with certainty who will die first so all the appreciated property can be placed in that spouse's name.

Now, here's a really shocking additional twist. For community property owned by couples in the nine community-property states, no matter whose name the property or stock is in, since the community is assumed to own an undivided interest in the whole, the basis of the entire property is adjusted no matter which spouse dies first.

Marital Property: Who, What, and *Where*

Our states follow two different types of marital property law, one deriving from English common law and the other from the Napoleonic code or civil law.

Common-law or Separate-property States
If you live in a separate-property state, the general rule is that each spouse's earnings belong to each individually. Each of you has the right to manage your own earnings. The property that each of you brought into the marriage belongs to you individually, as does any subsequent inheritance. You can dispose of your separate property by will.

If one spouse dies and doesn't leave a will, the surviving spouse is entitled to from a third to a half of the property of the deceased spouse, depending upon state law. Your right to continue to live in the family home would depend upon how title to the house is held.

If you divorce, you cannot count on being awarded half of the marital assets. Most separate-property states have moved to a system of equitable distribution, under which the assets are divided proportionately according to the ages of the two spouses, their individual earnings capacities, the number and ages of their children, and other criteria set by law in each of the various states. This system is usually better for women than the old system of common law, in which the wife's claim to any property not specifically in her name was limited.

Community-property States

In the nine community-property states—Arizona, California, Idaho, Louisiana, Nevada, New Mexico, Texas, Washington, and Wisconsin—each spouse owns an undivided 50 percent interest in the community, which includes all earnings and property acquired during the marriage and excludes individual inheritances and gifts and property you each brought into the marriage. In general, even if you kept all of your earnings separate, your spouse would be entitled to half of them, as you would be entitled to half of your spouse's earnings. If you buy property, your spouse will have a one-half interest in it unless you make a specific written agreement to the contrary.

The control of community assets, including your individual salaries, varies from state to state. Traditionally, although the wife owned half, management of the community was vested in the husband. Since the early 1970s, community-property laws have been changed to allow equal management rights in most states. California went one step further and gave either spouse the right to commit 100 percent of the community. In theory, if you lived in California and your spouse earned $100,000 a year, you would have the right to spend all of it down to the last penny—and your spouse would have equivalent rights over your earnings as well.

In community-property states, each spouse also has the right to will his or her half of the community property to any beneficiary of his or her choosing. Thus, if you want to protect your exclusive tenancy in the family home (which is usually community property), you had better make sure that your spouse does not will an interest in it to someone else.

Separate property that is held separately throughout the marriage can be disposed of by the original owner individually.

Upon the dissolution of a marriage in community-property states, half of the community property and assets are awarded to each spouse unless you have a binding legal agreement to the contrary.

You can write your state attorney general for a booklet on marital property rights.

Prenuptial Agreements

If you signed a prenuptial agreement, which has become more common for middle-class couples with second and third marriages, your estate planner should review the terms. You can choose to be more generous than the prenuptial agreement, but at minimum, you must meet the terms of your prenuptial agreement when you devise your property. For example, if you promised your spouse that she would inherit 10 percent of your estate and instead you have left the entire estate to your children, the family is headed for court.

Will Contracts

Normally, a person can change her will until death as long as the will is validly executed, but will contracts between spouses can bind the surviving spouse to an agreement made during marriage about the disposition of the marital property. Without a formal will contract or a Q-TIP spousal trust, the surviving spouse is free to dispose of her property as she sees fit, regardless of any prior oral agreements.

ANNUAL GIFTS: UTILIZING THE ESTATE TAX LOOPHOLE

For multimillion-dollar estates that face significant estate-tax liability, gift-giving during your lifetime presents important opportunities for tax savings. If you have a major estate and you feel time is on your side, now is the time to set up an irrevocable trust funded by annual tax-free gifts using the *Crummey powers* explained below. If you are instead in your later years and time prevents you from avoiding taxes through such a long-term estate plan, lifetime gifts can still reduce your total gift- and estate-tax liability.

There are three basic ways to give gifts during your lifetime that will reduce your estate- and gift-tax liability. Under IRC 2503(b), you are entitled to give $10,000 annually to any and all donees of your choosing tax free. In addition, without limitation, tuition fees and medical expenses can be paid directly to the provider on behalf of any person without incurring gift taxes. If you decide to pay for your grandchild's college tuition, remember that you must pay the school directly. Gifts paid directly to your grandchild in excess of $10,000 per year will incur a gift tax, even if the funds are earmarked for education. Gifts must be made outright and cannot include future interests to qualify for the annual exclusion.

Under IRC 2503(c), gifts may be made to minors in trust that qualify for the $10,000 annual exclusion (for married couples, a "split gift" totaling $20,000, $10,000 per person). To qualify, the trustee must be able to expend any and all of the principal and income of the trust on behalf of the minor. In addition, when the minor beneficiary reaches the age of twenty-one, all of the property is granted to him or her outright. No one other than the minor can be a beneficiary of the trust.

Finally, the courts have created Crummey powers, which may enable you to fund a trust tax free.

THE ULTIMATE ESTATE PLAN FOR LARGE ESTATES

If you will have a large estate, one that far exceeds the $600,000 estate tax exemption, early planning will enable you to take advantage of an amazing estate-tax loophole.

Let's say Melissa wanted to pass her million-dollar-plus estate tax free. In 1991, she gave $60,000 to the trustee of the $200,000 trust she had previously created. She also gave her two children, Nicole and Zachary, and her four grandchildren, Mitchell, Andrew, Jason, and Richard, the right to withdraw $10,000 each from the trust in April. Since none of the children exercised their right to withdraw, the money became part of the trust corpus, and in May the trustee used the money to buy life insurance. In 1992 and every year thereafter, Melissa did the same thing. By 2020, Melissa will have effectively put $1.8 million in the trust and the trustee would have purchased a large life insurance policy on Melissa. In this way, Melissa will have provided for her family for decades to come without incurring any gift- or estate-tax liability.

You may be asking: How was Melissa able to legally transfer a major estate tax free? The answer involves some complicated judicially and statutorily created rules. In 1968, in the case of *Crummey* v. *Commissioner*, the court concluded that the power to withdraw funds is equivalent to owning the funds for gift tax purposes. In other words, if you gave your son the legal right to withdraw $10,000 from a trust account, it is legally equivalent to your giving your son the $10,000. This rule holds true whether or not he withdraws the sum. This rule holds true even if he is only given a period of thirty days in which to exercise his right. In fact, this rule holds true even if he is an infant and has no practical ability to exercise his right.

Why is this important? Because you could give money each year to your trustee, with each of your children (and grandchildren) having the right to withdraw $10,000 of the gifted funds. Once given this right to withdraw, they are presumed to own the money for gift purposes. Since there is a gift-tax exclusion for gifts of up to $10,000 per person each year, your estate is never taxed on the theoretical transfer to the children. Because they will not withdraw the money, they are theoretically funding the trust, not you.

You can continue this routine each year for your entire life, without ever being taxed on the transfers. (Be aware that the donee will be taxed on *releases*, or the failure to exercise her right to withdraw, that exceed $5,000 or 5 percent of the corpus in any given year. This means that you need $200,000 in the trust to prevent the *children* from being taxed on their failure to exercise their rights to withdraw.) Since these same people to whom you give these Crummey powers will be the beneficiaries of the trust, they will not exercise their rights to withdraw.

You can then have the trustee buy life insurance with these funds each year. The trustee will designate the trust as the beneficiary of the life insurance policy. (There will be no tax on the payment of benefits from the life insurance policy.)

By the time you die, you will have created and funded a trust tax free with a value far in excess of your $600,000 estate tax exclusion.

But note: Because of the potential tax avoidance resulting from the use of the Crummey powers, particularly in light of the later cases decided based on Crummey, some experts believe that Crummey powers may be legislated out of existence. Check with advisors to update this area of tax law.

THE OTHER ANNUAL GIFT-TAX LOOPHOLE

Larry had drafted a will when he was thirty-five, but he never redesigned his estate plan to account for the millions of dollars he made in the music industry. At seventy-five, after his wife's death, Larry realized it was time to meet with his professional team to create a more effective estate plan. Unfortunately, it was too late in life to fully benefit from the use of Crummey powers even if he immediately began a program similar to Melissa's.

Instead, Larry would have to gift a portion of his estate during his lifetime. Two problems were created by this plan, both stemming from the fact that Larry could not precisely predict how long he would live. First, Larry would not want to gift away too much of his estate while he was still healthy enough to enjoy it himself. This problem is tempered by the fact that Larry has a multi-million dollar estate. Second, the tax benefit of some lifetime gifts may be lost if given within three years of death. Essentially, Larry wanted to make sure he didn't give his estate too soon *or* too late.

Table 10-1 shows Larry's potential estate tax liability were he not to give any lifetime gifts. Assuming a 50 percent estate tax rate, the federal government will take $2,505,000 from Larry's $5,610,000 estate.

TABLE 10-1: POTENTIAL ESTATE TAX LIABILITY

Net estate less applicable deductions	$5,610,000
Estate-tax exclusion	<600,000>
Taxable estate	5,010,000
Estate-tax rate	× .50
Estate-tax liability	2,505,000

Note: A 50% gift- and estate-tax rate is assumed to simplify this example, but different rates would apply in practice.

While alive, Larry can still reduce that tax burden significantly by gifting away $2,510,000, or almost half of his estate, to his son. Larry gets the annual $10,000 gift-tax exclusion for the gift to his son, but it provides little tax relief for the more than $2.5 million gift. In fact, Larry incurs a gift tax liability of $1,250,000 (see Table 10-2) since the gift is taxed at the same 50 percent rate his estate would face for the $2.5 million at his death. So aside from the $10,000 exclusion, where is the benefit?

TABLE 10-2: GIFT TAX LIABILITY

Gift	$2,510,000
Less gift-tax exclusion	<10,000>
Taxable gift	2,500,000
Gift-tax rate	× .50
Gift-tax liability	1,250,000

Note: A 50% gift- and estate-tax rate is assumed to simplify this example, but different rates would apply in practice.

The benefit comes in the form of the deduction for gift taxes paid. Although lifetime gifts must be included in the estate calculation to the extent that they exceed the annual $10,000 per donee exclusion, in this case $2.5 million, the $1.25 million in gift tax paid on the gift does not have to be added back if Larry survives for three years. As Table 10-3 shows, this deduction results in estate-tax savings of $630,000.

TABLE 10-3: ESTATE TAX SAVINGS

Taxable estate exclusive of gifts	$2,500,000
Plus lifetime gifts in excess of $10,000 gift-tax exclusion	2,500,000
Less gift-tax paid	<1,250,000>
Taxable gross estate (including taxable gifts)	3,750,000
Tax rate	× .50
Estate-tax liability	1,875,000
Potential estate-tax liability	2,505,000
Tax savings from the lifetime gift	630,000

Note: A 50% gift- and estate-tax rate is assumed to simplify this example, but different rates would apply in practice.

In effect, Larry is able to significantly reduce the total taxes paid by his estate by giving his beneficiaries their "inheritance" during his lifetime. Should Larry spread these gifts over more donees and more years, Larry could augment the tax savings with multiple $10,000 gift-tax exclusions. Larry is probably too late to pass his estate tax free the way Melissa did, but unless he dies during the next three years, he can still save on estate taxes by making gifts. (Note, most gifts within three years of death are *not* included in the gross estate but come into the estate tax calculation at "date of gift" values. All gift taxes paid on gifts within three years of death are included in the gross estate.)

Steppin' Up

Some tax loopholes must be used with caution. The new basis at death rule can actually increase the tax liability for major estates when the rule is blindly followed. Here's how it happens:

When the value of an asset appreciates, you are taxed on the capital gain or profit when you sell the asset. The capital gain is based on the difference between the sale price and the basis or cost of the asset. As explained in Chapter 5, the basis of your home would be the purchase price you paid for the house plus the costs of any permanent improvements or renovations to the house. When you sell the home, you are taxed on the capital gain, or the difference between its basis and the sale price.

New heirs receive what appears to be a windfall with the new basis at death rule. Instead of keeping the donor's basis in the asset, in this case the cost of the home plus renovations, the heir takes a new basis in the asset equivalent to the value of the asset on the day of the donor's death (or on the alternative valuation date six months later).

Although the new basis rule applies whether the asset has appreciated or depreciated, most accountants focus on the tax benefits of a stepped-up basis. Since the basis of an appreciated asset is stepped up to equal its price on the day of death, the new heir could sell an inherited asset without any capital gains tax liability, even if the heir's parent had paid far less for the asset than it was worth at the parent's death.

For example, let's say Steve purchased 10,000 shares of Neorx stock on the same day that his mother purchased 10,000 shares of the same stock for four dollars per share. If Steve inherits his mother's shares, valued at the day of her death at fourteen dollars per share, and he sells all 20,000 shares when the shares are worth fifteen dollars per share, the following tax liability would result:

	Steve's Shares	Inherited Shares
Original basis	$ 40,000	$ 40,000
Stepped-up basis	—	$140,000

Realized market value	$150,000	$150,000
Capital gain	$110,000	$ 10,000
Capital gain tax (assumed)	28%	28%
Tax liability on sale	$ 30,800	$ 2,800

At first glance, that looks like quite a tax loophole. Congress wanted to offer heirs a "fresh start." Although Steve's total tax bill for the sale of the stock would be $33,600 ($30,800 + $2,800), he gets a very generous tax break for the inherited shares.

However, the capital gains *will* show up in his mother's estate. If his mother's estate is already worth over $600,000, the estate will pay tax on the stock at the estate-tax rate (between 37 and 55 percent depending on the total value of her estate). At a 50 percent estate-tax rate, the estate will have a $50,000 tax bill for the $100,000 ($140,000 value at the day of his mother's death less the $40,000 original cost of the stock) in capital gains on the stock. In addition, Steve will still owe $2,800 for the appreciation in the stock between the time he received it and the time he sold it. That means the government will collect $52,800 from Steve's family for the capital gains on the stock he inherited. That is $22,000 ($52,000 − $30,800) more in taxes than if his mom had given Steve the stock in $10,000 annual increments (see Chapter 6) during her lifetime. Some loophole! Remember, for large estates, the benefits of a fresh start can be misleading.

Keep in mind that the new basis is mandatory. That means if stock were sold at twelve dollars a share, Steve would have a capital loss of $20,000 on the inherited shares even though there would be a capital gain of $80,000 on his original 10,000 shares. This same fresh start rule applies to inherited real estate as well.

CREATIVE USES OF LIFE INSURANCE IN ESTATE PLANNING

If you follow the financial press, you may have read about insurance trusts or the use of insurance to protect your estate. With insurance choices, two basic questions must always be answered:

1. Can I make more money by putting my investment elsewhere?
2. Is there a particular tax advantage to choosing insurance over the alternative investment?

1. PROVIDING LIQUIDITY IN AN ILLIQUID ESTATE

In many estates, the major assets are not liquid or readily convertible to cash. The family home is an example of an asset that the family might not wish to sell, but without cash in the estate, the executor may have no choice. In other cases, assets such as stocks are liquid, but due to market fluctuations, the estate may not want to sell.

Why would the estate need cash? The estate may owe many cash obligations, from administrative costs and probate fees to debt repayments, medical expenses, losses incurred during estate settlement, and burial costs. These costs are likely whether or not state and federal estate taxes are owed. Even if a living trust is utilized, where probate fees are forgone, trustee fees may be owed, as well as the other cash items connected with completing the transfer of assets. According to the *National Underwriter*, an insurance industry publication, these costs can eat up from 15 to 70 percent of an estate.

Insurance can be used to bridge the cash gap, leaving the bulk of the estate portfolio, including the family home, intact. Otherwise, assets such as your house may have to be sold in order to pay these expenses.

To determine the amount needed for this purpose, as distinct from providing funds for dependents, you'll need to estimate the costs of the various items. Here the challenge is not to project over a period of years, but to establish what will be needed in the nine months after your death to cover all of the estate's cash needs.

For example, assume Noah has an estate totaling $750,000. The first $600,000 will not be subject to federal taxes under the unified credit, so only $150,000 will be taxed. Noah's first cash need will be $55,000 for federal estate taxes without regard to deductions or tax credits which will reduce the federal estate tax bill. For this example, assume that the state death tax adds another $15,000. (Note: the federal government provides credit for state death taxes up to a certain limit and depending upon specific state law provisions.) Burial costs are $12,500; probate and administrative fees, $5,000; and his final medical expenses not covered by insurance cost $4,000. In addition, Noah's monthly docking charges for his Erikson 42 racing sloop over the nine-month period of estate settlement run to $4,500.

A total of $81,000 in cash is needed, but Noah's estate is all in land, business interests, and his yacht, none of which are liquid. Ideally, then, Noah's assets would include insurance to cover all these cash expenses.

Of course, neither you nor Noah know your final medical costs and other such items, but based upon the size of your assets now, you can estimate what cash might be needed. Periodically, you can review your position with your attorney and accountant to be sure you have accounted for changed circumstances.

As discussed in Chapter 9, insurance can be an expensive investment. Factoring in your age, earning capacity, and insurability, consider whether alternative liquid investments would be a financially preferable choice.

But in the case of a large estate like Noah's, the use of insurance over other liquid investments may have significant tax advantages. If Noah had saved the money, as distinct from putting it into insurance, additional estate taxes would have been owed on the savings. With a properly structured insurance plan, these taxes can be avoided.

2. SAVING ESTATE TAXES WITH AN INSURANCE TRUST

A number of writers, most notably Andrew Tobias, have pointed out the favored position of the insurance industry. The benign tax treatment afforded to life insurance placed in trust clearly supports this view. *Provided strict rules are followed, estate tax can be avoided altogether.* The key: To avoid taxes, set up the trust so that there is *no obligation* for the trust to pay estate debts or taxes.

Under normal circumstances, insurance is received by the estate. However, if insurance is not payable directly to the estate, but is instead receivable for the benefit of the estate, it is not part of the estate for estate tax purposes.

To gain the estate tax benefits of an insurance trust, you would normally set up an irrevocable trust with the insurance proceeds payable to the trust as beneficiary. The trust is also owner of the insurance. The trustee must have the power to engage in transactions that will accomplish the goal of paying the estate debts and taxes without specifically directing the trustee's behavior.

Normally, the trustee, with liquid assets from the insurance, is authorized to purchase from the estate illiquid assets, such as the family home. The two entities, the estate and the trust, will essentially swap assets. The estate becomes liquid and the trust takes the illiquid assets, such as the family home. The trust can then sell the illiquid assets or turn the assets over to the named beneficiaries.

Finally, there is one more hurdle to cross. In order to qualify for this attractive tax break (remember, so far the insurance is not taxed in the estate), the question of the putative and actual ownership of the insurance policy must be settled. That means the insured (and perhaps the spouse) may not retain any rights to the insurance policy. These rights include the following: the ability to name the beneficiary; to borrow against the policy; to surrender the policy for cash; and to exchange the policy for a different one. Preferably, the trust will apply for and own the insurance from the outset. If you transfer an existing policy, you must survive the transfer by three years (contemplation of death rule) or the policy proceeds will be back to be taxed in your estate. To ensure that you receive the benefits of an insurance trust, you must seek the advice of competent counsel.

If your head is spinning at this point, don't be surprised. These rules complicate rather than simplify matters, so unless your estate is over the magic $600,000 (single) or $1,200,000 (married) level, don't bother even thinking about it. If you are, you must seek the advice of competent counsel to ensure that you receive the benefits of an insurance trust.

CHARITABLE CONTRIBUTIONS AND TRUSTS

Once you have decided how much of your money to leave to your potential heirs, another area to consider is charitable contributions. The creation of a charitable trust should be given serious consideration if you have a major estate and do not have children or other dependents or are among the 29 percent of Americans who are likely to leave at least a portion of their estates outside of the "traditional" family. Charitable bequests enable you to give some part of your estate back to society. Charitable trusts may also help you to save on estate taxes since all assets transferred to charities in a qualifying manner are tax-exempt.

With charitable trusts, a benefactor can retain a lifetime of income for herself while leaving the remainder to the educational institution or other charity. These trusts, called *charitable remainder trusts*, have grown in popularity as institutions continue to hold seminars to explain them to alumni and other potential donors.

These charitable contributions enable you to reduce the taxable portion of your estate while allowing you to use the benefits of the contribution during your lifetime. With the *charitable remainder unitrust* or *annuity trust,* you can receive the income from your trust during your lifetime; in the case of *conservation easements,* you can retain the right to use the land for the rest of your life, although the uses to which the land can be put are limited.

Charitable Trusts

There are a number of trust devices that enable you to give to the charity or charities of your choice without forcing you to sacrifice significantly during your own lifetime. If this form of giving appeals to you, then you should seriously consider the various options and consult an advisor before creating the charitable trust of your choice.

The contribution can be made by a lifetime gift (if you are to be the beneficiary) or by a testamentary transfer (if your spouse or children will be the beneficiary). Depending on the type of charitable trust you create, the trustee pays the lifetime beneficiaries a fractional percentage of the trust each year and the remainder of the trust goes to the charity or educational institution of your choice.

Charitable Remainder Annuity Trusts

A charitable remainder annuity trust pays a fixed sum—based on a fixed percentage (not less than five percent) of the initial fair market value of the assets placed in the trust—to you or other individuals each year (or at more frequent intervals). The remainder goes to the designated charity. Since the fixed sum is paid whether or not the trust earns that high a yield, the sum should be based on market rates of return so that the remainder (the principal) is not reduced by the fixed payments.

Charitable Remainder Unitrusts

A charitable remainder unitrust pays a fixed percentage (not less than 5 percent) of the corpus of the trust to you or others each year. Since the percentage is based on the annual value of the trust and not its initial value, the unitrust better accounts for inflation and capital appreciation.

A charitable remainder income-only unitrust may provide that the amount distributed each year is the lesser of the fixed percentage of the value of the trust's assets or the amount of trust income. Therefore, distributions from the trust for any year would not exceed the trust's income, and the entire charitable remainder will remain intact.

POOLED INCOME FUND

Another method for making charitable contributions is the pooled income fund. A variety of donors make contributions to the fund. Each of the individual donors retains a lifetime income interest in the fund with the remainder to go to charity. Like a mutual fund, the amount of income received by participants is based on the aggregate earnings of the fund.

CONSERVATION EASEMENTS

Another currently popular device is the *conservation easement* or *qualified conservation contribution,* first introduced in 1969. The contribution of a perpetual, open-space easement to a land trust sets up a tax break equal to the fair market value of the easement or the difference between the fair market value of the pre-easement land and its current value.

This contribution can be made either in conjunction with an estate plan or simply as an income tax savings device. The easement deduction can be spread over a period of up to five years, providing an enormous benefit for income taxes, or it can reduce the total estate in a testamentary transfer by the amount of the deduction. Keep in mind that if you fall into the alternative minimum tax, you cannot take the conservation easement or any other appreciated property deductions for income tax purposes.

An example may help to explain this complicated tax maneuver. Consider Scott, who had inherited a thousand-acre farm from his grandmother that was bought in 1940 for $100 an acre. Situated on a wide stretch of the Tennessee River, the place includes pheasants, quail, and a large variety of small-animal life. For preserving open spaces, this one-thousand-acre parcel is ideal.

Scott must first determine the potential benefit of contributing the entire one-thousand-acre parcel. Since neighboring land sells for $2,000 an acre, the potential tax benefit of the conservation easement is a deduction of approximately $1,900,000 ($1,000 acres times the $2,000 an acre fair market value minus the $100 per acre cost). Because the conservation easement deduction can be spread over a period of five years and Scott's income is less than $400,000 per year, he would have no income tax liability for five years.

Unfortunately for Scott, the alternative minimum tax prevents any such tax benefit for him. Since Scott is subject to the AMT, he would lose the entire potential $1,900,000 deduction. Unfortunately for the environment, in this case the AMT takes away the financial incentive provided by the rules of conservation easements—to preserve land.

PROTECTING FAMILY BUSINESSES AND FAMILY FARMS

Family businesses and farms are given help to surmount estate tax burdens that would otherwise close the business or force the sale of the farm.

A new IRC Section (2032A) was added by Congress in 1976 and expanded by tax reforms in 1981. This *special use valuation* section permits a different valuation election for farm and small business real property than is available for other estate assets.

This special relief was provided because the normal concept of fair market value assumes a "highest and best use" of real estate, in other words, development. If the heirs of a farm wish to keep the land to use as a farm, or the owners of a small business want to keep a small office building rather than convert it to a large commercial complex, the heirs often will face taxes that exceed what they could pay and still keep the farm or business in operation. Under this special rule, the qualified property may be valued at its actual use, and not at its highest and best use, subject to a maximum reduction in value of $750,000 under 1995 law.

To qualify for the election, the property must have been used in the farm or small business and owned and operated by the decedent's family. It must also pass to a "qualified heir," that is, a member of the decedent's family.

If, within ten years of the decedent's death, the property is sold or the qualified use ceases, or if the qualified heir discontinues "substantial participation" in the business, the estate will be subject to a "recapture" tax. In other words, the tax previously saved will be tacked back on.

The procedure is essentially the same for both family businesses and family farms. We have chosen to provide an example using the family farm, given the importance of Section 2032A in protecting the last vestiges of this American tradition—maintaining the family farm through the generations.

Let's look at the case of a cattle ranch in Montana, a state popular with the West Coast urbanites for real estate investing. Because of the harsh winters and short growing season, most large Montana family agricultural businesses are cattle businesses. To graze enough cattle to produce adequate income for a family to live, as well as to pay property taxes and business expenses, such a ranch requires a minimum of 4,000 to 5,000 acres. In Montana, many such family ranching operations continue, raising and selling at market 200 to 250 head of cattle each year. At current prices, 200 head of beef cattle will command approximately $90,000 at the fall sale. Figuring a profit margin of 15 to 20 percent, the family's liquidity is limited to $15,000 to $20,000 in normal years.

But in Montana, the large acreage, open sky, and mellow lifestyle have attracted recreational investors from both coasts. Whereas at farm uses the land may be worth only $200 to $300 an acre, as "elbow room" for urbanites, a 5,000-acre ranch can sell for $500 an acre or more.

Because of the discrepancy in land values based on use, many ranchers face an estate tax problem when they attempt to keep the agricultural business in the family. If a married couple has to value their 5,000-acre farm at recreational use values of $500 an acre, the value of the farm is $2,500,000. By contrast, if the land is valued based on its farm use value of $200 an acre, it may be worth only $1,000,000. The difference in valuations could mean the difference between keeping the farm in the family or not. If the recreational use valuation was used, the couple's children would be forced to sell the farm to pay the estate taxes. But the special use valuation enables the children to keep the ranch in operation.

The tax break available with the special use valuation is limited to $750,000. If the land were the only asset in the parents' estate and the parents had preserved both of their estate tax exemptions through a marital trust, the taxable portion of the land would be as follows:

Valuation of the land	$2,500,000
Less the exemption for married couples	(1,200,000)
Less the farm valuation break	(750,000)
Taxable portion of the estate land	$550,000

Given the relative lack of liquidity of most such farms, this provision can spell the difference between the end of the property's use as a ranch or the continuance of a family business, depending upon the size and value of the property. Another break also available for qualified family businesses is an extension of the time period for payment of the estate tax. As opposed to the normal nine-month deadline for payment of estate taxes after death, qualified family businesses have up to five years of interest-only payments (at favorable rates) followed by ten years of annual tax payments, for a total timeline of fourteen years and nine months. To qualify, a business must be more than 35 percent of the gross estate less deductible expenses and debts. The business must also be "closely held," meaning that it is owned by a few people, whether or not they are related. If the business is incorporated, at least 20 percent of the voting stock must be in the estate to qualify. If the business is disposed of or terminated during the deferral period, the unpaid tax will be accelerated.

If you own a business or a family farm, be sure to take extra precautions in reviewing the potential asset base of the estate. If you want the business to survive, you should consider creating an insurance trust, described on pages 260–261, to cover the estate taxes if you do not otherwise have sufficient liquidity.

TYING IT ALL TOGETHER

Let's return to the example of the Montana farm family to see how all the various estate planning devices can work together to save taxes. The ranch couple's land and other assets appear in Table 10-4.

The couple has three children. One child is provided for and both the couple and the child agree that to keep the family business intact, she will bypass receiving any inheritance. However, situations change, so rather than making such an agreement, the

TABLE 10-4: RANCH COUPLE'S ASSETS

Cash and equivalents	$38,000
Ranch home and buildings	200,000
Livestock	114,000
Horses	6,000
Equipment	60,000
Insurance	350,000
Retirement funds	20,000
Land	2,500,000
Potential gross estate	$3,288,000

couple would be wise to leave some portion of their estate to their daughter who can then elect to disclaim her inheritance.

The couple's primary challenge was to keep the ranch intact by providing enough cash to cover the estate taxes without requiring a sale of the ranch and to provide an inheritance for each of the two children who would not participate in managing the ranch.

During the estate planning process, an opportunity arises for the couple to buy a neighboring parcel of land which would help their oldest son to continue the ranching operation. Although the couple is tempted to buy the land, a better move would be for the son to buy the land himself, thereby not adding to the parents' estate-planning problem.

We first wanted to determine where deductions and exemptions were available for the parents' estate. Looking at the asset list, we saw that the $350,000 in insurance can be placed in an insurance trust set up prior to death as part of the estate plan. In addition, the marital deduction or Q-TIP trust must be set up to preserve the full marital deduction.

The couple wanted to give the youngest son a small hundred-acre parcel at the edge of the ranch. Since no farm valuation is available for gifts, the gift would be valued at its recreational use at $500 per acre or $50,000. Because the couple can give a combined gift of $20,000 per recipient per year, the land should be gifted to their son over a period of three years to avoid any taxes relating to that transfer.

Under the current plans, the gross estate would change as shown in Table 10-5.

At current rates, the tax on this estate would amount to $341,120, an amount that would just be covered by the amount of cash in the insurance trust, thereby allowing the land to remain intact.

Because none of the alternatives are ideal, the family must keep one issue in mind: equity among the children. Despite their

---

TABLE 10-5: RANCH COUPLE'S PLANNED ASSETS

Cash and equivalents	$38,000
Ranch home and buildings	200,000
Livestock and horses	120,000
Equipment	60,000
Insurance	350,000
Less insurance to insurance trust	<350,000>
Retirement funds	20,000
Land	2,500,000
Less land gift to one son this year	<20,000>
Less maximum farm land deduction	<750,000>
Revised potential gross estate	$2,868,000
Less combined estate tax exemption amounts	<1,200,000>
Adjusted gross estate	$1,668,000

desire to preserve land that has remained in the family for over one hundred years, the couple would not want to keep the land intact at the expense of keeping the family intact.

One solution would be to divide the farm into three equal parts, leaving it to all three children but with a life estate for the two not managing the farm property, and a remainder to the grandchildren. This life estate would provide income, if any, but no right to sell or further divide the property until the next generation, which would then face the same problem of dividing historical family land.

Another choice would be to create a family-owned corporation and give shares of the corporation to each of the three children equally. The corporation could be structured to keep the management and control of the corporation in the hands of the chosen managing heir. (Problems might cause a forced sale, however.)

A final solution would be to place the assets in a limited partnership, with the chosen heir having the role of general partner. In this capacity, the limited partners (the other two heirs) would have no control and no liability, although they would own a share of the underlying land. The managing heir would act as general partner and have the right to run the farm as he saw fit.

None of these solutions—other than leaving the farm primarily to one heir—solves the problem of keeping the land intact for future generations. (But should the role of estate planning be to tie silver strings?) That, in addition to the economies of scale of agribusiness, is one reason family farms have been so difficult to maintain.

EXERCISING CONTROL

Whether dealing with its disposition at your death or its use during your life, the flow of capital from a major estate could have a significant impact on your family and the world around you. Because of this potential impact, you need to exercise control in your planning. Family conflicts left unresolved or created by a poor estate plan are magnified in proportion to the size of the estate. Similarly, the tax consequences of an improperly conceived estate plan are heightened for major estates, so professional advice should be sought. Regardless of the beneficiaries you ultimately choose, the conveyance of a major estate provides both an opportunity for the future and your gift from the past.

11

---○---

THE FLOW OF CAPITAL: MONEY, POWER, AND SOCIETY

THE FLOW OF CAPITAL affects all of our lives. For some, capital is the stream that funds their businesses. For others, capital is the source of their salaries. For new heirs, capital represents opportunity—the opportunity to assume the role of gatekeeper, controlling the flow and productive deployment of their own newfound reserve of capital.

The availability of control presents your greatest challenge as a new heir. You must learn to control your capital and direct its flow, or you risk becoming a victim of the money controlling you.

Although capital can be a great source of enjoyment and entertainment, its power extends far beyond personal gratification. When properly controlled, capital can build dreams into reality. At the same time, the wealthy are often disillusioned to find that money in itself is not satisfying. When lottery winners say that they expect to keep their jobs even after winning, they are expressing their realization that money alone does not provide for a day-to-day occupation of mind and spirit.

With capital, an individual can have a significant impact on public and personal life through investment, entrepreneurship, charitable donations, and political contributions. Although the modest inheritor must exercise caution when considering entering any of these potentially high-stakes endeavors, one of the pleasures, and responsibilities, of money, is to use it to accomplish the investment, social, charitable, and political goals you cherish.

SOCIALLY RESPONSIBLE INVESTING

The concept of using capital to control behavior probably reaches back into man's genetic code, for as long as man has amassed even the smallest vestige of wealth, he has used it to control others.

The first organized positive use of capital in the United States traces to the early Quaker resistance to slave trading and war in the seventeenth century. In the nineteenth century, churches refused to invest their funds in companies that produced alcohol or tobacco products. In the "Age of Reform" from 1890 to 1917, social change became a key part of the American agenda. After the Great Depression, providing for our citizens "from the cradle to the grave" was the watchword of the time, even though that level of security was a European ideal, not an American one.

A MODERN MOVEMENT IS BORN

The development of the modern socially responsible movement grew out of the energies of the sixties. When the first new heirs of that era came into wealth, they looked around and realized that they were part of the "enemy" that was being blamed for civil rights injustices and the war in Vietnam. Having inherited capital, they were now the new capitalists, and they didn't like it. These heirs reasoned that while they didn't want to give up their inheritances, they could direct their investments in ways that could make a difference. Building on this perspective, groups of civil rights leaders, religious leaders, and leaders of the new inherited wealth movement worked in concert first to boycott war materials producers and later to divest companies from South Africa.

When Congress passed legislation in the 1980s mandating that U.S. companies divest South African holdings, the socially responsible movement was legitimized and given new force. With the end of apartheid in South Africa, socially responsible investment leaders and investors confirmed their belief in the power of directing the flow of capital.

In addition to individual investors, groups have organized around investing or disseminating information about investing. The first modern socially responsible fund, the Pax Fund, appeared in 1970. Today, the largest such mutual fund, the Calvert Fund, totals more than $1 billion.

NEGATIVE SCREENS

Socially responsible investing first took hold in the financial world as a reactive screen against "sin" stocks. Negative screens prevented investment in liquor, tobacco, and gambling companies, as well as companies involved with disfavored foreign governments. These negative screens have had varying success in making their intended social impact. A General Motors' boycott resulted in the divestment of nuclear weapons production by that company. In contrast, most church portfolios, representing billions of dollars, won't touch tobacco or liquor, yet those industries continue to thrive. Many private investors created their own negative screens, often avoiding companies that have historically poor records on the employment or environmental fronts.

POSITIVE SCREENS

Today, with the emergence of more sophisticated *positive* screens, socially responsible investors are now rewarding companies for "doing good" as well as punishing companies for "doing bad." Environmentally friendly companies, innovative health companies, and companies led by women and minorities have now become targets for investors who want their capital to be a positive force for social change.

The success of many of these funds employing positive screens, combined with the increasing sophistication of investors and money managers, has led to more proactive, socially responsible investing. In addition to the potential risk and yield associated with investments or securities, investors are analyzing the performance of companies in relation to the environment, their human resource policies, and socially desirable objectives such as empowering women or cost-effectively improving sanitation in poverty-stricken regions. The popularity of socially responsible investing continues to grow with the proliferation of informed, socially conscious investors and professionals.

VENTURE CAPITAL

Venture capital investing is one of the most direct means of affecting social change. The allure of venture capital is high, rapid returns. The risk is the loss of even more than your initial investment.

Why would anyone want to consider investing in a situation where more than the investment could be lost? Because the promise of venture capital is not limited to rapid returns. Venture capitalists are enthralled with the pace and excitement of small businesses that have the potential for rapid expansion, job creation, and societal impact.

THE 4M FORMULA FOR SOCIALLY RESPONSIBLE INVESTING
If you plan on getting involved in socially responsible investments, you should keep two thoughts in mind. First, understand the principle that socially responsible investing is not charity. If the activity or proposed investment is not designed to turn a profit in the near future, it's not an investment. Be rigorous in your examination of any investment, and expect investments that pay social dividends to pay monetary ones as well. Second, start small.

———o———

MODEST
If your inheritance is under $50,000, don't leap into socially responsible venture capital or commit funds to a start-up company. Instead, explore one of the established mutual funds with stated social goals and a good track record.

———o———

MODERATE
If your inheritance is in the moderate range ($50,000 to $250,000), you could consider a socially responsible fund and perhaps $10,000 in a properly organized start-up business.

———o———

MAJOR
At the major level ($250,000 to $1,000,000), while you wouldn't want to be the sole investor in a startup venture, certainly you could afford to consider a $25,000 to $50,000 venture or growth stage business investment, recognizing that the money will be at risk and could be lost.

———o———

MILLIONS
At this level, you can seriously invest in venture capital. If you are starting out, you are well advised to join other emerging investors in a socially responsible investment group.

WHAT YOU GET

In exchange for critical infusions of capital, the investor or venture capitalist expects to own from 40 to 60 percent of the business. Although most entrepreneurs are hesitant to forgo any share of their creations, sacrifice to venture capitalists is necessary for the growth of many promising new businesses.

As an investor, you will find that venture capital presents both opportunity and risk. Any start-up or early-stage business can fail, and your exposure may not be limited to the funds you originally invest. Depending upon the covenants in the original deal, investors may find themselves involved with cash infusions and emergency management.

Before undertaking a venture capital investment, do your homework; in other words, do your *due diligence.*

DUE DILIGENCE

Due diligence is the process of checking to see that the business opportunity is as it has been presented in the business plan and that the legal and financial documents are in order. Since failure rates among start-ups are one in four or higher, venture capital investments require significant due diligence. The greater the proportion of your wealth you are investing, the more careful you'll want to be. Visit with the entrepreneur personally. Check out the place of business. Be sure that it meets your expectations in reality, not just on paper.

Most seasoned investors make the strength of the entrepreneur the primary basis for their venture capital investment decisions. The new venture lives or dies by the dedication of the entrepreneur, so make a thorough review of management your first priority.

You'll also want to look to the existing and proposed capitalization. Be sure that there is enough capital for the business to continue operating until it turns a profit.

Have your attorney look over the legal documents, including the offering memorandum and subscription agreement. Be sure that your potential loss is limited to the amount of capital you have laid on the table and does not include any "capital calls" or extra capital to be paid in.

If you don't understand the financial projections, ask your accountant if they seem reasonable under the particular circumstances. Of course, keep in mind that projections are just that —someone's optimistic hopes about what will happen, not a guarantee.

If it seems that a great deal of checking (and expense) is involved to invest in a business venture, you're right. Such activities basically are the preserve of millionaire inheritors. At that level, losing $25,000 to $100,000 would hurt, but it wouldn't be fatal to preserving one's inheritance fairly intact.

However, after you inherit, if family and friends are aware of your good fortune, you'll find yourself with numerous investment "opportunities." Just as almost everyone has one good movie script inside them just waiting to be written, almost every person bored with their job has one good "business" just waiting to be born.

Supporting entrepreneurship should not be discouraged, but don't invest alone. Make sure you have experienced co-investors. They can help shoulder the burden of maintaining the business through tough times.

If you are thinking about starting your own business with your inheritance, think twice. Without adequate preparation, starting a business from scratch is one of the easiest ways to lose money, next to a trip to Las Vegas. Bottom line: Don't put more money into your own business than you would be willing to lose in someone else's. It is better to earn the interest on your inheritance than to work in vain.

INVESTING, NOT GIVING

Socially responsible investing (SRI) is investing, not charitable giving. Studies have shown that socially responsible investments perform as well as or better than the Standard and Poor's 500. In fact, many financial experts maintain that companies that incorporate humanistic values will do better than those that do not. This concept should be intuitive. Companies that are focused on the needs of their employees, their environments, and their consumers are the companies most likely to prosper in the long run.

The Investors' Circle

In 1992, a national group of private investors formed the Investors' Circle to establish a marketplace for socially responsible venture deals. After trial and error the group set up a "deal flow," an organized process for circulating potential investments. An investors' committee looks over 200 to 300 deals forwarded, and selects ten to fifteen. This process culminates in a semiannual venture fair, with morning presentations by entrepreneurs seeking capital. The investors hear the presentations, and in the afternoon meet individually with the entrepreneurs and their teams. In the evening they share their impressions of the pros and cons of particular enterprises.

Investors then do their own due diligence, either directly or through their advisors, and make a decision whether or not to invest.

The Investors' Circle is one of several socially responsible investment groups that provide pre-screening, peer support, and potential partners for investors seriously interested in the world of venture capital.

Looking for strong socially responsible deals can take patience, but they exist. Even though you may not be a member of an investment group generating a flow of potential deals or investment opportunities, such as the Investors' Circle, you can locate deals and engage in a similar process for yourself. In addition, several computerized deal-flow "capital networks" have been created to match potential investors with capital-hungry start-up companies in their areas of interest.

CHARITABLE GIVING

Charitable donations are another way to achieve social goals with your capital. In 1993, Americans gave $126 billion to charity. Seven percent of that amount ($8.5 billion) was in the form of bequests.

Unlike investing, the rewards for charitable giving are personal and psychic, rather than financial. Of course, in higher tax brackets, the deduction for charitable contributions can provide tax breaks for up to 50 percent of income. And, as we have seen in estate planning, once fortunes reach a certain size, giving them away makes sense since estate taxes run 55 percent above $21 million.

But, you should still be demanding.

Set up a charitable budget for your giving, and hold the organizations you support responsible for performing their stated objectives. Watch that administrative expenses do not exceed reasonable amounts (usually no more than 25 percent of the organization's annual budget).

POLITICAL GIVING

Another form of exercising your money muscle is political giving. For the price of a cocktail or dinner ticket during an election season, you can dine with the President or spend lunch with a senator.

While the topic of campaign reform is one that deserves discussion, it is beyond our scope here. In the meanwhile, remember that you can use your access to candidates to influence positive social, economic, and political policies.

MONEY, POWER, AND SOCIETY

Throughout the book, we have looked at the psychological questions and issues surrounding wealth, especially inherited wealth.

Recently, the creator of a high-tech fortune spoke at an exclusive private school in Los Angeles. A teenager reported what most impressed him about the presentation: In answer to a question about how much he had made, the entrepreneur said he had so much money that he had stopped counting it. The teenager was so enraptured by the vision of the wealth that he could not recall the force that created it. The boy had given us a simple reminder that even at a young age, we allow wealth to become an end in itself. As a new heir, you must not become so enthralled with your wealth that you cannot see the power for change—in your life and in society—that it offers.

IS INHERITING GOOD?

A number of groups have been formed of second and later generation heirs with the purpose of putting money to more productive ends. These wealthy heirs have recognized the often debilitating effects that inheriting wealth can have on personal development and family functionality. These heirs have recognized that "the rich are different from you and me . . ." because they think they are.

The question remains whether the preservation and pursuit of wealth enhances or detracts from achieving and maintaining a healthy society with values that promote the worth of individual achievement and the collective good.

The answer, short of a radical redistribution of wealth through a restructuring of the inheritance tax system, appears to lie in educating those with resources about their wise and socially responsible use.

No matter the financial position of the family—from working class to wealthy—the control of money represents power and control within the family. In that respect, the family mirrors society.

The new heirs must shift the meaning of the control of capital. On a personal level, that goal translates into simpler, less consumptive lifestyles. On the societal level, the task centers on using wealth to create and maintain a positively functioning, unified society, free of the dysfunctionalities that for so long have held families and our society in thrall.

Wealth has passed through the generations. The revolution stirred by the inheritance boom is not led by the transfer of wealth, but by its transformation into a force for positive growth.

The danger of inherited wealth is that it confers power without discipline. The ultimate purpose of this book has been to bring that discipline to the new heir.

More than $11 trillion will be passed during the inheritance boom. Given that scale, the irresposible use of an inheritance—whether it be the result of sentimentality, temptation, or complexity—has dangerous implications for generations to come. The responsible deployment of an inheritance—by budgeting, allocating assets, planning estates, and controlling the flow of capital—can make a positive difference for us all.

APPENDICES

Appendix 1. Selected Tax Forms

Form **1040**	Department of the Treasury—Internal Revenue Service **U.S. Individual Income Tax Return**	(99)	IRS Use Only—Do not write or staple in this space.		OMB No. 1545-0074

For the year Jan. 1–Dec. 31, 1996, or other tax year beginning , 1996, ending , 19

Label (See page 11.)

Your first name and initial | Last name | Your social security number

If a joint return, spouse's first name and initial | Last name | Spouse's social security number

Use the IRS label. Otherwise, please print or type.

Home address (number and street). If you have a P.O. box, see page 11. | Apt. no.

City, town or post office, state, and ZIP code. If you have a foreign address, see page 11.

For help finding line instructions, see pages 2 and 3 in the booklet.

Presidential Election Campaign (See page 11.)

Do you want $3 to go to this fund? . . . .
If a joint return, does your spouse want $3 to go to this fund? . . . . . .

Yes | No | Note: Checking "Yes" will not change your tax or reduce your refund.

Filing Status

Check only one box.

1 Single
2 Married filing joint return (even if only one had income)
3 Married filing separate return. Enter spouse's social security no. above and full name here. ▶
4 Head of household (with qualifying person). (See instructions.) If the qualifying person is a child but not your dependent, enter this child's name here. ▶
5 Qualifying widow(er) with dependent child (year spouse died ▶ 19). (See instructions.)

Exemptions

6a ☐ Yourself. If your parent (or someone else) can claim you as a dependent on his or her tax return, **do not** check box 6a . . . .
b ☐ Spouse . . . .
c Dependents:

(1) First name Last name	(2) Dependent's social security number. If born in Dec. 1996, see inst.	(3) Dependent's relationship to you	(4) No. of months lived in your home in 1996

If more than six dependents, see the instructions for line 6c.

d Total number of exemptions claimed . . . .

No. of boxes checked on lines 6a and 6b
No. of your children on line 6c who:
• lived with you
• did not live with you due to divorce or separation (see instructions)
Dependents on 6c not entered above
Add numbers entered on lines above ▶

Income

Attach Copy B of your Forms W-2, W-2G, and 1099-R here.

If you did not get a W-2, see the instructions for line 7.

Enclose, but do not attach, any payment. Also, please enclose Form 1040-V (see the instructions for line 62).

7 Wages, salaries, tips, etc. Attach Form(s) W-2 . . . . | 7
8a Taxable interest. Attach Schedule B if over $400 . . . . . . | 8a
b Tax-exempt interest. DO NOT include on line 8a . . | 8b |
9 Dividend income. Attach Schedule B if over $400 . . . . . | 9
10 Taxable refunds, credits, or offsets of state and local income taxes (see instructions) . | 10
11 Alimony received . . . . | 11
12 Business income or (loss). Attach Schedule C or C-EZ . . . . . | 12
13 Capital gain or (loss). If required, attach Schedule D . . . . . | 13
14 Other gains or (losses). Attach Form 4797 . . . . | 14
15a Total IRA distributions . . | 15a | b Taxable amount (see inst.) | 15b
16a Total pensions and annuities | 16a | b Taxable amount (see inst.) | 16b
17 Rental real estate, royalties, partnerships, S corporations, trusts, etc. Attach Schedule E | 17
18 Farm income or (loss). Attach Schedule F . . . . | 18
19 Unemployment compensation . . . . | 19
20a Social security benefits . | 20a | b Taxable amount (see inst.) | 20b
21 Other income. List type and amount—see instructions ....
22 Add the amounts in the far right column for lines 7 through 21. This is your **total income** ▶ | 22

Adjusted Gross Income

If line 31 is under $28,495 (under $9,500 if a child did not live with you), see the instructions for line 54.

23a Your IRA deduction (see instructions) . . . . . | 23a
b Spouse's IRA deduction (see instructions) . . . . . | 23b
24 Moving expenses. Attach Form 3903 or 3903-F . . . | 24
25 One-half of self-employment tax. Attach Schedule SE . . | 25
26 Self-employed health insurance deduction (see inst.) . . | 26
27 Keogh & self-employed SEP plans. If SEP, check ▶ ☐ | 27
28 Penalty on early withdrawal of savings . . . . . | 28
29 Alimony paid. Recipient's SSN ▶ | 29
30 Add lines 23a through 29 . . . . | 30
31 Subtract line 30 from line 22. This is your **adjusted gross income** . . . . . ▶ | 31

For Privacy Act and Paperwork Reduction Act Notice, see page 7. | Cat. No. 11320B | Form **1040** (1996)

Form 1041
Department of the Treasury—Internal Revenue Service
U.S. Income Tax Return for Estates and Trusts

For calendar year 1996 or fiscal year beginning , 1996, and ending , 19

OMB No. 1545-0092

A Type of entity:
- ☐ Decedent's estate
- ☐ Simple trust
- ☐ Complex trust
- ☐ Grantor type trust
- ☐ Bankruptcy estate–Ch. 7
- ☐ Bankruptcy estate–Ch. 11
- ☐ Pooled income fund

Name of estate or trust (If a grantor type trust, see page 7 of the instructions.)

Name and title of fiduciary

Number, street, and room or suite no. (If a P.O. box, see page 7 of the instructions.)

City or town, state, and ZIP code

B Number of Schedules K-1 attached (see instructions) ▶

C Employer identification number

D Date entity created

E Nonexempt charitable and split-interest trusts, check applicable boxes (see page 8 of the instructions):
- ☐ Described in section 4947(a)(1)
- ☐ Not a private foundation
- ☐ Described in section 4947(a)(2)

F Check applicable boxes:
- ☐ Initial return ☐ Final return ☐ Amended return
- ☐ Change in fiduciary's name ☐ Change in fiduciary's address

G Pooled mortgage account (see page 9 of the instructions):
☐ Bought ☐ Sold Date:

Income

1	Interest income	1
2	Dividends	2
3	Business income or (loss) (attach Schedule C or C-EZ (Form 1040))	3
4	Capital gain or (loss) (attach Schedule D (Form 1041))	4
5	Rents, royalties, partnerships, other estates and trusts, etc. (attach Schedule E (Form 1040))	5
6	Farm income or (loss) (attach Schedule F (Form 1040))	6
7	Ordinary gain or (loss) (attach Form 4797)	7
8	Other income. List type and amount	8
9	**Total income.** Combine lines 1 through 8 ▶	9

Deductions

10	Interest. Check if Form 4952 is attached ▶ ☐	10
11	Taxes	11
12	Fiduciary fees	12
13	Charitable deduction (from Schedule A, line 7)	13
14	Attorney, accountant, and return preparer fees	14
15a	Other deductions NOT subject to the 2% floor (attach schedule)	15a
b	Allowable miscellaneous itemized deductions subject to the 2% floor	15b
16	**Total.** Add lines 10 through 15b	16
17	Adjusted total income or (loss). Subtract line 16 from line 9. Enter here and on Schedule B, line 1 ▶	17
18	Income distribution deduction (from Schedule B, line 17) (attach Schedules K-1 (Form 1041))	18
19	Estate tax deduction (including certain generation-skipping taxes) (attach computation)	19
20	Exemption	20
21	**Total deductions.** Add lines 18 through 20 ▶	21

Tax and Payments

22	Taxable income. Subtract line 21 from line 17. If a loss, see page 13 of the instructions	22
23	**Total tax** (from Schedule G, line 8)	23
24	Payments: a 1996 estimated tax payments and amount applied from 1995 return	24a
b	Estimated tax payments allocated to beneficiaries (from Form 1041-T)	24b
c	Subtract line 24b from line 24a	24c
d	Tax paid with extension of time to file: ☐ Form 2758 ☐ Form 8736 ☐ Form 8800	24d
e	Federal income tax withheld. If any is from Form(s) 1099, check ▶ ☐	24e
	Other payments: f Form 2439 ; g Form 4136 ; Total ▶	24h
25	**Total payments.** Add lines 24c through 24e, and 24h ▶	25
26	Estimated tax penalty (see page 13 of the instructions)	26
27	Tax due. If line 25 is smaller than the total of lines 23 and 26, enter amount owed	27
28	Overpayment. If line 25 is larger than the total of lines 23 and 26, enter amount overpaid	28
29	Amount of line 28 to be: **a Credited to 1997 estimated tax** ▶ ; **b Refunded** ▶	29

Please Sign Here

Under penalties of perjury, I declare that I have examined this return, including accompanying schedules and statements, and to the best of my knowledge and belief, it is true, correct, and complete. Declaration of preparer (other than fiduciary) is based on all information of which preparer has any knowledge.

▶ Signature of fiduciary or officer representing fiduciary | Date | EIN of fiduciary if a financial institution (see page 4 of the instructions)

Paid Preparer's Use Only

| Preparer's signature | ▶ | Date | Check if self-employed ▶ ☐ | Preparer's social security no. |
| Firm's name (or yours if self-employed) and address | ▶ | | EIN ▶ | ZIP code ▶ |

For Paperwork Reduction Act Notice, see page 1 of the separate instructions.
Cat. No. 11370H
Form **1041** (1996)

Form 1041 (1996)   Page **2**

Schedule A   **Charitable Deduction.** Do not complete for a simple trust or a pooled income fund.

1	Amounts paid for charitable purposes from gross income	**1**
2	Amounts permanently set aside for charitable purposes from gross income	**2**
3	Add lines 1 and 2	**3**
4	Tax-exempt income allocable to charitable contributions (see page 14 of the instructions)	**4**
5	Subtract line 4 from line 3	**5**
6	Capital gains for the tax year allocated to corpus and paid or permanently set aside for charitable purposes	**6**
7	**Charitable deduction.** Add lines 5 and 6. Enter here and on page 1, line 13.	**7**

Schedule B   **Income Distribution Deduction**

1	Adjusted total income (from page 1, line 17) (see page 14 of the instructions)	**1**
2	Adjusted tax-exempt interest	**2**
3	Total net gain from Schedule D (Form 1041), line 17, column (a) (see page 15 of the instructions)	**3**
4	Enter amount from Schedule A, line 6	**4**
5	Long-term capital gain for the tax year included on Schedule A, line 3	**5**
6	Short-term capital gain for the tax year included on Schedule A, line 3	**6**
7	If the amount on page 1, line 4, is a capital loss, enter here as a positive figure	**7**
8	If the amount on page 1, line 4, is a capital gain, enter here as a negative figure	**8**
9	**Distributable net income (DNI).** Combine lines 1 through 8. If zero or less, enter -0-	**9**
10	If a complex trust, enter accounting income for the tax year as determined under the governing instrument and applicable local law **10**	
11	Income required to be distributed currently	**11**
12	Other amounts paid, credited, or otherwise required to be distributed	**12**
13	Total distributions. Add lines 11 and 12. If greater than line 10, see page 15 of the instructions	**13**
14	Enter the amount of tax-exempt income included on line 13	**14**
15	Tentative income distribution deduction. Subtract line 14 from line 13	**15**
16	Tentative income distribution deduction. Subtract line 2 from line 9. If zero or less, enter -0-	**16**
17	**Income distribution deduction.** Enter the smaller of line 15 or line 16 here and on page 1, line 18	**17**

Schedule G   **Tax Computation** (see page 16 of the instructions)

1	Tax: a ☐ Tax rate schedule or ☐ Schedule D (Form 1041)	**1a**	
	b Other taxes	**1b**	
	c Total. Add lines 1a and 1b. ▶		**1c**
2a	Foreign tax credit (attach Form 1116)	**2a**	
b	Check: ☐ Nonconventional source fuel credit ☐ Form 8834	**2b**	
c	General business credit. Enter here and check which forms are attached: ☐ Form 3800 or ☐ Forms (specify) ▶	**2c**	
d	Credit for prior year minimum tax (attach Form 8801)	**2d**	
3	Total credits. Add lines 2a through 2d ▶		**3**
4	Subtract line 3 from line 1c		**4**
5	Recapture taxes. Check if from: ☐ Form 4255 ☐ Form 8611		**5**
6	Alternative minimum tax (from Schedule I, line 41)		**6**
7	Household employment taxes. Attach Schedule H (Form 1040)		**7**
8	**Total tax.** Add lines 4 through 7. Enter here and on page 1, line 23 ▶		**8**

Other Information

		Yes	No
1	Did the estate or trust receive tax-exempt income? If "Yes," attach a computation of the allocation of expenses. Enter the amount of tax-exempt interest income and exempt-interest dividends ▶ $		
2	Did the estate or trust receive all or any part of the earnings (salary, wages, and other compensation) of any individual by reason of a contract assignment or similar arrangement?		
3	At any time during calendar year 1996, did the estate or trust have an interest in or a signature or other authority over a bank, securities, or other financial account in a foreign country? See page 17 of the instructions for exceptions and filing requirements for Form TD F 90-22.1. If "Yes," enter the name of the foreign country ▶		
4	During the tax year, did the estate or trust receive a distribution from, or was it the grantor of, or transferor to, a foreign trust? If "Yes," see page 17 of the instructions for other forms the estate or trust may have to file		
5	Did the estate or trust receive, or pay, any seller-financed mortgage interest? If "Yes," see page 17 of the instructions for required attachment		
6	If this is a complex trust making the section 663(b) election, check here (see page 17 of the instructions) ▶ ☐		
7	To make a section 643(e)(3) election, attach Schedule D (Form 1041), and check here (see page 17). ▶ ☐		
8	If the decedent's estate has been open for more than 2 years, check here ▶ ☐		

Form 1041 (1996)   Page **3**

Schedule I	**Alternative Minimum Tax** (see pages 18 through 22 of the instructions)

Part I—Estate's or Trust's Share of Alternative Minimum Taxable Income

1	Adjusted total income or (loss) (from page 1, line 17)	**1**	
2	Net operating loss deduction. Enter as a positive amount	**2**	
3	Add lines 1 and 2	**3**	
4	**Adjustments and tax preference items:**		
a	Interest **4a**		
b	Taxes **4b**		
c	Miscellaneous itemized deductions (from page 1, line 15b) **4c**		
d	Refund of taxes . . . . **4d** ( )		
e	Depreciation of property placed in service after 1986 . . . . . **4e**		
f	Circulation and research and experimental expenditures **4f**		
g	Mining exploration and development costs **4g**		
h	Long-term contracts entered into after February 28, 1986 . . . . **4h**		
i	Amortization of pollution control facilities **4i**		
j	Installment sales of certain property **4j**		
k	Adjusted gain or loss (including incentive stock options). **4k**		
l	Certain loss limitations **4l**		
m	Tax shelter farm activities **4m**		
n	Passive activities **4n**		
o	Beneficiaries of other trusts or decedent's estates **4o**		
p	Tax-exempt interest from specified private activity bonds **4p**		
q	Depletion **4q**		
r	Accelerated depreciation of real property placed in service before 1987 **4r**		
s	Accelerated depreciation of leased personal property placed in service before 1987 . . . . **4s**		
t	Intangible drilling costs **4t**		
u	Other adjustments **4u**		
5	Combine lines 4a through 4u	**5**	
6	Add lines 3 and 5	**6**	
7	Alternative tax net operating loss deduction (see page 21 of the instructions for limitations). .	**7**	
8	Adjusted alternative minimum taxable income. Subtract line 7 from line 6. Enter here and on line 13	**8**	
	Note: *Complete Part II before going to line 9.*		
9	Income distribution deduction from line 27 . . . . **9**		
10	Estate tax deduction (from page 1, line 19) **10**		
11	Add lines 9 and 10	**11**	
12	Estate's or trust's share of alternative minimum taxable income. Subtract line 11 from line 8 .	**12**	

If line 12 is:
- $22,500 or less, stop here and enter -0- on Schedule G, line 6. The estate or trust is not liable for the alternative minimum tax.
- Over $22,500, but less than $165,000, go to line 28.
- $165,000 or more, enter the amount from line 12 on line 34 and go to line 35.

(continued on page 4)

Form 1041 (1996)

Part II—Income Distribution Deduction on a Minimum Tax Basis

13	Adjusted alternative minimum taxable income (from line 8)	13	
14	Adjusted tax-exempt interest (other than amounts included on line 4p)	14	
15	Total net gain from Schedule D (Form 1041), line 17, column (a). If a loss, enter -0-	15	
16	Capital gains for the tax year allocated to corpus and paid or permanently set aside for charitable purposes (from Schedule A, line 6)	16	
17	Capital gains paid or permanently set aside for charitable purposes from current year's income (see page 21 of the instructions).	17	
18	Capital gains computed on a minimum tax basis included on line 8	18 ( )	
19	Capital losses computed on a minimum tax basis included on line 8. Enter as a positive amount	19	
20	Distributable net alternative minimum taxable income (DNAMTI). Combine lines 13 through 19 .	20	
21	Income required to be distributed currently (from Schedule B, line 11)	21	
22	Other amounts paid, credited, or otherwise required to be distributed (from Schedule B, line 12)	22	
23	Total distributions. Add lines 21 and 22	23	
24	Tax-exempt income included on line 23 (other than amounts included on line 4p)	24	
25	Tentative income distribution deduction on a minimum tax basis. Subtract line 24 from line 23 .	25	
26	Tentative income distribution deduction on a minimum tax basis. Subtract line 14 from line 20 .	26	
27	**Income distribution deduction on a minimum tax basis.** Enter the smaller of line 25 or line 26. Enter here and on line 9	27	

Part III—Alternative Minimum Tax

28	Exemption amount		28	$22,500
29	Enter the amount from line 12	29		
30	Phase-out of exemption amount	30	$75,000	
31	Subtract line 30 from line 29. If zero or less, enter -0-	31		
32	Multiply line 31 by 25% (.25)		32	
33	Subtract line 32 from line 28. If zero or less, enter -0-		33	
34	Subtract line 33 from line 29		34	
35	If line 34 is: • $175,000 or less, multiply line 34 by 26% (.26). • Over $175,000, multiply line 34 by 28% (.28) and subtract $3,500 from the result		35	
36	Alternative minimum foreign tax credit (see page 21 of instructions).		36	
37	Tentative minimum tax. Subtract line 36 from line 35		37	
38	Regular tax before credits (see page 22 of instructions)	38		
39	Section 644 tax included on Schedule G, line 1b	39		
40	Add lines 38 and 39		40	
41	**Alternative minimum tax.** Subtract line 40 from line 37. If zero or less, enter -0-. Enter here and on Schedule G, line 6		41	

SCHEDULE D
(Form 1041)

Department of the Treasury
Internal Revenue Service

Capital Gains and Losses

▶ Attach to Form 1041 (or Form 5227). See the separate instructions for
Form 1041 (or Form 5227).

OMB No. 1545-0092

Name of estate or trust

Employer identification number

Note: *Form 5227 filers need to complete ONLY Parts I and II.*

Part I Short-Term Capital Gains and Losses—Assets Held One Year or Less

(a) Description of property (Example, 100 shares 7% preferred of "Z" Co.)	(b) Date acquired (mo., day, yr.)	(c) Date sold (mo., day, yr.)	(d) Sales price	(e) Cost or other basis (see instructions)	(f) Gain or (loss) (col. (d) less col. (e))
1					

2 Short-term capital gain or (loss) from Forms 4684, 6252, 6781, and 8824	**2**	
3 Net short-term gain or (loss) from partnerships, S corporations, and other estates or trusts . . .	**3**	
4 Net gain or (loss). Combine lines 1 through 3	**4**	
5 Short-term capital loss carryover from 1995 Schedule D, line 28	**5** ( )
6 Net short-term gain or (loss). Combine lines 4 and 5. Enter here and on line 15 below . . . ▶	**6**	

Part II Long-Term Capital Gains and Losses—Assets Held More Than One Year

7					

8 Long-term capital gain or (loss) from Forms 2439, 4684, 6252, 6781, and 8824	**8**	
9 Net long-term gain or (loss) from partnerships, S corporations, and other estates or trusts . . .	**9**	
10 Capital gain distributions	**10**	
11 Gain from Form 4797	**11**	
12 Net gain or (loss). Combine lines 7 through 11	**12**	
13 Long-term capital loss carryover from 1995 Schedule D, line 35	**13** ( )
14 Net long-term gain or (loss). Combine lines 12 and 13. Enter here and on line 16 below . . . ▶	**14**	

Part III Summary of Parts I and II

	(a) Beneficiaries' (see instructions)	(b) Estate's or trust's	(c) Total
15 Net short-term gain or (loss) from line 6, above **15**			
16 Net long-term gain or (loss) from line 14, above **16**			
17 Total net gain or (loss). Combine lines 15 and 16 . . . ▶ **17**			

Note: *If line 17, column (c), is a net gain, enter the gain on Form 1041, line 4. If lines 16 and 17, column (b) are net gains, go to Part VI, and DO NOT complete Parts IV and V. If line 17, column (c), is a net loss, complete Parts IV and V, as necessary.*

For Paperwork Reduction Act Notice, see page 1 of the Instructions for Form 1041.   Cat. No. 11376V   Schedule D (Form 1041) 1996

Schedule D (Form 1041) 1996   Page **2**

Part IV	**Capital Loss Limitation**

18 Enter here and enter as a (loss) on Form 1041, line 4, the smaller of:

   a The loss on line 17, column (c); **or**

   b $3,000 . . . . **18** |(   )

If the loss on line 17, column (c) is more than $3,000, OR if Form 1041, page 1, line 22, is a loss, complete Part V to determine your capital loss carryover.

Part V	**Capital Loss Carryovers From 1996 to 1997**

Section A.—Carryover Limit

19	Enter taxable income or (loss) from Form 1041, line 22.	**19**
20	Enter loss from line 18 as a positive amount	**20**
21	Enter amount from Form 1041, line 20	**21**
22	Adjusted taxable income. Combine lines 19, 20, and 21, but do not enter less than zero . . .	**22**
23	Enter the smaller of line 20 or line 22.	**23**

Section B.—Short-Term Capital Loss Carryover
(Complete this part only if there is a loss on line 6 and line 17, column (c).)

24	Enter loss from line 6 as a positive amount		**24**
25	Enter gain, if any, from line 14. If that line is blank or shows a loss, enter -0-	**25**	
26	Enter amount from line 23	**26**	
27	Add lines 25 and 26		**27**
28	**Short-term capital loss carryover to 1997.** Subtract line 27 from line 24. If zero or less, enter -0-. If this is the final return of the trust or decedent's estate, also enter on Schedule K-1 (Form 1041), line 12b		**28**

Section C.—Long-Term Capital Loss Carryover
(Complete this part only if there is a loss on line 14 and line 17, column (c).)

29	Enter loss from line 14 as a positive amount		**29**
30	Enter gain, if any, from line 6. If that line is blank or shows a loss, enter -0-.		**30**
31	Enter amount from line 23	**31**	
32	Enter amount, if any, from line 24	**32**	
33	Subtract line 32 from line 31. If zero or less, enter -0-		**33**
34	Add lines 30 and 33		**34**
35	**Long-term capital loss carryover to 1997.** Subtract line 34 from line 29. If zero or less, enter -0-. If this is the final return of the trust or decedent's estate, also enter on Schedule K-1 (Form 1041), line 12c.		**35**

Part VI	**Tax Computation Using Maximum Capital Gains Rate** (Complete this part only if both lines 16 and 17, column (b) are gains, and Form 1041, line 22 is more than $3,800.)

36	Enter taxable income from Form 1041, line 22.		**36**
37a	**Net capital gain.** Enter the smaller of line 16 or 17, column (b)	**37a**	
b	If you are filing Form 4952, enter the amount from Form 4952, line 4e .	**37b**	
c	Subtract line 37b from line 37a. If zero or less, stop here; you cannot use Part VI to figure the tax for the estate or trust. Instead, use the 1996 Tax Rate Schedule		**37c**
38	Subtract line 37c from line 36. If zero or less, enter -0-		**38**
39	Enter the greater of line 38 or $1,600		**39**
40	Tax on amount on line 39 from the 1996 Tax Rate Schedule. If line 39 is $1,600, enter $240.00 .		**40**
41	Subtract line 39 from line 36. If zero or less, enter -0-		**41**
42	Multiply line 41 by 28% (.28)		**42**
43	Maximum capital gains tax. Add lines 40 and 42		**43**
44	Tax on amount on line 36 from the 1996 Tax Rate Schedule		**44**
45	**Tax.** Enter the smaller of line 43 or line 44 here and on line 1a of Schedule G, Form 1041 . . .		**45**

✴

SCHEDULE J (Form 1041)	**Accumulation Distribution for a Complex Trust**	OMB No. 1545-0092

Department of the Treasury
Internal Revenue Service

▶ File with Form 1041.

▶ See the separate Form 1041 instructions.

Name of trust	Employer identification number

Part I Accumulation Distribution in 1996

Note: *See the Form 4970 instructions for certain income that minors may exclude and special rules for multiple trusts.*

1 Other amounts paid, credited, or otherwise required to be distributed for 1996 (from Schedule B of Form 1041, line 12) **1**

2 Distributable net income for 1996 (from Schedule B of Form 1041, line 9) . . . **2**

3 Income required to be distributed currently for 1996 (from Schedule B of Form 1041, line 11) **3**

4 Subtract line 3 from line 2. If zero or less, enter -0- **4**

5 Accumulation distribution for 1996. Subtract line 4 from line 1 . . . . **5**

Part II Ordinary Income Accumulation Distribution (Enter the applicable throwback years below.)

Note: *If the distribution is thrown back to more than five years (starting with the earliest applicable tax year beginning after 1968), attach additional schedules. (If the trust was a simple trust, see Regulations section 1.665(e)-1A(b).)*

		Throwback year ending 19	Throwback year ending 19	Throwback year ending 19	Throwback year ending 19	Throwback year ending 19 ....
6 Distributable net income (see page 24 of the instructions) .	**6**					
7 Distributions (see page 24 of the instructions)	**7**					
8 Subtract line 7 from line 6 .	**8**					
9 Enter amount from page 2, line 25 or line 31, as applicable	**9**					
10 Undistributed net income Subtract line 9 from line 8 .	**10**					
11 Enter amount of prior accumulation distributions thrown back to any of these years	**11**					
12 Subtract line 11 from line 10	**12**					
13 Allocate the amount on line 5 to the earliest applicable year first. Do not allocate an amount greater than line 12 for the same year (see page 24 of the instructions) . . .	**13**					
14 Divide line 13 by line 10 and multiply result by amount on line 9	**14**					
15 Add lines 13 and 14 . . .	**15**					
16 Tax-exempt interest included on line 13 (see page 24 of the instructions)	**16**					
17 Subtract line 16 from line 15	**17**					

For Paperwork Reduction Act Notice, see page 1 of the Instructions for Form 1041. Cat. No. 11382Z **Schedule J (Form 1041) 1996**

Schedule J (Form 1041) 1996   Page **2**

Part III   **Taxes Imposed on Undistributed Net Income** (Enter the applicable throwback years below.) (see page 24 of the instructions)
Note: *If more than five throwback years are involved, attach additional schedules. If the trust received an accumulation distribution from another trust, see Regulations section 1.665(d)-1A.*

If the trust elected the alternative tax on capital gains (repealed for tax years beginning after 1978), **SKIP** lines 18 through 25 and **COMPLETE** lines 26 through 31.		**Throwback year ending** 19	**Throwback year ending** 19	**Throwback year ending** 19	**Throwback year ending** 19	**Throwback year ending** 19 ....
18 Regular tax	18					
19 Trust's share of net short-term gain	19					
20 Trust's share of net long-term gain.	20					
21 Add lines 19 and 20. . . .	21					
22 Taxable income	22					
23 Enter percent. Divide line 21 by line 22, but do not enter more than 100%	23	%	%	%	%	%
24 Multiply line 18 by the percentage on line 23. . .	24					
25 Tax on undistributed net income. Subtract line 24 from line 18. Enter here and on page 1, line 9.	25					
Do not complete lines 26 through 31 unless the trust elected the alternative tax on long-term capital gain.						
26 Tax on income other than long-term capital gain . .	26					
27 Trust's share of net short-term gain	27					
28 Trust's share of taxable income less section 1202 deduction.	28					
29 Enter percent. Divide line 27 by line 28, but do not enter more than 100%	29	%	%	%	%	%
30 Multiply line 26 by the percentage on line 29. . .	30					
31 Tax on undistributed net income. Subtract line 30 from line 26. Enter here and on page 1, line 9	31					

Part IV   **Allocation to Beneficiary**
Note: *Be sure to complete* **Form 4970,** *Tax on Accumulation Distribution of Trusts.*

Beneficiary's name   Identifying number

Beneficiary's address (number and street including apartment number or P.O. box) City, state, and ZIP code		**(a)** This beneficiary's share of line 13	**(b)** This beneficiary's share of line 14	**(c)** This beneficiary's share of line 16
32 Throwback year 19	32			
33 Throwback year 19	33			
34 Throwback year 19	34			
35 Throwback year 19	35			
36 Throwback year 19	36			
37 Total. Add lines 32 through 36. Enter here and on the appropriate lines of Form 4970.	37			

✪

SCHEDULE K-1 (Form 1041) Department of the Treasury Internal Revenue Service	**Beneficiary's Share of Income, Deductions, Credits, etc.** for the calendar year 1996, or fiscal year beginning .... , 1996, ending .... , 19 .... ▶ **Complete a separate Schedule K-1 for each beneficiary.**	OMB No. 1545-0092

Name of trust or decedent's estate

☐ Amended K-1
☐ Final K-1

Beneficiary's identifying number ▶	Estate's or trust's EIN ▶
Beneficiary's name, address, and ZIP code	Fiduciary's name, address, and ZIP code

	(a) Allocable share item		**(b)** Amount	**(c)** Calendar year 1996 Form 1040 filers enter the amounts in column (b) on:
1	Interest.	1		Schedule B, Part I, line 1
2	Dividends	2		Schedule B, Part II, line 5
3a	Net short-term capital gain	3a		Schedule D, line 5, column (g)
b	Net long-term capital gain	3b		Schedule D, line 13, column (g)
4a	Annuities, royalties, and other nonpassive income before directly apportioned deductions	4a		Schedule E, Part III, column (f)
b	Depreciation	4b		⎫
c	Depletion	4c		Include on the applicable line of the
d	Amortization	4d		appropriate tax form
5a	Trade or business, rental real estate, and other rental income before directly apportioned deductions (see instructions) .	5a		Schedule E, Part III
b	Depreciation	5b		⎫
c	Depletion	5c		Include on the applicable line of the
d	Amortization	5d		appropriate tax form
6	Income for minimum tax purposes	6		
7	Income for regular tax purposes (add lines 1 through 3b, 4a, and 5a)	7		
8	Adjustment for minimum tax purposes (subtract line 7 from line 6).	8		Form 6251, line 12
9	Estate tax deduction (including certain generation-skipping transfer taxes)	9		Schedule A, line 27
10	Foreign taxes.	10		Form 1116 or Schedule A (Form 1040), line 8
11	Adjustments and tax preference items (itemize):			
a	Accelerated depreciation	11a		⎫ Include on the applicable
b	Depletion	11b		line of Form 6251
c	Amortization	11c		
d	Exclusion items	11d		1997 Form 8801
12	Deductions in the final year of trust or decedent's estate:			
a	Excess deductions on termination (see instructions)	12a		Schedule A, line 22
b	Short-term capital loss carryover	12b		Schedule D, line 5, column (f)
c	Long-term capital loss carryover	12c		Schedule D, line 13, column (f)
d	Net operating loss (NOL) carryover for regular tax purposes	12d		Form 1040, line 21
e	NOL carryover for minimum tax purposes	12e		See the instructions for Form 6251, line 20
f	....	12f		⎫ Include on the applicable line
g	....	12g		of the appropriate tax form
13	Other (itemize):			
a	Payments of estimated taxes credited to you . .	13a		Form 1040, line 53
b	Tax-exempt interest	13b		Form 1040, line 8b
c	....	13c		⎫
d	....	13d		
e	....	13e		Include on the applicable line
f	....	13f		of the appropriate tax form
g	....	13g		
h	....	13h		

For Paperwork Reduction Act Notice, see page 1 of the Instructions for Form 1041.   Cat. No. 11380D   **Schedule K-1 (Form 1041) 1996**

Form **706**		United States Estate (and Generation-Skipping Transfer) Tax Return			

(Rev. August 1993)

Department of the Treasury
Internal Revenue Service

Estate of a citizen or resident of the United States (see separate instructions). To be filed for decedents dying after October 8, 1990. For Paperwork Reduction Act Notice, see page 1 of the instructions.

OMB No. 1545-0015
Expires 12-31-95

Part 1—Decedent and Executor

1a	Decedent's first name and middle initial (and maiden name, if any)	1b Decedent's last name		2 Decedent's social security no.
3a	Domicile at time of death (county and state, or foreign country)	3b Year domicile established	4 Date of birth	5 Date of death
6a	Name of executor (see instructions)	6b Executor's address (number and street including apartment or suite no. or rural route; city, town, or post office; state; and ZIP code)		
6c	Executor's social security number (see instructions)			
7a	Name and location of court where will was probated or estate administered			7b Case number

8　If decedent died testate, check here ▶ ☐ and attach a certified copy of the will. 9 If Form 4768 is attached, check here ▶ ☐

10　If Schedule R-1 is attached, check here ▶ ☐

Part 2—Tax Computation

1	Total gross estate (from Part 5, Recapitulation, page 3, item 10)	1	
2	Total allowable deductions (from Part 5, Recapitulation, page 3, item 20)	2	
3	Taxable estate (subtract line 2 from line 1)	3	
4	Adjusted taxable gifts (total taxable gifts (within the meaning of section 2503) made by the decedent after December 31, 1976, other than gifts that are includible in decedent's gross estate (section 2001(b))	4	
5	Add lines 3 and 4	5	
6	Tentative tax on the amount on line 5 from Table A in the instructions	6	
7a	If line 5 exceeds $10,000,000, enter the lesser of line 5 or $21,040,000. If line 5 is $10,000,000 or less, skip lines 7a and 7b and enter -0- on line 7c .	7a	
b	Subtract $10,000,000 from line 7a	7b	
c	Enter 5% (.05) of line 7b	7c	
8	Total tentative tax (add lines 6 and 7c)	8	
9	Total gift tax payable with respect to gifts made by the decedent after December 31, 1976. Include gift taxes by the decedent's spouse for such spouse's share of split gifts (section 2513) only if the decedent was the donor of these gifts and they are includible in the decedent's gross estate (see instructions)	9	
10	Gross estate tax (subtract line 9 from line 8)	10	
11	Maximum unified credit against estate tax	11	192,800 00
12	Adjustment to unified credit. (This adjustment may not exceed $6,000. See page 6 of the instructions.)	12	
13	Allowable unified credit (subtract line 12 from line 11)	13	
14	Subtract line 13 from line 10 (but do not enter less than zero)	14	
15	Credit for state death taxes. Do not enter more than line 14. Compute the credit by using the amount on line 3 less $60,000. See Table B in the instructions and **attach credit evidence** (see instructions)	15	
16	Subtract line 15 from line 14	16	
17	Credit for Federal gift taxes on pre-1977 gifts (section 2012) (attach computation)	17	
18	Credit for foreign death taxes (from Schedule(s) P). (Attach Form(s) 706CE)	18	
19	Credit for tax on prior transfers (from Schedule Q)	19	
20	Total (add lines 17, 18, and 19)	20	
21	Net estate tax (subtract line 20 from line 16)	21	
22	Generation-skipping transfer taxes (from Schedule R, Part 2, line 10)	22	
23	Section 4980A increased estate tax (from Schedule S, Part I, line 17) (see instructions)	23	
24	Total transfer taxes (add lines 21, 22, and 23)	24	
25	Prior payments. Explain in an attached statement	25	
26	United States Treasury bonds redeemed in payment of estate tax	26	
27	Total (add lines 25 and 26)	27	
28	Balance due (or overpayment (subtract line 27 from line 24)	28	

Under penalties of perjury, I declare that I have examined this return, including accompanying schedules and statements, and to the best of my knowledge and belief, it is true, correct, and complete. Declaration of preparer other than the executor is based on all information of which preparer has any knowledge.

Signature(s) of executor(s)　　　　　　　　　　　　　　　　　　　　　Date

Signature of preparer other than executor　　　　　　　Address (and ZIP code)　　　　　　Date

Cat. No. 20548R

Form 706 (Rev. 8-93)

Estate of:

Part 3.—Elections by the Executor

Please check the "Yes" or "No" box for each question.

		Yes	No
1	Do you elect alternate valuation?		
2	Do you elect special use valuation? . . . . If "Yes," you must complete and attach Schedule A–1		
3	Do you elect to pay the taxes in installments as described in section 6166? . . . . If "Yes," you must attach the additional information described in the instructions.		
4	Do you elect to postpone the part of the taxes attributable to a reversionary or remainder interest as described in section 6163?		

Part 4.—General Information (Note: *Please attach the necessary supplemental documents.* **You must attach the death certificate.**)

Authorization to receive confidential tax information under Regulations section 601.504(b)(2)(i), to act as the estate's representative before the Internal Revenue Service, and to make written or oral presentations on behalf of the estate if return prepared by an attorney, accountant, or enrolled agent for the executor:

Name of representative (print or type)	State	Address (number, street, and room or suite no., city, state, and ZIP code)

I declare that I am the ☐ attorney/ ☐ certified public accountant/ ☐ enrolled agent (you must check the applicable box) for the executor and prepared this return for the executor. I am not under suspension or disbarment from practice before the Internal Revenue Service and am qualified to practice in the state shown above.

Signature		CAF number	Date	Telephone number

1 Death certificate number and issuing authority (attach a copy of the death certificate to this return).

2 Decedent's business or occupation. If retired, check here ▶ ☐ and state decedent's former business or occupation.

3 Marital status of the decedent at time of death:

☐ Married

☐ Widow or widower—Name, SSN, and date of death of deceased spouse ▶ ....

....

☐ Single

☐ Legally separated

☐ Divorced—Date divorce decree became final ▶

4a Surviving spouse's name	4b Social security number	4c Amount received (see instructions)

5 Individuals (other than the surviving spouse), trusts, or other estates who receive benefits from the estate (do not include charitable beneficiaries shown in Schedule O) (see instructions). For Privacy Act Notice (applicable to individual beneficiaries only), see the Instructions for Form 1040.

Name of individual, trust, or estate receiving $5,000 or more	Identifying number	Relationship to decedent	Amount (see instructions)

All unascertainable beneficiaries and those who receive less than $5,000 . . . . ▶	

Total	

(Continued on next page)

Page 2

Form 706 (Rev. 8-93)

Part 4.—General Information *(continued)*

Please check the "Yes" or "No" box for each question. | Yes | No

6 Does the gross estate contain any section 2044 property (qualified terminable interest property (QTIP) from a prior gift or estate) (see page 5 of the instructions)?

7a Have Federal gift tax returns ever been filed?
If "Yes," please attach copies of the returns, if available, and furnish the following information:

7b Period(s) covered | 7c Internal Revenue office(s) where filed

If you answer "Yes" to any of questions 8–16, you must attach additional information as described in the instructions.

8a Was there any insurance on the decedent's life that is not included on the return as part of the gross estate?

b Did the decedent own any insurance on the life of another that is not included in the gross estate?

9 Did the decedent at the time of death own any property as a joint tenant with right of survivorship in which (a) one or more of the other joint tenants was someone other than the decedent's spouse, and (b) less than the full value of the property is included on the return as part of the gross estate? If "Yes," you must complete and attach Schedule E.

10 Did the decedent, at the time of death, own any interest in a partnership or unincorporated business or any stock in an inactive or closely held corporation?

11 Did the decedent make any transfer described in section 2035, 2036, 2037, or 2038 (see the instructions for Schedule G)? If "Yes," you must complete and attach Schedule G.

12 Were there in existence at the time of the decedent's death:
a Any trusts created by the decedent during his or her lifetime?
b Any trusts not created by the decedent under which the decedent possessed any power, beneficial interest, or trusteeship?

13 Did the decedent ever possess, exercise, or release any general power of appointment? If "Yes," you must complete and attach Schedule H

14 Was the marital deduction computed under the transitional rule of Public Law 97-34, section 403(e)(3) (Economic Recovery Tax Act of 1981)?
If "Yes," attach a separate computation of the marital deduction, enter the amount on item 18 of the Recapitulation, and note on item 18 "computation attached."

15 Was the decedent, immediately before death, receiving an annuity described in the "General" paragraph of the instructions for Schedule I? If "Yes," you must complete and attach Schedule I.

16 Did the decedent have a total "excess retirement accumulation" (as defined in section 4980A(d)) in qualified employer plans and individual retirement plans? If "Yes," you must complete and attach Schedule S

Part 5.—Recapitulation

Item number	Gross estate	Alternate value	Value at date of death
1	Schedule A—Real Estate		
2	Schedule B—Stocks and Bonds		
3	Schedule C—Mortgages, Notes, and Cash		
4	Schedule D—Insurance on the Decedent's Life (attach Form(s) 712)		
5	Schedule E—Jointly Owned Property (attach Form(s) 712 for life insurance)		
6	Schedule F—Other Miscellaneous Property (attach Form(s) 712 for life insurance)		
7	Schedule G—Transfers During Decedent's Life (attach Form(s) 712 for life insurance)		
8	Schedule H—Powers of Appointment		
9	Schedule I—Annuities		
10	Total gross estate (add items 1 through 9). Enter here and on line 1 of the Tax Computation		

Item number	Deductions	Amount
11	Schedule J—Funeral Expenses and Expenses Incurred in Administering Property Subject to Claims	
12	Schedule K—Debts of the Decedent	
13	Schedule K—Mortgages and Liens	
14	Total of items 11 through 13	
15	Allowable amount of deductions from item 14 (see the instructions for item 15 of the Recapitulation)	
16	Schedule L—Net Losses During Administration	
17	Schedule L—Expenses Incurred in Administering Property Not Subject to Claims	
18	Schedule M—Bequests, etc., to Surviving Spouse	
19	Schedule O—Charitable, Public, and Similar Gifts and Bequests	
20	Total allowable deductions (add items 15 through 19). Enter here and on line 2 of the Tax Computation	

Page 3

Form **709**	**United States Gift (and Generation-Skipping Transfer) Tax Return**	
(Rev. November 1993)	(Section 6019 of the Internal Revenue Code) (For gifts made after December 31, 1991)	OMB No. 1545-0020
Department of the Treasury Internal Revenue Service	**Calendar year 19** .... ▶ **See separate instructions. For Privacy Act Notice, see the Instructions for Form 1040.**	Expires 5-31-96

Part 1—General Information

1 Donor's first name and middle initial	**2** Donor's last name	**3** Donor's social security number
4 Address (number, street, and apartment number)		**5** Legal residence (Domicile) (county and state)
6 City, state, and ZIP code		**7** Citizenship

		Yes	No
8	If the donor died during the year, check here ▶ ☐ and enter date of death.................................., 19		
9	If you received an extension of time to file this Form 709, check here ▶ ☐ and attach the Form 4868, 2688, 2350, or extension letter		
10	Enter the total number of separate donees listed on Schedule A—count each person only once . . . . ☐		
11a	Have you (the donor) previously filed a Form 709 (or 709-A) for any other year? If the answer is "No," do not complete line 11b .		
11b	If the answer to line 11a is "Yes," has your address changed since you last filed Form 709 (or 709-A)?		
12	Gifts by husband or wife to third parties.—Do you consent to have the gifts (including generation-skipping transfers) made by you and by your spouse to third parties during the calendar year considered as made one-half by each of you? (See instructions.) (If the answer is "Yes," the following information must be furnished and your spouse must sign the consent shown below. **If the answer is "No," skip lines 13–18 and go to Schedule A.**)		
13	Name of consenting spouse **14** SSN		
15	Were you married to one another during the entire calendar year? (see instructions)		
16	If the answer to 15 is "No," check whether ☐ married ☐ divorced or ☐ widowed, and give date (see instructions) ▶		
17	Will a gift tax return for this calendar year be filed by your spouse?		
18	**Consent of Spouse**—I consent to have the gifts (and generation-skipping transfers) made by me and by my spouse to third parties during the calendar year considered as made one-half by each of us. We are both aware of the joint and several liability for tax created by the execution of this consent.		

Consenting spouse's signature ▶   Date ▶

Part 2—Tax Computation

1	Enter the amount from Schedule A, Part 3, line 15	**1**		
2	Enter the amount from Schedule B, line 3	**2**		
3	Total taxable gifts (add lines 1 and 2)	**3**		
4	Tax computed on amount on line 3 (see Table for Computing Tax in separate instructions). .	**4**		
5	Tax computed on amount on line 2 (see Table for Computing Tax in separate instructions). . .	**5**		
6	Balance (subtract line 5 from line 4)	**6**		
7	Maximum unified credit (nonresident aliens, see instructions)	**7**	192,800	00
8	Enter the unified credit against tax allowable for all prior periods (from Sch. B, line 1, col. C) . .	**8**		
9	Balance (subtract line 8 from line 7)	**9**		
10	Enter 20% (.20) of the amount allowed as a specific exemption for gifts made after September 8, 1976, and before January 1, 1977 (see instructions)	**10**		
11	Balance (subtract line 10 from line 9)	**11**		
12	Unified credit (enter the smaller of line 6 or line 11)	**12**		
13	Credit for foreign gift taxes (see instructions)	**13**		
14	Total credits (add lines 12 and 13)	**14**		
15	Balance (subtract line 14 from line 6) (do not enter less than zero)	**15**		
16	Generation-skipping transfer taxes (from Schedule C, Part 3, col. H, total)	**16**		
17	Total tax (add lines 15 and 16)	**17**		
18	Gift and generation-skipping transfer taxes prepaid with extension of time to file	**18**		
19	If line 18 is less than line 17, enter BALANCE DUE (see instructions)	**19**		
20	If line 18 is greater than line 17, enter AMOUNT TO BE REFUNDED	**20**		

Under penalties of perjury, I declare that I have examined this return, including any accompanying schedules and statements, and to the best of my knowledge and belief it is true, correct, and complete. Declaration of preparer (other than donor) is based on all information of which preparer has any knowledge.

Donor's signature ▶   Date ▶

Preparer's signature
(other than donor) ▶   Date ▶

Preparer's address
(other than donor) ▶

Attach check or money order here.

For Paperwork Reduction Act Notice, see page 1 of the separate instructions for this form.   Cat. No. 16783M   Form **709** (Rev. 11-93)

Form 709 (Rev. 11-93) | Page **2**

SCHEDULE A Computation of Taxable Gifts

Part 1—Gifts Subject Only to Gift Tax. *Gifts less political organization, medical, and educational exclusions—see instructions*

A Item number	B • Donee's name and address • Relationship to donor (if any) • Description of gift • If the gift was made by means of a trust, enter trust's identifying number and attach a copy of the trust instrument • If the gift was of securities, give CUSIP number	C Donor's adjusted basis of gift	D Date of gift	E Value at date of gift
1				

Part 2—Gifts That are Direct Skips and are Subject to Both Gift Tax and Generation-Skipping Transfer Tax. You must list the gifts in chronological order. *Gifts less political organization, medical, and educational exclusions—see instructions. (Also list here direct skips that are subject only to the GST tax at this time as the result of the termination of an "estate tax inclusion period." See instructions.)*

A Item number	B • Donee's name and address • Relationship to donor (if any) • Description of gift • If the gift was made by means of a trust, enter trust's identifying number and attach a copy of the trust instrument • If the gift was of securities, give CUSIP number	C Donor's adjusted basis of gift	D Date of gift	E Value at date of gift
1				

Part 3—Taxable Gift Reconciliation

1	Total value of gifts of donor (add column E of Parts 1 and 2)	1	
2	One-half of items .... attributable to spouse (see instructions)	2	
3	Balance (subtract line 2 from line 1)	3	
4	Gifts of spouse to be included (from Schedule A, Part 3, line 2 of spouse's return—see instructions) .	4	

If any of the gifts included on this line are also subject to the generation-skipping transfer tax, check here ▶ ☐ and enter those gifts also on Schedule C, Part 1.

5	Total gifts (add lines 3 and 4)	5	
6	Total annual exclusions for gifts listed on Schedule A (including line 4, above) (see instructions) . . .	6	
7	Total included amount of gifts (subtract line 6 from line 5)	7	

Deductions (see instructions)

8	Gifts of interests to spouse for which a marital deduction will be claimed, based on items .... of Schedule A	8		
9	Exclusions attributable to gifts on line 8	9		
10	Marital deduction—subtract line 9 from line 8	10		
11	Charitable deduction, based on items .... to .... less exclusions .	11		
12	Total deductions—add lines 10 and 11		12	
13	Subtract line 12 from line 7		13	
14	Generation-skipping transfer taxes payable with this Form 709 (from Schedule C, Part 3, col. H, Total) .		14	
15	Taxable gifts (add lines 13 and 14). Enter here and on line 1 of the Tax Computation on page 1 . . .		15	

(If more space is needed, attach additional sheets of same size.)

DO NOT PRINT — DO NOT PRINT — DO NOT PRINT — DO NOT PRINT

Form 709 (Rev. 11-93)   Page **3**

SCHEDULE A   **Computation of Taxable Gifts** *(continued)*

16 **Terminable Interest (QTIP) Marital Deduction.** (See instructions for line 8 of Schedule A.)

If a trust (or other property) meets the requirements of qualified terminable interest property under section 2523(f), and

a. The trust (or other property) is listed on Schedule A, and

b. The value of the trust (or other property) is entered in whole or in part as a deduction on line 8, Part 3 of Schedule A,

then the donor shall be deemed to have made an election to have such trust (or other property) treated as qualified terminable interest property under section 2523(f).

If less than the entire value of the trust (or other property) that the donor has included in Part 1 of Schedule A is entered as a deduction on line 8, the donor shall be considered to have made an election only as to a fraction of the trust (or other property). The numerator of this fraction is equal to the amount of the trust (or other property) deducted on line 10 of Part 3. The denominator is equal to the total value of the trust (or other property) listed in Part 1 of Schedule A.

If you make the QTIP election (see instructions for line 8 of Schedule A), the terminable interest property involved will be included in your spouse's gross estate upon his or her death (section 2044). If your spouse disposes (by gift or otherwise) of all or part of the qualifying life income interest, he or she will be considered to have made a transfer of the entire property that is subject to the gift tax (see Transfer of Certain Life Estates on page 3 of the instructions).

17 **Election out of QTIP Treatment of Annuities**

☐ ◀ Check here if you elect under section 2523(f)(6) **NOT** to treat as qualified terminable interest property any joint and survivor annuities that are reported on Schedule A and would otherwise be treated as qualified terminable interest property under section 2523(f). (See instructions.)
Enter the item numbers (from Schedule A) for which you are making this election ▶

SCHEDULE B   **Gifts From Prior Periods**

If you answered "Yes" on line 11a of page 1, Part 1, see the instructions for completing Schedule B. If you answered "No," skip to the Tax Computation on page 1 (or Schedule C, if applicable).

A Calendar year or calendar quarter (see instructions)	**B** Internal Revenue office where prior return was filed	**C** Amount of unified credit against gift tax for periods after December 31, 1976	**D** Amount of specific exemption for prior periods ending before January 1, 1977	**E** Amount of taxable gifts

1	Totals for prior periods (without adjustment for reduced specific exemption) **1**	
2	Amount, if any, by which total specific exemption, line 1, column D, is more than $30,000 . . . . . **2**	
3	Total amount of taxable gifts for prior periods (add amount, column E, line 1, and amount, if any, on line 2). (Enter here and on line 2 of the Tax Computation on page 1.) **3**	

(If more space is needed, attach additional sheets of same size.)

Form 709 (Rev. 11-93)   Page **4**

SCHEDULE C **Computation of Generation-Skipping Transfer Tax**

Note: *Inter vivos direct skips that are completely excluded by the GST exemption must still be fully reported (including value and exemptions claimed) on Schedule C.*

Part 1—Generation-Skipping Transfers

A Item No. (from Schedule A, Part 2, col. A)	B Value (from Schedule A, Part 2, col. E)	C Split Gifts (enter ½ of col. B) (see instructions)	D Subtract col. C from col. B	E Nontaxable portion of transfer	F Net Transfer (subtract col. E from col. D)
1					
2					
3					
4					
5					
6					

If you elected gift splitting and your spouse was required to file a separate Form 709 (see the instructions for "Split Gifts"), you must enter all of the gifts shown on Schedule A, Part 2, of your spouse's Form 709 here.	Split gifts from spouse's Form 709 (enter item number)	Value included from spouse's Form 709	Nontaxable portion of transfer	Net transfer (subtract col. E from col. D)
In column C, enter the item number of each gift in the order it appears in column A of your spouse's Schedule A, Part 2. We have preprinted the prefix "S-" to distinguish your spouse's item numbers from your own when you complete column A of Schedule C, Part 3. In column D, for each gift, enter the amount reported in column C, Schedule C, Part 1, of your spouse's Form 709.	S-			
	S-			
	S-			
	S-			
	S-			
	S-			
	S-			
	S-			

Part 2—GST Exemption Reconciliation (Code section 2631) and Section 2652(a)(3) Election

Check box ▶ ☐ if you are making a section 2652(a)(3) (special QTIP) election (see instructions)

Enter the item numbers (from Schedule A) of the gifts for which you are making this election ▶ ....

1	Maximum allowable exemption	**1**	$1,000,000
2	Total exemption used for periods before filing this return	**2**	
3	Exemption available for this return (subtract line 2 from line 1)	**3**	
4	Exemption claimed on this return (from Part 3, col. C total, below)	**4**	
5	Exemption allocated to transfers not shown on Part 3, below. You must attach a Notice of Allocation. (See instructions.)	**5**	
6	Add lines 4 and 5	**6**	
7	Exemption available for future transfers (subtract line 6 from line 3)	**7**	

Part 3—Tax Computation

A Item No. (from Schedule C, Part 1)	B Net transfer (from Schedule C, Part 1, col. F)	C GST Exemption Allocated	D Divide col. C by col. B	E Inclusion Ratio (subtract col. D from 1.000)	F Maximum Estate Tax Rate	G Applicable Rate (multiply col. E by col. F)	H Generation-Skipping Transfer Tax (multiply col. B by col. G)
1					55% (.55)		
2					55% (.55)		
3					55% (.55)		
4					55% (.55)		
5					55% (.55)		
6					55% (.55)		
					55% (.55)		
					55% (.55)		
					55% (.55)		

Total exemption claimed. Enter here and on line 4, Part 2, above. May not exceed line 3, Part 2, above	**Total generation-skipping transfer tax.** Enter here, on line 14 of Schedule A, Part 3, and on line 16 of the Tax Computation on page 1	

(If more space is needed, attach additional sheets of same size.)

Appendix 2. Estate Tax Rates

	UNIFIED RATE SCHEDULE		
(A)	**(B)**	**(C)**	**(D)**
		Tax on amount in Column A*	Tax rate on excess over amounts in Column A*
Amount Subject to Tentative Tax			
exceeding	but not exceeding		Percent
$ —	$10,000	$—	18
10,000	20,000	1,800	20
20,000	40,000	3,800	22
40,000	60,000	8,200	24
60,000	80,000	13,000	26
80,000	100,000	16,200	28
100,000	160,000	23,800	30
160,000	250,000	36,800	32
250,000	500,000	70,800	34
500,000	750,000	155,800	37
750,000	1,000,000	248,300	39
1,000,000	1,250,000	345,800	41
1,250,000	1,500,000	448,300	43
1,500,000	2,000,000	555,800	45
2,000,000	2,500,000	780,800	49
2,500,000	3,000,000	1,025,800	53
3,000,000	—	1,290,800	55

*Before credits and phase-out of graduated rates.

Appendix 3. Will Execution Requirements by State

A STATE-BY-STATE SUMMARY

A. At what age may you make a will?
B. How many persons must witness* your will?
C. Are holographic wills† recognized as valid?

	A.	B.	C.
ALABAMA	18	2	no
ALASKA	18	2	yes
ARIZONA	18	2	yes
ARKANSAS	18	2	yes
CALIFORNIA	18	2	yes
COLORADO	18	2	yes
CONNECTICUT	18	2	no (5)
DELAWARE	18	2	no
DC	18	2	no
FLORIDA	18	2	no
GEORGIA	14	2	no
HAWAII	18	2	no (6)
IDAHO	18	2	yes
ILLINOIS	18	2	no
INDIANA	18 (1)	2	no
IOWA	18	2	no
KANSAS	18	2	no
KENTUCKY	18	2	yes
LOUISIANA	16	2, 3, or 5 (4)	yes
MAINE	18	2	yes
MARYLAND	18	2	no (7)

MASSACHUSETTS	18	2	no
MICHIGAN	18	2	yes
MINNESOTA	18	2	no
MISSISSIPPI	18	2	yes
MISSOURI	18	2	no
MONTANA	18	2	yes
NEBRASKA	18	2	yes
NEVADA	18	2	yes
NEW HAMPSHIRE	18 (2)	2	no
NEW JERSEY	18	2	yes
NEW MEXICO	18	2	no
NEW YORK	18	2	no (7)
NORTH CAROLINA	18	2	yes
NORTH DAKOTA	18	2	yes
OHIO	18	2	no
OKLAHOMA	18	2	yes
OREGON	18 (2)	2	no
PENNSYLVANIA	18 (3)	2	yes
PUERTO RICO	14	3 or 5 (4)	yes
RHODE ISLAND	18	2	no (7)
SOUTH CAROLINA	18 (2)	2	no (5)
SOUTH DAKOTA	18	2	yes
TENNESSEE	18	2	yes
TEXAS	18 (1&2)	2	yes
UTAH	18	2	yes
VERMONT	18 (1)	2	no
VIRGIN ISLANDS	18	2	no (7)
VIRGINIA	18	2	yes
WASHINGTON	18	2	no
WEST VIRGINIA	18	2	yes
WISCONSIN	18	2	no (5)
WYOMING	18	2	yes

*Most states require that witnesses be disinterested (not benefiting from will), of legal age (which may be different than the age one may write a will), and of sound mind.

†For purposes of this chart, a holographic will is defined as a will written either entirely or substantially in the person's own handwriting that is signed and dated by the person making it, but not signed by any witnesses.

(1) or younger than 18 if on actual military duty in the armed services.
(2) or younger than 18 if lawfully married.

(3) usual but not necessary (however two witnesses are required when will is signed by mark or by person other than testator).

(4) plus notary, depending on type of will.

(5) unless validly executed out of state.

(6) except foreign-made wills that are valid where executed may be admitted to probate.

(7) except if made by a person on actual military duty in the U.S. armed services.

Source: Martindale-Hubbell Law Digest, *Published by Martindale-Hubbell, a Reed Reference Publishing Company (USA).* 1995 Edition.

Disclaimer: This chart is meant only as a general reference and not a substitute for legal counsel. Every effort was made to provide accurate information; however, state laws are constantly under revision and may have changed by the time this book was published.

Appendix 4. Resources

To reach Emily Card and Adam Miller, write Box 3725, Santa Monica, CA 90403. Please enclose a self-addressed stamped envelope. Visit the authors at http://www.womenmoney.com or e-mail at ownmoney@aol.com.

Social Security Administration. 1-800-772-1213. To order a record of your earnings and estimate of future retirement benefits and other information. Automated 24-hour service.

Veteran's Affairs. 1-800-827-1000. To obtain burial and flag information.

National Association of Personal Financial Advisors. 1130 W. Lake Cook Rd.1, #150, Buffalo Grove, IL 60089-1974. 1-800-366-2732. Fee-only financial planners. Call for a directory.

Insurance Analysis: Consumer Federation of America, Insurance Group, 1424 16th Street, N.W., #600, Washington, D.C. 20036. Enclose self-addressed stamped envelope.

Sources

INTRODUCTION: THE BASICS OF INHERITED WEALTH
Avery, Robert B., and Michael S. Rendall, "Inheritance and Wealth," Cornell University for Presentation at the Philanthropy Roundtable, November 11, 1993. "The Cornell Study."

Avery, Robert B., and Michael S. Rendall, "Estimating the Size and Distribution of Baby Boomers' Prospective Inheritances." Cornell University for Presentation at the Philanthropy Roundtable, November 11, 1993. "The Cornell Study." The bequests of $10.4 trillion by 2040 had been projected in 1989 dollars. In 1995, the dollar had already inflated by twenty percent, so the eventual total of the bequests possibly will vary in nominal terms, depending upon the cause of inflation.

CHAPTER 1. AVOIDING INHERITANCE PITFALLS
The Christian Science Monitor, September 10, 1992, p. 8.

Domini, Amy L., with Dennis Pearne and Sharon L. Rich, *The Challenges of Wealth*. Homewood, Ill.: Dow Jones-Irwin, 1988.

Fields, Rick, with Peggy Taylor, Rex Weyler, and Rick Ingrasci, *Chop Wood, Carry Water*. New York: Putnam, 1984.

Levy, John L., "Coping with Inherited Wealth," unpublished paper, 1986.

Lapham, Lewis H., *Money and Class in America*. New York: Ballantine Books, 1988.

Rand, Ayn, *The Fountainhead*. New York: Signet, 1993.

Wojahn, Ellen, "Share the Wealth, Spoil the Child?" *Inc.*, August 1989, pp. 64–77.

CHAPTER 2. FAMILY MATTERS

Adler, Bill, *Great Lawyer Stories*. New York: Carol Publishing Group, 1992.

Cunningham, Roger A., William B. Stoebuck, and Dale A. Whitman, *The Law of Property*, 2nd ed. St. Paul: West Publishing, 1993.

Davies, Robertson, *The Manticore*. New York: Penguin, 1976.

Dukeminier, Jesse, and Stanley M. Johanson, *Wills, Trusts and Estates*, 4th ed. Boston: Little, Brown, 1990.

Gubernick, Lisa, and Alexander Parker, "The Outsider." *Forbes*, October 26, 1987, pp. 38–42.

McGovern, William M., Jr., Sheldon F. Kurtz, and Jan Ellen Rein, *Wills, Trusts and Estates Including Taxation and Future Interests*. St. Paul: West Publishing, 1988.

Mennell, Robert L., *Wills and Trusts in a Nutshell*. St. Paul: West Publishing, 1979.

Mitchell, Margaret, *Gone with the Wind*. New York: Macmillan, 1936, p. 38.

Nash, Alanna, "The Woman Who Overturned an Empire." *Ms.*, June 1986, pp. 44–46+.

CHAPTER 3. ACCEPTING THE INHERITANCE

Black's Law Dictionary, 5th ed. St. Paul: West Publishing, 1979.

Dacey, Norman F., *How to Avoid Probate*, 5th ed. 1993.

Dukeminier, Jesse, and Stanley M. Johanson, *Wills, Trusts and Estates*, 4th ed. Boston: Little, Brown, 1990.

Dunn, Don, "First Things First: A Last Will and Testament." *Business Week*, December 9, 1991, pp. 108–109.

Hutton, Cynthia, "Keeping It in the Family." *Fortune*, Fall 1987, pp. 111–24.

Manning, Jerome A., *Estate Planning: How to Preserve Your Estate for Your Loved Ones*. New York: Practising Law Institute, 1992.

McNulty, John K., *Federal Estate and Gift Taxation in a Nutshell*, 4th ed. St. Paul: West Publishing, 1989.

CHAPTER 4. BENEFITING FROM A TRUST

Bittker, Boris, Lawrence Stone, and William Klein, *Federal Income Taxation*, 6th ed. Boston: Little, Brown, 1984.

Hutton, Cynthia, "Keeping It in the Family." *Fortune*, Fall 1987, pp. 111–24.

McGovern, William M., Jr., *Wills, Trusts and Future Interests: An Introduction to Estate Planning Cases and Materials.* St. Paul: West Publishing, 1983.

McNulty, John K., *Federal Income Taxation of Individuals in a Nutshell,* 4th ed. St. Paul: West Publishing, 1988.

Samansky, Allan J., *Charitable Contributions and Federal Taxes.* Charlottesville: Michie Company, 1993.

CHAPTER 5. MONEY MANAGEMENT

Bamford, Janet, Jeff Slyskal, Emily Card, and Aileen Jacobsen, *The Consumer Reports Money Book.* Yonkers: Consumers Union, 1992.

Bittker, Boris, Lawrence Stone, and William Klein, *Federal Income Taxation,* 6th ed. Boston: Little, Brown, 1984.

Card, Emily, *The Ms. Money Book.* New York: E. P. Dutton, 1990.

McNulty, John K., *Federal Income Taxation of Individuals,* 4th ed. St. Paul: West Publishing, 1988.

Tax Loopholes: Everything the Law Allows. New York: Boardroom Reports, 1993.

Tyson, Eric, *Personal Finance for Dummies.* San Mateo, Calif.: IDG Books, 1994.

CHAPTER 6. ALLOCATING YOUR ASSETS

Card, Emily, *The Ms. Money Book.* New York: E. P. Dutton, 1990.

Evans and Archer, "Diversification and the Reduction of Dispersion: An Empirical Analysis." *Journal of Finance,* December 1968.

Perritt, Gerald, and Alan Lavine, *Diversify Your Way to Wealth.* Chicago: Probus Publishing Company, 1994.

Wall, Ginita, *The Way to Invest.* New York: Henry Holt, 1995.

CHAPTER 8. ADVICE ON ADVISORS

Bamford, Janet, Jeff Slyskal, Emily Card, and Aileen Jacobsen, *The Consumer Reports Money Book.* Yonkers: Consumers Union, 1992.

Card, Emily, "Expert Advice: What a Financial Planner Can and Can't Do for You." *Ms.,* October 1986, pp. 40–43.

Card, Emily, "How to Complain." *Ms.,* September 1985, pp. 26+.

Fisher, Roger, and William Ury, *Getting to Yes: Negotiating Agreement Without Giving In.* New York: Penguin, 1981.

CHAPTER 9.   PLANNING YOUR ESTATE

Card, Emily, "Planning Your Parents' Estate." *Working Woman*, August 1992, p. 39.

Card, Emily, "Writing Your Will." *Ms.*, July 1984, pp. 88–92.

Dukeminier, Jesse, and Stanley M. Johanson, *Wills, Trusts and Estates*, 4th ed. Boston: Little, Brown, 1990.

Gamble, Richard H., "Estate Planning for the Unmarried Person," *Trusts and Estates*, vol. 25, April 1986, pp. 25–28.

Hutton, Cynthia, "Keeping It in the Family." *Fortune*, Fall 1987, pp. 111–24.

Living Trusts. New York: Boardroom Classics, 1993.

Manning, Jerome A., *Estate Planning*, 4th ed. New York: Practising Law Institute, 1991.

McGovern, William M., Jr., *Wills, Trusts and Future Interests: An Introduction to Estate Planning Cases and Materials.* St. Paul: West Publishing, 1983.

McNulty, John K., *Federal Income Taxation of Individuals in a Nutshell*, 4th ed. St. Paul: West Publishing, 1988.

Mooney, F. Bentley, Jr., *Preserving Your Wealth.* Chicago: Probus, 1993.

Peat, W. Leslie, and Stephanie J. Willbanks, *Federal Estate and Gift Taxation: An Analysis and Critique.* St. Paul: West Publishing, 1991.

Samansky, Allan J., *Charitable Contributions and Federal Taxes.* Charlottesville: Michie Company, 1993.

Schwartzberg, Harold, and Jule E. Stocker, *Stocker on Drawing Wills*, 10th ed. New York: Practising Law Institute, 1987.

Ibid., 1990 Supplement.

Tax Loopholes: Everything the Law Allows. New York: Boardroom Reports, 1993.

Gottlieb, Carrie, and Richard I. Kirkland, Jr., "Should You Leave It All to the Children?" *Fortune*, September 29, 1986, pp. 18–26.

Gamble, Richard H., "Estate Planning for the Unmarried Person." *Trusts and Estates*, April 1986, pp. 25–28.

CHAPTER 10.   MINIMIZING ESTATE TAXES

American Demographics, vol. 15, no. 5, May 1992, pp. 46–49.

Card, Emily, "Before—or Even After—You Say 'I Do': Designing an Economic Partnership," in *Ms.*, June 1984, pp. 72–78.

Condon, Gerald, and Jeffrey Condon, *Beyond the Grave.* New York: HarperBusiness, 1995.

Dukeminier, Jesse, and Stanley M. Johanson, *Wills, Trusts and Estates,* 4th ed. Boston: Little, Brown, 1990.

First, David M., "Wills: Importance of Tax Apportionment Clauses." *CPA Journal,* April 1989, pp. 71–72.

The Guide to Gifts and Bequests, 1995–1997. New York: The Institutions Press, 1995.

Hunt, James, Life Insurance Actuary, Board of Consumer Federation of America, Insurance Group, interview.

Hutton, Cynthia, "Keeping It in the Family." *Fortune,* Fall 1987, pp. 111–24.

Living Trusts. New York: Boardroom Classics, 1993.

Manning, Jerome A., *Estate Planning: How to Preserve Your Estate for Your Loved Ones.* New York: Practising Law Institute, 1992.

McGovern, William M., Jr., *Wills, Trusts and Future Interests: An Introduction to Estate Planning Cases and Materials.* St. Paul: West Publishing, 1983.

McNulty, John K., *Federal Income Taxation of Individuals in a Nutshell,* 4th ed. St. Paul: West Publishing, 1988.

Peat, W. Leslie, and Stephanie J. Willbanks, *Federal Estate and Gift Taxation: An Analysis and Critique.* St. Paul: West Publishing, 1991.

Planning Your Estate. Berkeley: Nolo Press, 1994.

Samansky, Allan J., *Charitable Contributions and Federal Taxes.* Charlottesville: Michie Company, 1993.

Schwartzberg, Harold, and Jule E. Stocker, *Stocker on Drawing Wills,* 10th ed. New York: Practising Law Institute, 1987.

Ibid., 1990 Supplement.

Tax Loopholes: Everything the Law Allows. New York: Boardroom Reports, 1993.

Ware, Robert C., "How to Explain the Importance of a Will." *Insurance Sales,* June 1986, pp. 35–36.

CHAPTER 11.   THE FLOW OF CAPITAL

Bavaria, Joan, "Insight." *Investing for a Better World,* September 15, 1994, p. 1.

Brecher, Jeremy, John Brown Childs, and Jill Cutler, eds., *Global Visions: Beyond the New World Order.* Boston: South End Press, 1993.

Luch, Christopher, and Nancy Pilotte, "Domini Social Index Performance." *Barra Newsletter* #145. November/December, 1992.

Domini, Amy L., and Peter D. Kinder, *Ethical Investing: How to Make Profitable Investments without Sacrificing Your Principles.* Reading: Addison-Wesley, 1986.

Kaplan, Anne E., ed., *Giving USA 1994 Edition.* Published by AARFC Trust for Philanthropy (American Association of Fund Raising Councils).

Kaufman, Iva, and Debbie Tompkins, "Passing It On: Making A Philanthropic Plan." unpublished paper presented at the Ms. Foundation, June 1989.

Kelly, Margery, "To Tell the Truth." *Business Ethics,* September/October 1994, pp. 6–7.

Kinder, Peter D., Steven D. Lydenberg, and Amy L. Domini, eds., *Social Investment Almanac: A Comprehensive Guide to Socially Responsible Investing.* New York: Henry Holt, 1992.

Kinder, Peter D., Steven D. Lydenberg, and Amy L. Domini, *Investing for Good: Making Money While Being Socially Responsible.* New York: HarperBusiness, 1993.

"The Renaissance of Values." *The Green Money Journal,* vol. 3, pp. 1, 13.

Schelling, Thomas C., *Micromotives and Macro Behavior.* New York: W.W. Norton, 1978.

Index

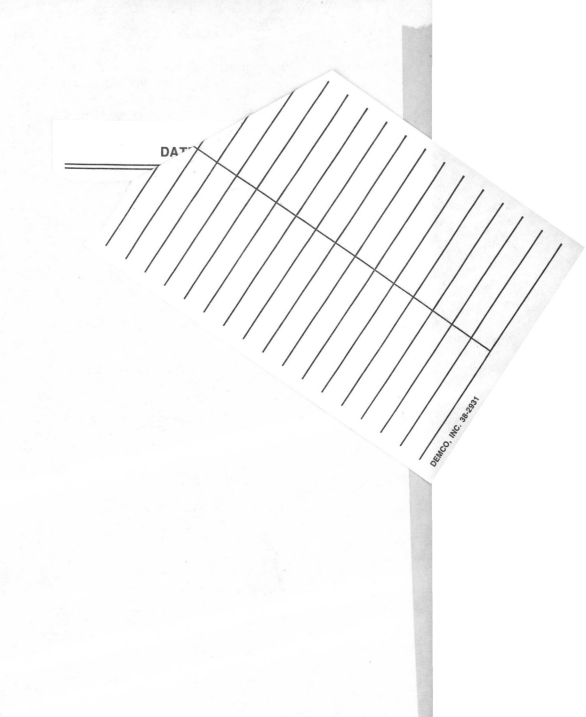

DATE

DEMCO, INC. 38-2931